D0770575

The New England Women's Diaries Series
New Year
Edited with an introduction by Karen Robert

in Cuba

Mary Gardner Lowell's Travel Diary, 1831–1832

Massachusetts Historical Society

Northeastern University Press

Boston

Library of Congress Cataloguing-in-Publication Data

Lowell, Mary Gardner, 1802–
New year in Cuba : Mary Gardner Lowell's travel diary, 1831–1832 /
edited with an introduction by Karen Robert.
p. cm.
Includes bibliographical references and index.
ISBN 1-55553-558-5 (pbk. : alk. paper) — ISBN 1-55553-559-3 (cloth : alk. paper)
1. Cuba—Description and travel. 2. Plantation life—Cuba. 3. Slaves—Cuba—Social conditions—19th century. 4. Cuba—Race relations. 5. Lowell, Mary Gardner, 1802– —Journeys—Cuba. I. Robert, Karen, 1966– II. Title.
F1763 .L69 2003
917.29104'5—dc21 2002015463

Book design and typography in Quadraat by Christopher Kuntze.
Printed and bound by Maple Press, York Pennsylvania.
The paper is Sebago Antique, an acid-free stock.

MANUFACTURED IN THE UNITED STATES OF AMERICA
07 06 05 04 03 5 4 3 2 1

For Rodrigo

ACKNOWLEDGMENTS

My first thanks must go to my graduate mentor Rebecca J. Scott, who introduced me to the coordinators of the New England Women's Diaries Project and, by extension, to Mary Gardner Lowell's diary. The manuscript benefited greatly from the assistance of my editors, Ondine LeBlanc at the Massachusetts Historical Society and Elizabeth Swayze at Northeastern University Press. Ondine in particular was as much collaborator as editor at various stages in the research and writing. The thoughtful suggestions offered by Laurel Thatcher Ulrich and the anonymous reviewer contributed to the rigor of the final version, though any remaining weaknesses are of course my own. My dear friends, colleagues, and neighbors Brad Cross and Christine Cook Cross also provided helpful advice at various stages, and Margie Reed did a cheerful and meticulous job formatting the final manuscript. Institutional support included a research stipend from Frederick Ballou and the Massachusetts Historical Society, and a course release grant from St. Thomas University. The library staff at the Massachusetts Historical Society, the Baker Library at Harvard University, the New England Historic Genealogical Society and the Harriet Irving Library at the University of New Brunswick were always extremely helpful. Special thanks to Esperanza B. de Varona, director of the Cuban Heritage Collection at the Otto G. Richter Library of the University of Miami, for her generous last-minute assistance in locating the Cuban illustrations reprinted here. The most important support came from my family—Beverley and Elston Robert, Nestor Gutiérrez and Beatriz Hermelo, my dear son Lucas, and, as always, Rodrigo Gutiérrez Hermelo.

Contents

ILLUSTRATIONS

Preface ❦ *The New England Women's Diaries Series*

I walked into the Massachusetts Historical Society for the first time in the early 1970s. When I told the woman at the desk that I wanted to write about women in colonial New England, she said, "Good luck. You won't find much." Neither at the MHS nor at any of the other archives I visited were there any guides to women's papers. My only recourse was to sift through various collections of family papers, page by page, looking for material relevant to my project.

All that has changed. One of the consequences of the renaissance in women's history over the past thirty years is that archives all over the United States now have finding aids to women's papers. In the process of preparing one such guide, Ondine LeBlanc decided that the time had come to share with a larger public the extraordinary collection of women's diaries at the Massachusetts Historical Society. More than two hundred diaries, ranging from the colonial period to the late twentieth century, document an astonishing range of female activity, from ocean travel to spiritual exploration. The authors include farmwives, teachers, urban activists, household servants, literati. Their stories encompass a panorama of social experience, from the frontlines of World War I to the plantations of nineteenth-century Cuba.

The forms of the diaries also vary. Some are taciturn, others expansive. Some focus on interior life, others on daily labor. Some are as steady as a clock or an almanac; others episodic, ebbing and flowing with the tides of event or emotion. Some are travel journals filled with local color and ethnographic observation. Others, originating as personal communications to a trusted friend, belong to that familiar mixed genre the "letter journal." Whatever the form, they fit the classic definition of the diary as a personal account of daily (if not every day) experience.

The New England Women's Diaries Series is a joint venture of the Massachusetts Historical Society and Northeastern University Press. Our intended audience is the proverbial "general reader." As a consequence, we have chosen diaries for their intrinsic interest as well as for their value as historical sources. Introductions, written by scholars with expertise in the period, place, or general subject matter of the diaries, provide rich contextual introductions but keep scholarly apparatus to a minimum. Wherever possible, we present each diary in its entirety.

Preface

The words "diary" and "journal" are both rooted in the notion of the daily unfolding of events human or heavenly. Thus, in Old French, variations on the word "journal" could connote both the movement of the sun across the sky and the amount of land a team of oxen could plough in a day. The reader of a diary sees a life unfold as it happens, bit by bit, with all the unrealized plots, dead ends, and confusions of ordinary life. There is predictability—the sun comes up, the sun goes down, fields are planted, journeys begun and ended, sentences move across the page, persons are born, grow old or fall ill, and die. Yet diaries, like life, are filled with the suspense of unrealized aspiration. What new joy or terror lies just around the corner? A good diary provides many of the satisfactions of a good novel. It lets the reader inside another person's life, offering the intimacy of a vicarious friendship. Yet because diaries, unlike novels, develop incrementally, the stories are always cluttered with incidentals and never complete. Sometimes events come to a satisfying resolution; more often they sputter to an end in half-finished sentences on a still empty page. Introductions, footnotes, maps, photographs, and occasional selections from other texts can help explain "what happened," but these devices can never provide the resolution—or the artifice of fiction.

A good diary keeps its secrets. That is its challenge and its charm.

Laurel Thatcher Ulrich
Series Editor

New Year in Cuba

Introduction

"Set forth with my husband, little George & nurse (Lorenza Stephens) upon my travels," wrote Mary Gardner Lowell on the first page of a new diary on December 18, 1831. Mary spent the next six months carefully recording the details of a voyage that carried her young family some four thousand miles before bringing them safely back to the comforts of their home in Boston's aristocratic Beacon Hill. Their travels swept them through the outposts of commercial Boston's distant hinterlands. From Boston Harbor they sailed southward to Cuba, where they spent three months touring the cities of Havana and Matanzas and visiting a number of American-owned slave plantations. In the early spring of 1832 they crossed the Gulf of Mexico to New Orleans, where they boarded a steamboat that carried them through the new boomtowns along the Mississippi and Ohio Rivers as far as Pittsburgh. Here they caught a stagecoach to Philadelphia, where Mary's diary entries ended.

Mary Gardner Lowell was one of a handful of Anglo-American female travelers to record impressions of Latin America in the early nineteenth century. Political independence on the mainland and loosening trade restrictions in the remaining Spanish colonies of Cuba and Puerto Rico opened up the continent to European and North American merchants, diplomats, naturalists, and explorers after 1810. Yet few women risked the dangers of shipwreck, piracy, and insurrection that plagued travelers to Latin America in these early years, and even fewer left written records of their experiences.[1] The male author of a Cuban travel account that Mary carried with her in 1831 warned of the dangers found in the island's interior: "It is not without good cause that men go armed; and in spite of arms, disasters are frequent; and if American editors could draw from Cuba springs, the horribles would be multiplied a thousand fold."[2] Mary's own diary catalogs many of the discomforts that faced a privileged white woman who ventured into the Caribbean or even the North American interior in the 1830s: crippling seasickness, frightening advances by Spanish men, threats of slave uprising, choking dust in New Orleans, and fears of explosion on the Mississippi steamboats.

The rough frontiers of the Cuban and North American interiors also exposed Mary to unfamiliar and often uncomfortable social situations. The three months in Cuba marked her first trip outside English-speaking North America and her first experience of a slave plantation society. The confined quarters of her New Orleans hotel and Mississippi steamboat forced her to rub shoulders—probably for the first time in her life—with "common" shopkeepers, boatmen, and homesteaders. All of these settings required her to evaluate and adapt to new gender, class, and race relations, even while she continued to benefit from her own status as a white woman escorted by her wealthy and influential husband.

Travel may have entailed risk, but it also brought the rare thrill of mobility outside the strict domestic confines that bound the lives of elite women in the early nineteenth century. As she moved through different social settings, Mary explored the changing norms governing women's behavior. She learned to ride horseback in rural Cuba and, as she reported to her sister Elizabeth, was "quite astonished to find myself so much at home in the saddle."[3] Such liberty contrasted sharply with the gender conventions she discovered in Havana, which were even more rigid than in Boston. Spanish rules of respectability prohibited elite women from traveling by carriage without a male relative and forced them to screen their faces from public view. As a tourist, Mary chose to flout such conventions on more than one occasion, exposing her honor in ways that would have been unthinkable closer to home. As a North American sure of her own culture's superiority, she concluded that such exaggerated control over women's behavior only confirmed the underlying "immorality" of Spanish Cuban society.

While Mary's concerns appear limited to domestic and personal issues, when understood within its historical moment, her diary provides insights into broader questions of race, slavery, gender, and imperialism that informed the relationship between the "free" northern United States and the plantation societies of the American South and the Caribbean. Mary's travels kept her close to the waves of slave unrest and abolitionist debate that rippled along the eastern seaboard from Boston to the Caribbean in 1831, a year that marked a crucial turning point for the institution of slavery in the Americas. At the beginning of that year William Lloyd Garrison launched his radical abolitionist newspaper, the *Liberator*, in the African American neighborhood located on the north slope of Beacon Hill, just a few blocks from the elite enclave where Mary and her family lived. In 1831 Garrison became the first white antislavery activist in the United States to demand immediate and unconditional freedom for all slaves. On August

21, 1831, eight months after the *Liberator*'s first appearance, Nat Turner led the bloodiest slave rebellion in United States history, which resulted in the deaths of some fifty-five whites in Virginia and ignited a backlash of repression and restrictive legislation against African Americans, free and enslaved. A new round of debate ensued over the problem of slavery in American society. Not wanting to admit to the brutality of the regime they ruled, Virginia slaveholders blamed the Nat Turner Rebellion on the inflammatory arguments coming out of New England.[4]

Turner's execution came on November 5, six weeks before Mary embarked on her first visit to a slave-holding region. In her diary Mary never explicitly mentioned Nat Turner or the broader political debates surrounding slavery—no doubt deferring to the rules of propriety that circumscribed female writing to "private" and domestic concerns. Yet in a year as charged as 1831, the themes of slavery and violence inevitably erupted through the surface of Mary's rather conventional descriptions of social gatherings, especially as rumors reached the American travelers of another revolt—the Jamaican insurrection known as the "Baptist War." While visiting the provincial town of Matanzas, Cuba, in January 1832, Mary wrote about "the insurrection in Jamaica, the news of which reached us a fortnight since," adding that "It seems the blacks have driven back the soldiers and there is every prospect of their ultimately obtaining possession of the island." Though mistaken in her prediction, Mary captured the sense of urgency and doom shared by slavery's supporters in the early 1830s. The aftermath of the Baptist War raged in Jamaica—Britain's most important Caribbean slave colony—through early February 1832, while the Lowells and their party were touring the slave districts of nearby Cuba. Eventually, news of the violence in the Caribbean would spread to England and fuel abolitionist lobbying that resulted in the British Emancipation Act of 1833.[5]

From the first news of the Jamaican insurrection through the end of her Cuban visit, Mary wrote in ever more detail about the living and working conditions of slaves, the mechanisms of discipline used by slaveholders, and the constant threat of violence that pervaded plantation life. With a kind of morbid fascination, she recorded in detail the stories she heard about attacks on white planters or overseers. Her husband's friend Mr. Griswold, an administrator on an American-owned plantation, had been assaulted in his sleep two months before the Lowells' arrival: "He was aroused by a slight noise in the next room about two o'clock in the morng when he received a blow" and was "left for dead." The Sages, her hosts on the Santa Ana coffee plantation, shared details of an insurrection that had occurred five years earlier in their area of Matanzas while they were visiting the United States. "It is probable both [Mr.] Sage & [his wife] Hepsy would have been murdered had they not been absent," wrote Mary in her diary, adding on the same page that she had "persuaded [her] husband to purchase a sword."[6] One night, the sound of screaming coming from the courtyard of her rooming house threw Mary into a panic: "The first idea excited in my mind by these sounds, as usual in Cuba when any thing out of the way happens at night, was that of insurrection, and I could not help feeling how defenceless we were without even a pistol to make a show of resistance."

Though not explicitly acknowledged in the diary, raging debates about the viability, morality, and future of slavery probably account for Mary's careful cataloging of plantation life and labor in a diary otherwise dedicated to more conventional "feminine" concerns. As Mary's worries about self-defense suggest, her curiosity about plantation life did not amount to a denunciation of slavery or an identification with the slaves' plight. As a member of one of Boston's most privileged families, Mary took for granted her right to enjoy a level of luxury and comfort that could be sustained only by the labor of others. In one diary entry, she describes a single breakfast offered by her hosts, the Wilsons, on the San Juan estate that included "roast turkey, oysters, omelet, apple pies, plantains, funche, cakes, tea & coffee." Just five days earlier she had described the weekly food rations offered to slaves on the same plantation: "four mackerel . . . plantains & some corn." Mary's accounts of her leisurely tourist routines—horseback riding, garden strolls, and evenings of card games or waltzing—also contrast starkly with her descriptions of the work regime in the sugar mills:

> It is perfectly marvelous to see how the negroes who skim the syrup can avoid scalding themselves and every one in their vicinity. It is as hot as fire can make it & is thrown up without any apparent caution; but I presume habit gives a slight of hand which renders the operation harmless; it is said the blacks are never scalded in this way. occasionally one drowns himself in a fit of despair or temper in the boiling liquid. Those who feed the mill with cane frequently injure their hands very severely between the rollers.

In fact, the solidly enforced social hierarchies of slavery seem to have represented one of Cuba's greatest attractions for expatriates from Jacksonian America, where revolutionary politics and frontier opportunities had eroded the old colonial norms of deference between poor whites and their social superiors.[7] Mrs. Williams, the sister of an American planter who owned three estates and over four hundred slaves in Cuba, assured Mary that "she considered the good servants one of the greatest advantages of living upon the island." As Mary reported to her diary, "Of course they require a steady hand and superintendance but when once you have established your authority but little discipline is necessary."

Mary's refined Bostonian gaze also provides rich insights into perceptions of national identity in the Jacksonian period. The new settlements in the Mississippi Valley appear to her nearly as strange and exotic as the streets of Havana, and she writes with the same curiosity—and sometimes distaste—about the customs of the middling folks who share with her the cramped quarters of the Mississippi steamboat. Writing about an evening of fiddle music, she describes one of the musicians in terms that reveal her disdain: "One of these *harmonisers* was the most ludicrous figure, he sat perfectly self satisfied, with his hat drawn down on one side & his black thick hair forming a bush on the other, with one foot drawn up on to the other knee and drawing his bow with an air of entire independance, stopping for nothing hit or miss." Overall, in fact, Mary seems to enjoy herself far more in Cuba—Spanish, colonial, slaveholding, and patriarchal—than she does in the rough, democratic frontier of her own young country. The American interior leaves her out of sorts. She loathes New Orleans, is dismayed by the muddy waters and muddier towns of the Mississippi, and writes with relief once her travels take her into Ohio, whose more picturesque and manicured landscape reminds her of home: "I bade adieu to the Mississippi with right good will. The scenery, throughout, has been extremely monotonous, and upon a second trip would be exceedingly uninteresting to me, indeed I think no small consideration would induce me to take the voyage again, although I am very glad to have seen the Father of waters for myself."[8]

Mary Gardner Lowell crossed many boundaries in her six months of traveling: between the Anglo-American and Spanish worlds, between abolitionist Boston and slave-owning Cuba, between the parlor and the sugar mill, between the refined East Coast American city and the new western and Caribbean hinterlands. Stories of arrogant Spanish men, shipwrecks, and slave revolts provided ripe material for the kind of vivid travel writing she achieved in this diary. The polite veneer of her formal style could not disguise the extent to which the experience had changed Mary, giving her a heightened sense of her place in the wider world. Yet we still might ask what would have prompted a young woman from one of Boston's leading families to forsake the luxuries of home and face such risks, especially with a toddler in tow. To answer this question and to make the most of this diary's rich insights we must view Mary within the webs of personal and social relationships that bound her Boston world to the slave plantations of rural Cuba and the river towns of the Mississippi.

THE COMFORTS OF HOME

Mary was born in 1802 into two intertwined families, which, in the course of her growth into adulthood, took their places at the center of a new and self-conscious Boston elite, a group whose aristocratic tastes and clannish loyalties would later win it the epithet "Brahmin."[9] Her own full married name—Mary Lowell Gardner Lowell—stands as evidence of the endogamous tendencies within the small group of families who made up her social circle. She was the second of six children born to Samuel Pickering Gardner (1767–1843) and Rebecca Russell Lowell (1779–1853). (The couple also raised an adopted daughter, Eliza Cabot Blanchard, after she lost her parents to tuberculosis in 1814.) Like most other families who rose to ascendancy in Boston in the decades following the War of 1812, both the Gardners and the Lowells were relative newcomers to the city and unconnected to Boston's colonial elite. Samuel Pickering Gardner hailed from a Salem sea trading family with long connections to the West Indian sugar and slave trades. Both Mary's paternal grandfather, John Gardner, and her uncle of the same name had been ship captains who plied the waters between the Caribbean slave islands during the 1700s, and as a young man her father had helped to run a trading house in Charleston, South Carolina, before settling in Boston in 1793.[10]

Mary's mother, Rebecca Russell Lowell, came from another line of seafaring merchants, originally based in Newburyport, Massachusetts, though the Lowells are now best remembered as pioneering American industrialists. Francis Cabot Lowell I, Mary's maternal uncle, introduced factory production to the United States in the 1810s after pirating and adapting designs for textile machinery he had observed while on a convalescence in Britain. Lowell's Boston Manufacturing Co., founded in 1813 in Waltham, Massachusetts, initiated the industrialization of American society, described by one American historian as "a transformation fully as dramatic as the one that swept across England in the half century prior to 1815."[11]

The history of Boston's early manufacturing elite usually conjures up the names of male entrepreneurs such as Francis Cabot Lowell, Nathan Appleton, and Patrick Jackson, and such masculine institutions as the Suffolk Bank, the Boston Athenaeum, and Harvard University. Yet, as the historical sociologist Betty G. Farrell has demonstrated, women such as Mary and her mother, Rebecca Russell Lowell functioned as crucial marriage brokers within this world where business relationships were "embedded in extended families, or broad kinship networks."[12] Successful family alliances ensured the success of Boston's earliest industrial ventures through the private financing provided by carefully chosen shareholders. Men related by birth or marriage invariably stocked the boards of directors overseeing the city's banks and enterprises. Thus, though the Lowell name remains most closely associated with early Massachusetts manufacturing, the Lowells' early alliance with the Gardner family extended the family's institutional network in the crucial period between 1820 and 1840.[13]

Mary further cemented her place within this powerful clan five years before her trip to Cuba by marrying her first cousin, Francis Cabot Lowell II, who was just one year her senior. Far from scandalous, this marriage between cousins followed a general pattern among the Lowells, especially while the family was consolidating its fortune in the early years of the nineteenth century: "[For] three generations the Lowell men seldom sought relaxation in female society outside the tribal boundaries," writes one family historian. "The weekly reunions at Bromley Vale [the estate owned by Francis Cabot Lowell II's uncle John], Colonnade Row, and Pemberton Square, or on Bedford, Park, and Beacon Streets [in newly fashionable Beacon Hill], gave the young men both their social and their sentimental education."[14] Thus, Mary and Francis (Frank) must have grown up in close contact from early childhood, and their marriage in 1826 demonstrated their adherence to family business and sentimental priorities. At the time of the Lowells' Cuba trip, twenty-eight-year-old Francis, by reputation a quiet and serious man, was already director of the Columbian Bank and of the Merchants Insurance Company and managed the family trusts and real estate holdings.[15] The couple's first child, Francis III, died in July 1830, before reaching his third birthday.[16] Their second son, George, was less than two years old when they all set out for Cuba in December 1831.

The importance of female domestic life and sociability within Beacon Hill helps to explain Mary's laborious accounting of visits, parties, and invitations in the diary. Among the Boston elite, "women's central role in their families was one of 'kin-keeping,' of keeping up the most meaningful social connections in the kinship network."[17] A constant routine of visits and social gatherings lubricated these relationships. Women managed and enforced loyalty within a huge kin group that included distant cousins and in-laws. They also helped to arrange marriages and ostracized any who broke the rules of decorum and courtship. (Readers will note Mary's gossip about the widow Mrs. Kilgore, who had been cut off by Cincinnati society after breaking off an engagement to become "Mrs. DeWitt.")

Such extended family loyalties were especially important to the great merchant-industrial families of Boston, whose far-flung trading networks sent relatives to manage affairs in outposts such as Cincinnati, New Orleans, Havana, Hamburg, St. Petersburg, and even Bombay.[18] Throughout her travels, Mary regularly received letters from her sisters and mother that kept her abreast of the most important deaths, births, and marriages back in the United States. As her sister Sarah reported to her by the mail from Boston, "Our cousin Miss Catharine Pickman is engaged to Mr Richard Fay brother to Harriet & it is said her sister has followed her example & is engaged to Mr Crowninshields second son. You are not acquainted with these young ladies, but as they are relations it is proper you should feel a laudable interest."[19]

Mary used her journal not only as a means to practice her skills at literary description and storytelling but also as a ledger in which to record the complex patterns of visiting and introductions that made up her social life. More than two hundred names appear in the diary; markers identifying family connections and professional distinctions or commenting on respectability accompany them all. These markers specify the subjects' place within Mary's upper-class peer group. Thus her party welcomed a Mr. Merrick, who was spending the winter in Havana for his health, because he was a former business partner to a close acquaintance. Mr. Lowber, of Philadelphia, was embraced as "a lawyer of some distinction & one of the first families in the place." The free-spirited young heiress Miss Bumstead joined the travel party in Cuba thanks to an introduction letter from her Boston physician, Dr. Jackson—probably Mary's cousin James Jackson, one of the founders of the Massachusetts General Hospital.

Ironically, Mary was better able to manage her social contacts in Cuba than in the United States. The Lowells traveled to the Caribbean with a party of close family and friends, with whom they kept up their regular social activities: teas, dinners, dancing, and card games. The group included William Gorham, whose family was connected to both the Lowells and the Gardners, as well as the Boston merchant David Sears Sr. and his two daughters, Harriet and Cordelia. Dr. Horatio Robinson of Salem, Massachusetts, a Harvard classmate of Francis Cabot Lowell II, also accompanied the Lowells, as did Richard S. Sullivan and his daughter Eliza, who were also related to Mary through her mother (and described in the diary as being connected to the "best society" in Havana).

The same rules that governed association with other travelers also put the Lowells in contact with prominent American families in Cuba. Mary's mother wrote her from Boston in February of 1832 that she and her husband had "walked to your uncle Lowell's this afternoon to procure a letter of introduction for you to Mr. Fellows."[20] That letter, and the Lowells' association with the well-connected Sullivan family, earned Mary and her husband entry to the huge Fellows estate outside Havana. Such connections drew Havana into the cozy, exclusive orbit of Beacon Hill and made even rural Cuba seem like a familiar world, where Boston's rules of decorum applied. Such comfortable routines broke down in the American leg of the journey, especially in the Mississippi steamboat journey and Mary's New Orleans hotel, which forced her into close quarters with "very second rate looking sort of men, probably shopkeepers and other men of business." In the newer settlements of the Mississippi and the cramped confines of the steamboat, the elaborate rituals controlling social contacts did not obtain, and genteel ladies of Mary's status could not shield themselves from contact with members of the middle and lower classes.

Domestic details also figure prominently in Mary's diary, once again indicating the extreme importance of home comforts and family routines in her own life. The women of Mary Gardner Lowell's social circle in Boston lived a life of extraordinary luxury and leisure by the standards of Jacksonian America, though their roles as caregivers and marriage brokers meant that they were no mere ornaments or parasites on their husbands' wealth.[21] When most Americans lived in undecorated clapboard houses of two or three rooms, Mary and her peers lived in mansions equipped with abundant gas lighting, adequate heating, elegant chandeliers, and large, amply furnished parlors for receiving guests. By the 1830s consumer goods such as manufactured carpets and wood stoves began to appear in middle-class homes, and the popularity of new domestic advice books indicated an incipient moral concern with domesticity. Yet virtually no one outside of neighborhoods like Beacon Hill could afford to live up to the ideal of the elegant home.[22]

Throughout her diary Mary evaluates her surroundings according to her own standards of domesticity, whether describing a plantation manor, a slave hut, or a homesteader's cabin on the Mississippi. In a letter to her sister Elizabeth, she writes with some surprise about the heavy domestic burdens faced by her hostess Mrs. Sage, an American planter's wife in Cuba, who shared with her counterparts in the American South a wide range of physical chores and responsibilities on the plantation:

> [Mrs. Sage's] time seems constantly occupied she is obliged to do all her own & her husbands sewing as well as that for the house negroes. She takes the entire direction of all family arrangements, visits and administers to all the sick slaves. She takes care of the poultry yard which is by no means a small affair upon a plantation makes her own preserves which are very delicious, knows the name, nature & use of every plant flower & tree on the estate and besides all her affairs has her house filled with company in the winter season.

Commenting on her first glimpses of American homes as her boat approached New Orleans, Mary writes: "We feel among old friends, now that we see thatched and shingled cottages and chimneys too to which our eye for the last three months has been entirely unaccustomed. Most of the small farmhouses have piazzas and present a picturesque appearance. It seems to me every where more regard is paid to the ornamental than in New England, where it is a very rare thing to see any thing like taste in the establishments of the lower orders." Like so many women writers of the nineteenth century, Mary exercises her authority by focusing on the interior and garden scenes that are most familiar to her even while attributing moral, cultural, and class values to the domestic arrangements she encounters.

Extended family trips like the one recorded in Mary's diary fit a common pattern within the "sea-going, well-travelled, and cosmopolitan [Lowell] family."[23] The drive for material success pushed most of the Lowell men to exhaustion and illness in the nineteenth century, forcing them to take extended convalescent breaks. In fact, as a young boy Mary's husband, Francis, had accompanied his own father on the trip to England and Scotland, where the senior Francis—a notorious workaholic—had spent his time studying textile mill machinery instead of resting. The most intrepid

Lowell traveler, Francis Cabot Lowell II's brother John, died in India in 1836 while on an epic journey to retrace Marco Polo's route to China—yet he undertook this trip alone while mourning the loss of his young wife and two daughters to scarlet fever.[24] Most of the Lowell clans confined their travels to the eastern and middle states or the mandatory grand tour of Europe.

By the 1830s Cuba was beginning to take its place as a healthy winter haven for wealthy Americans seeking to escape their work-filled lives as well as the diseases that plagued their cities. While the weakest visitors to the island sometimes found themselves confined to a Havana hotel, most, according to Mary's descriptions, appear to have sought refuge and sunshine on one of the plantations outside Havana and Matanzas. Tuberculosis ravaged even comparatively clean and healthy cities like Boston in the antebellum period, accounting for as many as one-quarter of the deaths in the Northern States. According to the historian Jack Larkin, "Probably no single disease accounted for more deaths before the Civil War."[25] From the perspective of the early twenty-first century, it is striking to note the way disease and death haunted even the sheltered world of Mary's upper-class peers. In 1830, just before Mary began this diary, she and Francis had lost their first child as well as Francis's brother Edward Jackson Lowell and sister-in-law Georgina Amory.[26] During their voyage to Cuba, through the winter of 1831–32, Mary received letters from Boston with news of an influenza epidemic attacking the city: "The influenza still prevails in town & has in some instances prov'd fatal," reported Mary's mother in December. "My three women have had it in different degrees. Lydia was quite sick—but has now recovered—Sarah & Eliza have as yet escap'd. Little Pelham Curtis is dangerously ill but to day the Dr has some hopes of him. Mrs Codman is dead & Miss Charlotte Perkins."[27] Alarmed by such accounts, Mary wrote home that the black sealing wax used by her sister Elizabeth on her correspondence, which could be taken as a sign of mourning in the nineteenth century, had "frightened me every time until the last when I had begun to be accustomed to it."[28]

The terror instilled by consumption and other contagious diseases accounts for the obsessive discussion of drafts and dews in Mary's diary, which might otherwise strike the modern reader as nothing but affectations of feminine frailty. "It is astonishing to see the imprudence of all the invalids who come here for their health," Mary complained in March 1832. "They expose themselves to hot suns & night dews, which are exceedingly heavy; & to every sort of fatigue." Several members of Mary's own traveling party had suffered from respiratory disease. The diary includes several mentions of a Mrs. Cunningham, a Boston acquaintance afflicted with tuberculosis, who arrived in Havana along with the Lowells in late 1831. Though Mary described notable improvements in her condition over the course of their Cuba visit, in the spring of 1832 she recorded news of Mrs. Cunningham's death during the arduous trip back to Boston. Mary's close traveling companion Eliza Sullivan, who also seemed revived by the air and exercise in Cuba, died within two years of her return home.

It was probably a sense of family obligation and fears of "exposure" that pushed Mary to accompany her husband to Cuba in the first place. Francis had traveled to Cuba alone on business once before, from March to early May of 1831. As he prepared for that earlier trip, Mary received a written scolding from her sister Elizabeth, who urged her to attend to her wifely duties and watch over her husband. Elizabeth herself had been exiled to Europe for her health, and she wrote with urgency to Mary: "I know my dear Mary, you will excuse the liberty I take. If it is *practicable* I would say go by all means with Mr. Lowell. I think you might find the expedition a very beneficial one. I should feel that there was much less danger to be apprehended from the severity of our own winter with home comforts & a wife to amuse him than from the great chances of a very great exposure to which he would be liable as a solitary traveller."[29] Elizabeth's wording appears to be deliberately cryptic, leaving us to wonder whether an element of sexual danger perhaps augmented the health risks facing a man left to his own devices in Cuba.

NEO-COLONIAL LANDSCAPES

As travelers, the Lowells formed part of a growing wave of migration between the United States and Cuba during the nineteenth century, when trade ties increasingly challenged the island's colonial loyalties to Spain.[30] In 1831 the Cuban-American relationship was still immature. Despite the American expatriate community's prominence in Mary's diary, the population of permanent North American residents on the island probably numbered no more than one thousand, and American interests could not yet claim to dominate the island's economy as they would in the latter half of the century.[31] In fact, business relationships between Cuba and the United States had only recently achieved some legal stability. For most of the fifty-five years since American independence, Spanish policy had wavered between permitting and banning trade between Cuba and the United States until Spain finally removed all restrictions on the island's foreign trade in 1818.[32]

Yet interconnected processes of economic transformation and growth —industrialization in the northeastern states, the expansion of slavery in the plantation belt running from the South to Cuba, and the opening of new frontiers on the island and in the North American interior—were already drawing Cuba and the United States together by 1831. As already noted through the history of Mary Gardner Lowell's own family, Boston stood at the epicenter of the industrial transformation of American life that began after the War of 1812. By 1831 the textile mills founded by Francis Cabot Lowell I on the Merrimack River had hundreds of smaller rivals throughout the Northeast. The paper and lumber industries also grew in the early nineteenth century, as did the number of grain mills and iron-works. Eastern cities such as New York and Philadelphia were developing complex and diverse industrial economies organized through factories, small-scale workshops, sweatshops, and home manufacturing. Labor struggles were also becoming a regular feature of the country's political life. Female textile workers and tailoresses had launched strikes in Dover, New Hampshire, and New York City in the previous five years, and the first Working Men's Party had been founded in Philadelphia in 1828.[33]

The strong demand for slave-produced sugar and coffee coming from the newly industrialized economies of western Europe and the United States drove Cuba's own economic boom in the first third of the nineteenth century. The island's elites profited enormously from the Haitian Revolution of the 1790s, a massive slave rebellion and anti-colonial war against France that had destroyed Haiti's export economy by the turn of the century. Surviving French planters had fled Haiti for nearby Cuba, taking their slaves, capital, and technical know-how with them, and Cuba's own fledgling plantation economy surged ahead in subsequent decades.[34] By 1831 Cuba was already challenging Jamaica to become heir to Haiti's status as the Caribbean's most successful sugar and coffee exporter.

Slave imports to Cuba multiplied through the early nineteenth century as local Spanish- and Cuban-born elites seized the opportunities offered by high international sugar and coffee prices and founded new plantations in the western end of the island. Scholars estimate that some 325,000 newly enslaved Africans were imported to the island between 1790 and 1820. Fully 100,000 of these arrived between 1817 and 1820 alone, when the Atlantic slave trade intensified in response to the end of the Napoleonic Wars and the signing of the first Anglo-Spanish treaty (1817), which threatened to abolish the trade. Pronounced imbalances of the sexes and brutal conditions kept Cuba's African population from reproducing itself. As Mary noted to her diary, "It is a rare thing to see a very old negro" in Cuba. The census of 1827 calculated the island's slave population at 286,942, with a sex ratio of 64 males to every 36 females. These slaves were divided roughly evenly into four sectors of the economy: sugar plantations *(ingenios)*, coffee farms, urban occupations, and miscellaneous other agricultural ventures, including cattle ranches and tobacco farms *(vegas)*.[35] Roughly 15,000 newly enslaved Africans had arrived in Cuba in the twelve months prior to Mary's arrival in January 1832.

For the Cuban planter class, fears of slave insurrection always tempered the thrill of sugar and coffee prosperity. Cuban elites never forgot the specter of Haiti, and successive Caribbean slave revolts in the first quarter of the nineteenth century instilled in them a kind of siege mentality, which is apparent in Mary's own diary entries. Economic expansion could be double-edged, since the new efficiencies brought by technical improvements in mill machinery and transportation only drove the demand for more slaves to do the brutal, unmechanized work of cutting cane. The 1827 census figures made amply clear to Cuban elites their own vulnerability as a slave-owning class, since the combined population of slaves and free people of color (286,946 and 106,494 respectively) considerably outnumbered the island's white population of 311,051.[36] In the newest plantation districts in the region of Matanzas, where the Lowells spent much of their visit, such ratios were even more pronounced, with African slaves alone accounting for somewhere between half and three-quarters of the population.[37]

Fear mixed with greed assured the Cuban elites' political conservatism and continued loyalty to the Spanish crown in the 1810s and 1820s, when, one by one, each of Spain's mainland colonies overthrew colonial control in a series of prolonged and savage wars for independence. By 1831 Spain had lost nearly all of its vast three-hundred-year-old American empire, which had spanned the continent from Mexico to the southern regions of South America; it retained only the islands of Puerto Rico and Cuba, which now earned the title "the ever-faithful isle." Yet in spite of its continued political ties to Spain, Cuba's economic priorities were already shifting northward to the nearby markets of the United States, which not only had a voracious appetite for Cuba's plantation products but also offered a greater range of foods and manufactures to Cuban buyers. In exchange for its sugar, cocoa, tobacco, molasses, and coffee exports, Cuba purchased textiles, casks, barrels, flour, rice, and other staples. These flowed into Havana harbor on American merchant ships that set sail from the ports of Boston, New York, Philadelphia, Savannah, and New Orleans. Just over six hundred American ships unloaded goods in Cuba in 1800, but by 1826 that number had nearly tripled to 1,702.[38]

Havana's growing wealth fueled frontier expansion into the Cuban interior. Matanzas had been cleared to make way for coffee and sugar in the four decades before Mary Gardner Lowell made her visit. The original impetus for developing this region's coffee and sugar sectors came from Havana-based planters who were well connected to Spanish colonial institutions. Yet American entrepreneurs had undertaken port improvements in Matanzas as early as 1809, and by the 1820s, as Spanish authorities tried to put down the independence movements on the mainland, American merchant ships dominated the city's import trade.[39] Mary's diary provides rare insights into the small number of American plantation owners who were also making inroads in Matanzas in the early part of the century, some of whom would become powerful players in the regional economy decades later.

Even at this early date in the long and intimate relationship between the United States and Cuba, Mary Gardner Lowell's diary brings to light stories of the many people who were knitting together a broad hinterland that ranged from the industrial North southward into the slave plantations of the Caribbean and westward into the new settlements of the Mississippi Valley. Already in the 1830s ambitious white Americans looked to Havana and Matanzas alongside New Orleans and Cincinnati as viable places to start new ventures, and Mary's gossipy accounts provide multiple insights into their choices. Her interest in domestic arrangements offers a unique perspective on the experiences of American women such as Mrs. Harper, who had opened a boardinghouse in Matanzas after finding herself stranded in Cuba a few years earlier. She and her husband had moved first from Philadelphia to New Orleans, where they had enjoyed a period "in good society" until her husband's business failed, whereupon they relocated to Cuba. Within a few years her husband died and left her "entirely destitute with several children." Following a pattern common to widows in the nineteenth century, Mrs. Harper turned to the role of landlady as one of the few respectable business options open to a woman of some social standing. She had recovered much of her wealth and prestige by catering to American business interests in Matanzas, as is proven by Mary's willingness to include her in the social activities of the Boston travel party.

The diary also stands as a reminder of the many business choices that knitted the free North to the slave-holding South and Caribbean islands, exposing as myth the idea of an open antagonism between free labor and slave interests in the antebellum period. Early Northern industrialists like Mary's husband, Francis Cabot Lowell II, also traded in tropical goods produced by slave labor, selling Cuban coffee and sugar in markets as far away as Hamburg and St. Petersburg.[40] Others, such as the brothers Gardiner Greene Howland and Samuel Shaw Howland of New York, built their fortunes as shipping merchants partly through this trade in slave-produced coffee and as investors in Cuban plantations. The powerful DeWolf family of Bristol, Rhode Island, who figure in the diary mainly as subjects of gossip, had been leading North American slave traders in the eighteenth century before they shifted their plantation investments to Cuba after 1800.

In the first decades of the nineteenth century, as ambitious white planters pushed Cuba's plantation territory eastward across the island, white settlers on the North American mainland "moved westward at an unprecedented speed, vigorously and often violently expanding the territorial limits of their society almost threefold."[41] By the spring of 1832, as Mary Gardner Lowell traveled up the Mississippi, that river had come to symbolize the other racial rift within Jacksonian political life—the territorial struggle between white settlers and American Indians. From the beginning of the century a combination of pressures from white migrants and government policies of warfare and Indian removal had been driving the native population of the United States westward. Whereas some 125,000 Indians lived in the east in 1820, by 1844 this number collapsed to roughly 30,000, with most eastern tribes relocated west of the Mississippi.[42]

Mary's river trip in 1832 coincided with one of the most infamous chapters in this long process—the controversy surrounding the passing of Andrew Jackson's 1830 Indian Removal Act. The act provided the federal government with the authority to consolidate its ad hoc efforts under a single relocation policy applicable to all eastern tribes, treating the displacement of the Indians as an inevitable fact that should be resolved once and for all. The Mississippi River was to be the line separating the territories of white and Native Americans. The act sparked widespread opposition and debate, particularly among supporters of the so-called civilized tribes like the Cherokee, who had adopted Christianity and the English language decades earlier. In February 1832, just before the Lowells began their Mississippi trip, the Supreme Court tabled a controversial ruling in favor of the Cherokee Nation's rights to maintain its territory in Georgia. Yet Jackson's political strength made the Court's ruling moot, and within three years federal troops moved against the "civilized" Cherokee, driving them across the Mississippi with other eastern tribes.[43]

On this struggle over land, ethnicity, and national identity, the diary is more telling for its silences than for its details. Though Mary demonstrates a curiosity about African-American racial identities as well as regional distinctions among "white" settlers in the United States interior, she betrays no interest in the American Indian presence in the Mississippi Valley. In fact, the only inkling of an indigenous presence in North America came near the very end of Mary's trip, when she stayed at an inn in Bedford, Pennsylvania. The owners had decorated the inn with crafts collected by their son-in-law, who had been employed as an Indian agent. "Here we had an excellent dinner," wrote Mary approvingly, "in a hall hung with Indian ornaments of various sorts, pouches, wampum belts, beautiful pipe stems decorated with feathers, swords, birch canoes & etc. all arranged with great taste." Following a pattern laid down a century earlier in the northeast, Mary viewed North American Indian identity as a relic of the past to be collected and displayed rather than as a vital issue of relevance to the nation's present and future.[44]

GENDER, AUTHORITY, AND IMPERIALISM

What of Mary's role as a writer? How can we discover her self-perception and her intentions in keeping this diary, and what significance, if any, should we attach to her perspective as a female traveler? We know for certain that she had been raised in a family that placed a high value on serious literature, apparently for girls as well as boys. One family history quotes a set of instructions prepared by Sam Gardner for his sons, urging them to "read with great attention, and more than once" the works of Herodotus, Polybius, Thucydides, and others. The same account describes Mary's mother, Rebecca Russell Lowell Gardner, as a woman of "intellectual tastes" who "tried to inspire the same in her grandchildren by rewarding them for committing to memory long speeches from Shakespeare, Milton,

&c."[45] Such rigorous training would account for the strength and clarity of Mary's writing.

Mary has left us some clues of her own that she was writing with a public in mind, which is not surprising given that travel letters and diaries at this time commonly circulated among intimate friends even when they did not make it to press. In the personal letters she wrote home from Cuba, she repeatedly urged her family members to keep her correspondence to themselves: "It seems almost like affectation to request all my correspondents not to show my letters out of the family or rather like vanity for it looks as if I thought them worthy of being shown but the truth is I should be so annoyed to have my scrawls seen by other people that I venture to make the request at the hazard of being charged with want of humility."[46] Such coyness was a typical convention of female writing in the nineteenth century, when women often apologized for presuming to take on the authority of the writer's voice.

Though Mary's voyage through the Caribbean and Mississippi Valley may have been quite unusual for her day, it does not necessarily follow that she was an exceptional or particularly liberated woman. As we have seen, she probably undertook the trip out of a sense of family obligation more than a yearning for adventure, even while she clearly delighted in many of her new experiences. She remained wedded to social and class conventions throughout her travels, making every effort to maintain the exclusionary rituals and formal decorum that governed her life at home in Boston. Moreover, as a wealthy white woman from Boston's trading and manufacturing elite, Mary herself was implicated in the very systems of labor exploitation and racism that she witnessed during her travels. She counted as her peers in Cuba the same American slaving interests with whom her husband did business, and in her descriptions of labor relations she tended to elide slavery and servitude, assimilating domestic slavery to the kinds of household hierarchies she was used to at home and diminishing the fact that slaves were human property.

Other circumstances blinded Mary to many aspects of the societies she visited on this trip. In Cuba, not only language barriers but also rules of etiquette limited her contacts mainly to the expatriate American business community. As a female visitor Mary could not even claim special insights into the cloistered world of elite Spanish women, who were prohibited from socializing with any foreigners, including even American women of her class. Mary was unique among female travelers writing about Latin

America in that she ventured into rural Cuba, where she came into contact not only with slaves and planters but also with members of the island's poor free population.[47] Still, without knowing Spanish, she remained an outsider, unable to communicate effectively with most of the people she encountered and prone to reproduce many stereotypes about Cuba's "indolent" women and "immoral" men. As noted above, class and racial prejudices and ideas about civility similarly colored Mary's perceptions of life in the American interior, which, even more than Cuba, she viewed mainly as a hurried tourist who clung to the limited comforts of the steamboat while looking forward to reaching home.

In spite of such caveats, unique patterns of emphasis do set Mary's account apart from many male travelers' descriptions and underscore the value of this source. Most obvious is Mary's interest in domestic and family matters, especially though not exclusively in relation to the early American community in Cuba. Whereas male travel writers tended to emphasize public matters of trade and diplomatic policy, as well as descriptions of public institutions and settings, Mary's most revealing insights pertain to personal and family concerns.[48] She displayed a surprising lack of discretion in many of her descriptions of the people she met, perhaps indicating the importance of gossip as a function of "kin-keeping" among the women of her class.

About the expatriate community in Cuba, Mary reported that "almost every man past the middle age of life in this part of the country (foreigners I mean, for the Spaniards are temperate) is addicted to the bottle and almost every individual is in debt." Her frankness stood in stark contrast to the circumspection of the one Cuban travel account that we know she had read, the Reverend Abiel Abbot's *Letters Written in the Interior of Cuba*, which Mary carried with her on her trip. Though Abbot had visited several of the same planter families as the Lowells, he avoided using full names in his letters and was careful to omit gossip. As he explained to one correspondent, "A hundred anecdotes may be very proper in fugitive and evanescent conversation, which are questionable, put down in indelible ink."[49] Thankfully for the contemporary reader, Mary ignored Abbot's warnings and reproduced in her diary stories about scandalous marriages, business deals gone bad, and violent revolts on slave plantations.

Whether or not this work did in fact circulate widely among Mary's peers in Boston, it is perhaps best understood within the context of nineteenth-century travel literature and specifically alongside travel accounts written by women. Virtually as soon as the Spanish colonies established their independence from Spain in the 1820s, descriptions of Latin America took their place as some of the most popular works within the lucrative genre of travel literature published in North America and Europe. Latin America was suddenly "opened up" to English-speaking businessmen and readers alike. Though Cuba's planter class remained aloof from the independence movements, as Spain lifted the island's shipping controls Cuba became a mandatory stopping-off point for foreign travelers to South America and "visitors to Cuba were among the most prolific contributors" to the travel writing genre.[50]

Though rare, the earliest women's travel descriptions of Latin America can be fruitfully studied alongside the first British women's accounts of the new imperial possessions in West Africa, Asia, and the South Pacific. In fact, according to the literary critic Mary Louise Pratt, by the time of Mary Gardner Lowell's trip to Cuba in 1831, "A literature was emerging to create a specifically female relationship to North European expansionism, a female domestic subject of empire, and forms of female imperial authority in the contact zone."[51] Mary's diary—with its intimate descriptions of domestic life, its slightly indiscreet gossip, and its exploration of gender, class, and racial interactions—can best be appreciated as an artifact of this specific historical moment and set of preoccupations.

By knitting together in one account the family and business networks that linked the mansions of Beacon Hill to the slave dwellings of Matanzas and the homesteaders' cabins along the Mississippi, Mary's diary helps us to understand the continuity of white American expansionism both westward and southward. Though the Caribbean could not yet be described as a neo-colonial extension of the United States, a kind of "American lake," the many personal stories that appear in Mary's diary remind us that individual ambitions and strategies for success would gradually build that neo-colonial relationship through the nineteenth century. In Mary's day family networks defined the economic ties between the industrial North and its hinterlands even more than government initiatives, and, as the diary amply illustrates, elite women played a key role in fostering such networks through their policing of social interactions and marriage practices.

Readers of the diary might also explore the gendered qualities of Mary's gaze as it scanned the landscapes of Cuba and North America. While Pratt defines male travel writers of the 1820s and 1830s as a "capitalist vanguard" who evaluated the Latin American terrain with a utilitarian eye to possibilities of exploitation and profit, Mary instead followed English romantic literary conventions by emphasizing the landscape's picturesque qualities.[52] The value she placed on domesticated nature—the formal garden as superior to either the "untamed" wilderness or the functional farm—shaped many of the contrasting descriptions in her diary. In Louisiana she complained that

> no regard whatever is paid to ornamenting the plantations, and we frequently pass those of great extent where there is not the slightest attempt at any cultivation except the raising of sugar cane, and the rudest fences divide the fields. This is particularly striking to us who have come from the splendid coffee estates of Cuba where for miles perhaps you may ride on the grounds of a private gentleman which present throughout the cultivation of a garden.

Though Mary may have been a fairly conventional matron of the Boston elite, she was anything but a conventional writer. As the reader will now discover, she wrote with fine precision, a critical eye, and a good dose of humor about her experiences throughout this trip. At each location she exercised her natural inquisitiveness, exploring not only matters of fashion, decoration, and etiquette, but botany, education, architecture, religious practices, and the living conditions of slaves and settlers. The diary reads as an intimate conversation directed perhaps to Mary's sisters, an invitation to share vicariously in her adventures. They demanded as much of her in their own letters. "I imagine you to be safely in harbor, several days since," wrote Mary's sister Sarah in early January 1832, "and I hope if it is in retrospection that you have now a store of hair breadth escapes to present to our wondering & horror struck imaginations."[53] As a writer Mary made every effort to oblige. One can almost picture the ladies gathered back in Boston, heads bowed over the pages, sharing in the diary's detailed descriptions, bits of gossip, and sarcastic asides.

NOTES TO INTRODUCTION

1. The historian June Hahner estimates that women writers penned only one in ten published travel accounts of Latin America in the nineteenth century, and most of the descriptions written by women appeared in the second half of the century with improved transportation and political stability. Hahner's bibliography of female travel accounts includes only a handful of works from the 1820s and 1830s. Mary Dundas Graham (Lady Calcott) published two volumes: *Journal of a Residence in Chile During the Year 1822 and a Voyage from Chile to Brazil in 1823* (London: Longman, Hurst,

Rees, Orme, Brown, and Green, and J. Murray, 1824) and *Journal of a Voyage to Brazil, and Residence There, During Part of the Years 1821, 1822, 1823* (London: Longman, Hurst, Rees, Orme, Brown, and Green, and J. Murray, 1824). Another early account is Flora Tristán, *Peregrinations of a Pariah, 1833–1834*, trans. and ed. Jean Hawkes (Boston: Beacon Press, 1986). See June E. Hahner, *Women Through Women's Eyes: Latin American Women in Nineteenth-Century Travel Accounts* (Wilmington, Del.: SR Books, 1998), xii–xiii. For a sample of another American woman's Cuba journal, see Claire M. Badaracco, "Sophia Peabody Hawthorne's Cuba Journal: Volume Three, 31 October 1834–15 March 1835," *Essex Institute Historical Collections* 118 (1982): 280–315.

2. Rev. Abiel Abbot, *Letters Written in the Interior of Cuba Between the Mountains of Arcana, to the East, and of Cusco, to the West, in the Months of February, March, April, and May, 1828* (Boston: Bowles and Dearborn, 1829), 215.

3. Mary Gardner Lowell to Mrs. J. C. Gray, St. Juan plantation, Camarioca, Feb. 12, 1832, Francis Cabot Lowell II Papers, box 2, folder 1832–1834, Massachusetts Historical Society (hereinafter MHS).

4. On Garrison and Turner, see Louis P. Masur, *1831: Year of Eclipse* (New York: Hill and Wang, 2001), 9–34.

5. Michael Craton, "Slave Revolts and the End of Slavery," in David Northrup, ed., *The Atlantic Slave Trade* (Lexington, Mass.: D. C. Heath, 1994), 211–17. See also Abigail B. Bakan, *Ideology and Class Conflict in Jamaica: The Politics of Rebellion* (Montreal: McGill-Queen's University Press, 1990), 50–67.

6. Detailed correspondence concerning this insurrection may be found in Ebenezer William Sage Papers, box 2, folder 1825, MHS.

7. Jack Larkin, *The Reshaping of Everyday Life, 1790–1840* (New York: Harper and Row, 1988), 13–31, 155–56.

8. On the rough masculine culture of the American interior and its impact on visitors from the East, see Elliott J. Gorn, "'Gouge and Bite, Pull Hair and Scratch': The Social Significance of Fighting in the Southern Backcountry," *American Historical Review* 90 (Feb. 1985): 18–43.

9. Oliver Wendell Holmes coined the term "Boston Brahmins" in his novel *Elsie Venner: A Romance of Destiny*, published in 1861; Betty G. Farrell, *Elite Families: Class and Power in Nineteenth-Century Boston* (Albany: State University of New York Press, 1993), 1.

10. Elizabeth Gardner Amory, "The Gardner Family of Salem and Boston" (typescript, June 1908), Gardner Family Papers, Ms. S-4, MHS.

11. Robert F. Dalzell Jr., *Enterprising Elite: The Boston Associates and the World They Made* (Cambridge: Harvard University Press, 1987), 3. See also Walter Licht, *Industrializing America: The Nineteenth Century* (Baltimore: Johns Hopkins University Press, 1995).

12. Farrell, *Elite Families*, 1.

13. Farrell, *Elite Families*, 68.

14. Ferris Greenslet, *The Lowells and Their Seven Worlds* (Boston: Houghton Mifflin, 1946), 113.

15. Farrell, *Elite Families*, 67.

16. Delmar R. Lowell, *The Historic Genealogy of the Lowells of America from 1639 to 1899* (Rutland, Vt.: Tuttle, 1899), 223. This first child is absent from published Lowell genealogies and family histories.

17. Farrell, *Elite Families*, 82.

18. Greenslet, *Lowells*, 214, mentions a branch of the Lowell family that had settled in Bombay.

19. S. R. G. [Sarah Russell Gray] to MGL, Dec. 23, 1831, Lowell II Papers, box 2, folder 1831.

20. R. R. Gardner to MGL, Boston, Feb. 11, 1832, Lowell II Papers, box 2, folder 1832.

21. Farrell, *Elite Families*, 79.

22. Larkin, *Reshaping of Everyday Life*, 131–48.

23. Greenslet, *Lowells*, 113.

24. Greenslet, *Lowells*, 199–214.

25. Larkin, *Reshaping of Everyday Life*, 79.

26. Mary's line-a-day diary for the year 1830 includes the following poem, probably dedicated to the child she had lost:

> Joy leads to communion with man who
> can share it; Grief to communion with God who alone can relieve
> it.
> Though my soul's hope hung on thy breath
> Thou to so bright a world art gone
> I would not make thee, sweet from death
> Tho loved in life. Sleep on. Sleep on.

Mary Gardner Lowell, "Line-a-Day Journal and Almanac," 1830, Lowell II Papers, box 2.

27. Rebecca Russell Lowell Gardner to MGL, Dec. 18, 1831, Lowell II Papers, box 2, folder 1831.

28. MGL to Eliza Blanchard, Camarioca, Cuba, March 4, 1832, Lowell II Papers, box 2, folder 1832–1834.

29. E. H. [?] Gray to Mary Gardner Lowell, n.d., Lowell II Papers, box 2, folder 1831.

30. On the growing relationship between Cuba and the United States in the nineteenth century, see Louis A. Pérez Jr., *Cuba and the United States: Ties of Singular Intimacy* (Athens: University of Georgia Press, 1990) and *On Becoming Cuban: Identity, Nationality, and Culture* (Chapel Hill: University of North Carolina Press, 1999).

31. The North American population in Cuba numbered 1,256 in 1846 and rose to 2,500 by 1862. Cuba, Centro de Estadistica, *Notas estadisticas de la isla de Cuba, en 1862* (Havana, 1864), cited in Pérez, *Cuba and the United States*, 19.

32. Pérez, *Cuba and the United States*, 5–13.

33. Licht, *Industrializing America*, chapter 2.

34. For a discussion of the impact of the Haitian revolution on Cuba's plantation economy, see Manuel Moreno Fraginals, *The Sugarmill: The Socioeconomic Complex of Sugar in Cuba, 1760–1860*, trans. Cedric Belfrage (New York: Monthly Review Press, 1976).

35. On slave imports through the turn of the nineteenth century, see David Eltis, *Economic Growth and the Ending of the Transatlantic Slave Trade* (New York: Oxford University Press, 1987), 245. For the 1827 figures, see Francisco Dionisio Vives, *Cuadro estadístico de la siempre fiel isla de Cuba correspondiente al ano de 1827* (Havana: Imprenta del Gobierno y de la Capitania General, 1829). Estimates on the distribution of the slave population are drawn from Laird W. Bergad, Fe Iglesias García, and María del Carmen Barcia, *The Cuban Slave Market, 1790–1880* (Cambridge: Cambridge University Press, 1995), 27.

36. Louis A. Pérez Jr., *Cuba: Between Reform and Revolution* (New York: Oxford University Press, 1988), 86. Pérez's figures for 1827 are adapted from Ramón de la Sagra, *Historia económico-política y estadística de la isla de Cuba* (Havana: Imprenta de las Viudas de Arazoza y Soler, 1831).

37. Laird W. Bergad, *Cuban Rural Society in the Nineteenth Century: The Social and Economic History of Monoculture in Matanzas* (Princeton: Princeton University Press, 1990), 33.

38. Pérez, *Cuba and the United States*, 13.

39. Bergad, *Cuban Rural Society*, 59.

40. For examples of such transactions see Lowell II Papers, box 2, and Sage Papers, box 2.

41. Larkin, *Reshaping of Everyday Life*, xiv.

42. Michael Paul Rogin, *Fathers and Children: Andrew Jackson and the Subjugation of the American Indian*, 2d ed. (New Brunswick, N.J.: Transaction Publishers, 1991), 4.

43. On Indian removal see Rogin, *Fathers and Children*; Masur, *1831*, 115–35.

44. See Ruth B. Phillips, *Trading Identities: The Souvenir in Native North American Art from the Northeast, 1700–1900* (Seattle: University of Washington Press, 1998).

45. Elizabeth Gardner Amory, "The Gardner Family," 51–52.

46. MGL to Mrs. J. L. Gardner, St. Juan plantation, Camarioca, Feb. 12, 1832, Lowell II Papers, box 2, folder 1832–34.

47. See Hahner, *Women Through Women's Eyes*, xix.

48. The reader might contrast Mary's diary with the widely available account written by the American traveler Joseph Dimock two decades later. See Louis A. Pérez, ed., *Impressions of Cuba in the Nineteenth Century: The Travel Diary of Joseph J. Dimock* (Wilmington, Del.: Scholarly Resources, 1998).

49. Abbot, *Letters*, 187.

50. Louis A. Pérez Jr., ed., *Slaves, Sugar, and Colonial Society: Travel Accounts of Cuba, 1801–1899* (Wilmington, Del.: Scholarly Resources Press, 1992), xxv.

51. Mary Louise Pratt, *Imperial Eyes: Travel Writing and Transculturation* (London: Routledge, 1992), 170.

52. Pratt, *Imperial Eyes*, 146–55; Elizabeth A. Bohls, *Women Travel Writers and the Language of Aesthetics, 1716–1818* (Cambridge: Cambridge University Press, 1995).

53. Sarah Russell Gray to MGL, Jan. 2, 1832, Lowell II Papers, box 2, folder 1832–1834.

EXPLANATION OF EDITORIAL METHOD

In the transcription of the diary, every effort has been made to remain as close as possible to the original manuscript and to keep annotations to a minimum. Spelling has not been modernized. Square brackets in the text indicate words whose spelling is unclear in the original or offer corrections of misspelled words only in cases where meaning is unclear. Angle brackets indicate parts of the text that are lost or unreadable as well as the location of blank pages and light pencil sketches in the diary. Contractions have been left in their original form except for rare cases, which are clarified in an endnote. Words crossed out in the original manuscript have been omitted, and all superscripts have been brought down to the line. Punctuation has been left in its original form, with the exception of the dash-like marks used frequently in the diary, which have been deleted or modified as commas or periods to clarify meaning. In other cases, periods have been added only when the diarist has used the edge of the page as a sentence stop, which was also a common practice in the nineteenth century. No other punctuation marks have been added to the text. Paragraph breaks have been introduced at logical intervals in longer diary entries. Dates have also been added to entries when these are absent or unclear for periods of over two weeks. Endnotes contain additional information on literary works, persons, or places mentioned in the diary; corrections of unclear or mistaken date entries; comments or symbols added to the diary in a different hand; explanation of contractions that have been modified. A separate biographical key provides more detailed information about the principal characters mentioned in the diary. Unfamiliar terms or words in Spanish are defined in the glossary.

The Diary

1832

March 15th Thursday. This morning I had a better opportunity of looking about the place than yesterday, having in some degree slept away my fatigue. The house is situated rather low with hills on all sides; the boheas in a semicircle on one side have a very comfortable appearance; a small house is appro-priated to the children too small to work and there you may see from ten to twenty little creatures enjoying themselves under the charge of an experienced negress. I was invited to look at a pair of twins a few days old, the drollest little creatures imaginable and a rare sight among the blacks— Some buildings, the stables &c occupy the centre of the yard; the volante house, coffee mill, Mayorals rooms &c being attached to the house. Opposite the back piazza is the hospital, a building indispensable on all large plantations, underneath which are store rooms, ironing room and kitchen. On the other side the house the coffee dryers extend a long distance giving the idea of large crops — At the further end, up the hill, is the hen house, quite a large building. — Mrs Jenckes says she sends to her son an hundred eggs every week; the fowls are examined each morning and those which are going to lay kept confined until after dinner when they are suffered to roam at large — Two pigeon houses stand in front of the hen establishment and the flock is immense indeed — we have found plenty every where, Mr Sage I believe has two or three thousand. — The large bell which is rung at stated intervals stands on one side; near the house is a small kitchen garden

Diary entry for March 15, 1832. Mary Gardner Lowell Diary, March 15–June 3, 1832. Francis Cabot Lowell Papers II, vol. 78. Courtesy of the Massachusetts Historical Society.

December 18th 1831, Set forth with my husband, little George & nurse (Lorenza Stephens) upon my travels. Left my Fathers house about 11 o'clock in the morning and came on board the ship Coliseum, Captn Windsor, where we found Mr Sears & family consisting of two daughters & two servants already established. W. Gorham had also preceded us. Mr Gorham, Mr Bowen, W. [P.] Mason, W. Amory, Papa and George came on board to bid us farewell. We had a very smooth sail out of the harbour but the weather was so intensely cold I could not remain long enough on deck to observe the city as we left its shore. I was glad to seat myself by the little cabin stove which burned extremely well and gave no trouble on account of smoke; this comfort however was soon denied us all, for at two o'clock we bid adieu to each other and retired to our berths where we were soon inclined to wish ourselves at home.

I was quite sea sick for two or three days & feverish as many more. Cider & hot lemonade during this time were more acceptable than any other nourishment. Papa's cider I found peculiarly good and his St. Germaine pears were relished by every person on board. To my infinite surprise the baby was sick, very much so for one day & languid & disposed to lay in his berth until Saturday when he went upon deck a short time. It was happy for the poor little fellow that he was ill as he would have been entirely left to his own resource, had he been able to run about for Lorenza, most unexpectedly to herself, was almost unable to lift her head and Mr. Lowell, being more sick than upon any former voyage, could only occasionally get out of his berth to see that we were not suffering. This extreme illness he attributed to a previous indisposition of the last few weeks. William Gorham made a pretty good sailor being able to keep on deck most of the time. Mr Sears did not leave his state room for several days, and the young ladies not 'till the Sunday. (Christmas day) The first part of our passage was extremely rough & the ship a slow sailor, her last passage to Havana was 32 days, she possesses the advantage, however, of being a remarkably sweet vessel & has a fine deck.

Saturday I crawled upon deck for an hour or two, during which time it was raining. I was enveloped in my cloak & hood & enjoyed the fresh air. Sunday morng the Steward wished us a "merry Christmas" and after dressing for the first time since I came on board I joined the Miss Sears's on deck. Although I had not felt sea sick for several days, lying in my berth, yet the exertion of sitting up made me frequently so. I still could not bear to relinquish the fine air, besides our cabin was undergoing the act of scouring, an ablution it greatly needed. After a short time Mr Sears had some oysters opened & a plate of Mother's gingerbread was produced. I sat up until quite exhausted and then lay down on a mattress at one corner of the deck & remained there until night obliged me to return again to the close cabin. Mr Sears brought with him some brown bread which we all found extremely good and I would never again go to sea without it. This eveg Mr Jacksons cheese was produced & much liked. Our principal variety in life has hitherto been in the change from one sort of diet to another. I read through the 2nd volume of the Bravo[1] while I lay in my berth & now anticipate better things.

Monday morng. To day came in with rain which soon cleared away & I resolved to rise & go upon deck but afterwards determined to remain in my berth feeling most miserably; it showered again in the course of the afternoon. Mr Lowell and Miss Harriet Sears played a game of piquet. Little George fretful. This evening as I lay in my berth, I heard the Captn talking at the tea table with the gentlemen about St. Petersburg where he was last year during the time the cholera raged there; he said it was thought to be the India cholera as far as the difference of climate permitted and was not considered contagious. He said it was attributed to the wind, which had blown constantly from the east for three months, and the want of rain. It was so very dry that in sailing up the Baltic the shore could not be discerned more than in a thick fog; the water of the Baltic at this time had a most peculiar appearance Captain Windsor frequently sounded thinking himself on a shoal, the water had so shiny, muddy an appearance; it resembled exactly our shores where they wash fish before they are laid on the flats. A day or two before he left the wind changed to the west & the cholera abated. Excessively hot in our cabin tonight. Began Anne of Geierstein.[2]

Tuesday. Lovely weather. The baby was on deck all day with no covering upon his arms & neck, he has been very happy. I was sea sick got upon deck where I lay on a matress all day eat a few grapes which made me more sick, & sent some of Elizabeths quince jelly to the Miss Searss' which proved very nice. Miss Harriet came & talked with me very agreeably as I lay in my little corner I was unable to read much. George when undressed for the night seemed to have an attack of cramp in his foot, he continually screamed out & drew up his foot we rubbed it with [apedildoc] and in a few minutes he was relieved we attributed it to the exertion he made in attempting to walk on deck. To day the thermometer has stood at '72.

Thursday Faint in the morng. I felt miserably all day & did not go upon deck. Head winds & heavy sea. The Capt says hardly one voyage in an hundred in these latitudes is so rough. It has been excessively hot in the cabin. Read a little.

Friday. Lay upon deck until eveg I find no exertion will conquer the miserable feeling which possesses me when I attempt to move. this sea sickness is by no means agreeable. Finished Anne of Geierstein. Saw to day a sailor washing his clothes in a novel manner, he threw them down on one side of the deck where the sea water had washed in &, having his shoes on, jumped up & down upon them. Once or twice he took one of them up & rubbed for a moment with his hands, but the greater part of the ablution was performed with his feet.

Saturday. Delightful weather, trade wind as mild as summer. I lay upon deck all day feeling extremely well when not sitting up. Read Tremaine.[3] At tea (from my little nook) heard the gentlemen talking about dishes. Capt said the liver of the cod fish was a great delicacy, very rich; it is impossible to keep it more than three hours & in consequence is little known; it is usually thrown into barrels when the fish is taken and becomes oil. Mr Sears remarked that the comb of the cock made a fine dish, it is only cooked at one place in Boston, the Tremont house. In France they possess either the art of artificially swelling them or the fowls have them of larger size. Capt said in Genoa he had seen fowls with combs of immense size.

Sunday January 1st 1832. Lay upon deck all day the weather so warm as to require nothing thrown over me. I read a little in Abbot's Cuba.[4] Kept baby with me at night in consequence of Lorenza's having the sick headach. it was excessively warm we actually suffered from heat.

Monday Lorenza still ill. Mr Lowell came into my state room in the morng and informed me that we had received signals from a ship in distress and were making preparations to render her assistance. By the time I reached the deck she was entirely in sight and proved to be a schooner bound from Nassau, an English Island, to New York. She had been within 12 miles of Sandy Hook and had been blown off the coast in a gale of wind and obliged to scud back again before the wind the crew had been forced to keep the pumps going night & day she filled so fast & this morning her rigging had been laid flat and only one mast remained which was split so that it was impossible for her to get back to Nassau. We took 9 men from the wreck. 5 of them blacks one a New York pilot who had been taken from a wreck by this same vessel. They brought nothing on board but their chests and trunks of clothes. Two of the men were passengers one a man by the name of Stetson a merchant of New York the other an Irishman who had been overseer upon some plantation & was returning with the intention of taking passage to his own country. These men informed us they had left about 500 dollars worth of goods in the cabin of the wreck which would have belonged to our ship had the Capt thought it best to stop for it; but he said it would be so cut up that each share would be small and that the delay would be three or four hours. We regretted some fine fruit they were taking to New York the vessel was laden with salt and would have found a good market. We observed a bark which was behind us stop and she probably made all these things her prize. The poor captain of the lost ship slept but little at night he was greatly troubled at the idea of returning to his owner (Mr. Wildgoose) without his ship. Nassau is a famous place for shells and they have the art there of making them up into most beautiful ornaments of various descriptions. The New York pilot shewed us an extremely pretty wreath for the head composed entirely of small white shells and which had much the effect of pearls. Being near the "hole in the wall" a place we have long hoped to see the Captain thought it prudent to lay by tonight there being no moon.

Tuesday. Warm rain all day. Made little progress five and twenty miles perhaps. Saw land at a distance; lay by again at night. Almost a dead calm thermometer in the cabin at tea time 74°. Mr Sears says on the 1st of January it was near 80° on deck. To day William Gorham made a discovery among his stores which were extremely acceptable. Baby in better humour today. He finds it very tedious to be obliged to sit still all day and we are afraid to let him walk about the deck lest the strain upon his limbs should occasion cramp.

Wednesday. Passed hole in the wall before I was up.

Thursday. We made considerable progress in the morning but the Captain finding we were getting into the gulf Stream was obliged to return to the place we left when we first began to move in the morng; he was in a great fume and chastised one of the sailors who stood at the helm. I could not understand what was the man's misdemeanor but he at length displeased the Captain to such a degree as to be sent forward. To day we have had a shower but the weather so mild I lay on deck during the whole of it. The mate caught a <*illegible*> which was pronounced very fine & we had soup for dinner made of a turtle translated from the wreck, & which was well enough concocted to have charmed Mr Trueman. I did not go down stairs until after nine in the eveg & had no outer garment excepting a cloak thrown over my feet; the scene was extremely pleasant the moon appeared as a crescent & the stars most brilliant. The Captain says he never before, in any part of the water, has experienced such cold weather in these latitudes as now. He has not usually been able to wear a thick coat upon deck. To us it is almost oppressively warm but we have come from the frigid zone. I was interested this eveg in observing the little bright spots resembling sparks of fire caused by the motion of the vessel through the water.

Friday. Extremely warm, thermometer 80° on deck. we sailed four or five knots an hour, passed the Bemini Islands on our left, near enough to be cheered by the sight of the green fields and trees. There is but one house upon them, the abode of wreckers and fishermen. We today saw several porpoises and one turtle who with head aloft seemed to be taking an observation. The Captn observed he was so far from land he had probably lost his reckoning. We have not yet met with any whales. For some distance this morng the bottom was distinctly visible and the water of a most beautiful shade between blue & green.

This afternoon Capt Windsor hoisted our flag with the hope of inducing a wrecker to approach & take off Capt Young & crew who wished to go to Nassau but one signal produced no effect and we were obliged to discharge our canon three times when four schooners engaged in the wrecking business came in sight in hopes, I presume that we were sufficiently in distress to need their kind assistance & help in disposing of our goods. One bore down to meet us and upon learning our wish dispatched two boats to relieve us of our burthen. The whole scene was most picturesque the sailors in the schooner the "Favorite" of Nassau, were all in the most graceful attitudes, dressed in white; one would think they had studied effect. These small vessels are constantly cruising about in search of wrecks. The law allows them half the cargo they save, the remainder belongs to the owner. The Captain said his brother had just made 4000 dollars in the business, he also told us that three New York vessels bound to New Orleans had just been stranded and although not entirely lost forced to put into port for repairs. So that, in these troubled times, we may esteem our lot a fortunate one. After we had dispatched Captn Young & his men all of whom except the three passengers left us, another wrecker came alongside & asked Captn Windsor for news who related what he had just done; the whole crew were as swarthy as Indians, dressed in white, with large straw hats. The negroes in the first schooner seemed to recognise those on board our ship and welcomed them with a laugh & grin. I was quite surprised to find George's serenity unruffled by the canons he seemed only amused which I consider quite an advance on the road to courage.

To day we fished up some gulf sea weed quite unlike that near shore, the color brown and filled with small shells. This evening has been most delightful, the moon shining on the waves and Jupiter almost rivalling her in brilliancy. We have had no remarkably fine sunsets the sun having usually, when the weather has been good, sunk into the ocean in an unobtrusive manner leaving only a bright light behind him. The sky has been unusually free from clouds.

Saturday Very hot. We have today seen great numbers of flying fish and one or two large men of war birds who followed the ship most gracefully; the plumage of this bird is jet black with the exception of the head & breast which are white. Their claws are formed to grapple with the rocks where they live. They probably subsist upon fish.

Sunday. Fine day. While I lay in my berth I heard the mate & others talking about sharks, he related an anecdote of a boy on the western coast of S. America, a native, who was fishing; a shark got hold of his bait and made off line and all. The boy retained his grasp and followed out to sea until at length the shark snapped the rope & the boy came crying back to land because he had lost his line. The wind today having been unfavorable we did not come in sight of land until sundown, we now have the pleasing anticipation of arriving tomorrow saw today a nautilus upon the surface of the water the sailors call it a "Portuguese Man of War" The sun set beautifully this evening and the night has been most brilliant. The thermometer in the middle of the day stood at 80° and our suffering from heat was so severe we were greatly surprised to find it no higher.

Monday. A pleasant day, the sun being obscured which our friends at the north would hardly realize as a desirable circumstance on the 9th of January. We have been in sight of Cuba the greater part of the day.

<drawing>

The green fields and trees were a most cheering sight for us. About sunset we were opposite Havana but the Captn thought it not prudent to enter the harbour until morng as the navigation is dangerous.

<drawing>

We have been out 22 days. I trust tomorrow will see us well housed. I think the voyage would have been pleasant to me had my health been as good as on shore.

Tuesday Every person on board was busy at an early hour in preparation for departure from our prison house. Lorenza was so much occupied in packing that I could not have her assistance in dressing and was obliged to remain in my berth until the ship had passed the Moro, a circumstance I regretted as it is a scene well worth witnessing. I came upon deck just after the custom house officers were there, and never shall I forget the astonishment & delight experienced at the scene which burst upon my view. Every thing buildings, trees, boats, men, costumes, were unlike any I had before seen; the whole had the effect of magic. On one side the city with the shipping drawn up to the wharves and strange figures of every sort. On shore, on the other buildings of fanciful forms intersperced among the trees producing the most picturesque view. The Moro castle & fortifications of the Cabanas standing about an eighth of a mile apart occupy a conspicuous situation at the entrance of the harbour. Directly under our bows were the barges of the custom house officers rowed by marines in the service of government (twelve to each boat) in an uniform of white drilling with blue collars, faced with blue at the pocket holes & round the ankle and black hats with a black ribbon band and long ends carefully tied on one side I was particularly struck with the extreme neatness of their dress the boats resemble the pictures I have seen of Italian gondolas having an awning at one end covered with blue cloth with seats & cushions for the gentlemen.

<drawing>

The boat men resting upon their oars surveyed us in the true Spanish style none of them were blacks, the deck was crowded with officers of Custom house very civil looking gentlemen. We were informed the Grotius had arrived three days since and that our names had already been in the papers as expected. Our friends here in consequence of the length of our passage had experienced some anxiety respecting our welfare & had at length come to the conclusion we had struck upon the bank and should be taken off by a wrecker.

We were delighted to hear Mr Sullivan had arrived and he soon himself appeared on board and brought the pleasing intelligence that Eliza had taken no cold in the journey to Charleston & was much improved since her arrival in Cuba; they had a voyage of eight days. Left Mrs Derby quite ill she said, however, that to save her life she would not take the sail to Havana. Mrs Rogers was also there very much out of health, but extremely imprudent in going out she likewise refused to come. William Swett soon appeared under the stern of our ship in a boat. Said he was quite well and enjoyed himself more than last year. After a slight delay we were deposited in a barge sent for us and in a few moments landed at a wharf covered with a roof as (indeed) were all I saw, and filled with men of various ranks all dressed in white drilling pantaloons white vests & coats of various colors. Among gentlemen black hats universal and most of them smoking vehemently A soldier stood at the landing place with a drawn sword the hilt in one hand & point in another Mr Lowell said he presumed it to be a mark of respect to the ladies. We were packed into two volantes, (the most singular affairs hereafter to be described) and a few minutes ride brought us in view of the gouvernor's square a beautiful garden filled with trees and flowering shrubs, roses, pomegranites, &c. We had no leisure to examine any thing all struck us as new & most marvelous. The people as they sat in their shops seemed very sociable and nodded and smiled as we passed.

We stopped at Mrs Howard's where we found lodgings engaged for us by Mr Sullivan, himself & Mr Sears being forced to go to another house to sleep; the entrance is through a courtyard and the house built in the Old Spanish fashion with rooms round the square opening upon a gallery We were shewn in to a fine dining room very large and extremely lofty, the floor a sort of plaster painted; much in use here, the walls white with a painted border, the ceiling which became pointed in the centre taking the form of the roof of wood pannelled or carved; from a gilt ornament in the middle was suspended a lamp. The furniture two sideboards fitted into corners with marble slabs covered with porcelain & cut glass, a sofa, chairs tables & col'd prints in frames (the death of Priam and the scene in which Coriolanus is besought by his family to return). Here we found Eliza Sullivan looking extremely well, to me, who had not seen her since her illness she appeared almost in her usual state of health. Our accommodations here are exceedingly good Eliza's room opens with folding doors into the dining hall & in the same manner on the balcony in front of the house which faces a large tobacco factory divided from us by a street not more than <*word missing*> feet wide; on the other side the Miss Searss chamber communicates with double doors mine opens into theirs in the same manner and the baby Isabella & Lorenza occupy the next. After talking with Eliza a while and eating dinner, I borrowed of her pen ink & paper and wrote letters to Papa and Elizabeth quite lengthy epistles and after tea one to Mrs Rogers to go tomorrow by a vessel to sail for Charleston. I was agreeably welcomed on my arrival by a short letter from G. P. Gray, brought by Dr. Robinson of Salem who sailed a few days after us, it informed me that Mother was recovering from influenza & that all other friends were well; there is no pleasure so great in travelling as that which proceeds from the perusal of letters from home; what we should there consider the most insignificant incidents, become very important. I went to bed at twelve o'clock and, suffering from the effects of too strong a cup of tea, lay awake the greater part of the night listening to the coughing of Mr Burke, a sick gentleman in the next room, the stamping of the horse and to a cock which crowed most unseasonably every half hour. I have always before regarded Chanticleer as the harbinger of morning but by a strange perversity the strain of this gentleman ceased only with the dawn.

January 11, 1832

Wednesday Eliza Sullivan has not appeared so well today, she apparently suffers from over fatigue and excitement yesterday. This morng we took Mrs Howards volante and drove to the warm bath where we found neat & commodious rooms and were well served. We were obliged to have recourse to the language of signs having no one to interpret for us. Having left my apartment sooner than the other ladies I took a chair in the yard & amused myself in observing the scene around me; at a window sat a bevy of fair dames smoking cigars, one or two of them certainly not more than twenty years of age all with heads crowned with the most immense shell combs, indeed I have not seen a woman or child (above the rank of a common laborer) white or black who has not been adorned with an enormous piece of tortoise shell, some of these combs are beautifully cut and very costly.

After conveying the young ladies home I went in pursuit of Eliza

Sullivan who had gone to visit Mrs John Cunningham, who is here extremely ill. I fortunately encountered Mr Lowell on my way who jumped into the volante and saved me some awkwardness as the calesero from some misapprehension of my direction carried me to the wrong boarding house (Mrs Lloyd's) where I marched directly up stairs and should have followed Eliza's instructions to enter the first chamber on the left, had we not met the landlady, and Mr L. knowing her, enquired for Mrs Cunningham we were informed she was at Madam Rouilliets whither we bent our steps; her house seemed to me vastly inferior to Mrs Howards although it is said, on account of its locality, to command a higher rent. Mrs Howard pays two thousand five hundred dollars a year, two of the lower apartments she lets again one to a barber & the other for some other purpose. For these I believe she receives about fifty dollars a month.

Mrs Cunningham seemed to me very ill, she has no nurse but her daughter a little girl of twelve who appears extremely discreet and capable for her years; she accompanied her mother to Brazil some time ago and at that time learned to depend much upon herself and now she is extremely devoted to her sick parent. Mrs Cunningham desired me to say (if I mentioned her in any of my letters home) that she was better; she was fearful her friends might become anxious about her. In the afternoon Mr Cunningham called with his daughter to see us. After his departure I intended to have written a long letter to go by a vessel which will sail tomorrow for Boston but was prevented by the arrival of my baggage from the ship, some of it, particularly my band box so abused by the porters as to require immediate attention, and I had only time to scribble a few lines to Sarah. My equanimity was assailed on opening the bandbox for I found the Steward had placed a jar of preserves among my fine ruffles which had (in consequence of the various revolutions it performed in its trip from the ship), been broken to pieces and the syrup was meandering gracefully through my finery. I vented my wrath in an ebullition of scolding for which I felt much better and repaired the evil as far as possible.

After tea I accompanied the Miss Searss & the gentlemen to the Square to hear the fine band which performs every Wednesday evening. Ladies of rank usually ride there in volantes and walk in the garden until nine o'clock when the music ceases; this evening, however, only the more common sort of people were seated on the benches or lounging about for the black clouds and occasional sprinkling of rain confined the high bred dames to their houses. Those females who were there seemed to disregard the weather although their dresses were ill prepared to contend with the elements. Thin muslins and short sleeves are universally worn here. I could hardly realize that I was actually standing against a hedge of limes and on the 11th of January was exposed with head uncovered in the open air surrounded by roses and other beautiful plants in full bloom. A heavy cloud obliged us to seek shelter under the portico of the Intendant's house where we sat comfortably upon a bench listening to the band environed with Spaniards of every description chattering like so many magpies. I fancy our right to remain where we were was at least doubtful for we were very closely eyed by the guard upon watch and indeed, as far as we understood, ordered to depart but some gentlemen near, seeing us rise to obey the command, interfered and by signs requested us to keep our seats. A few ladies were also under the portico, besides ourselves, but we were induced to imagine from the smallness of the number that they were members of the Intendant's family. The music struck me as good but as it was all new to me I could not form a very correct judgement of its merits; one must be tolerably well acquainted with a piece of music, particularly one that is scientific, to find it extremely agreeable. One of the instruments, indeed the only one I could see, appeared to me peculiar in its form & operation <*blank space*> it united in sound the drum & tamborine but was louder than either. we were rather too near to find it a pleasing accompaniment to the band I think it would have been a great addition to the effect at a distance. The Spaniards are a most musical people I should suppose, from what I have seen, that not a family in this City, of any tolerable pretensions, is without its piano or guitar or perhaps both. We returned home much pleased with our evenings excursion.

Thursday I called in the morning to see Mr. Burke who occupies the next room to us; he is a young man from New Orleans who is here with his wife for his health. His family have many of them been consumptive and he has himself suffered for a long time from complaints of the lungs, he passed last summer here and derived much benefit from the air but returned in the fall to bring his wife and has since then become more ill. This he attributes to fatigue on the voyage & other circumstances; at present his case seems extremely precarious. He coughs incessantly & has many other disagreeable symptoms. I carried him some pearl sage which is not to be procured here and which all the invalids in the house prefer to any thing else. I was fortunate enough to have a large quantity left of my

The Plaza de Armas, Havana. From ALBUM PINTORESCO DE LA ISLA DE CUBA (HAVANA: B. MAY, [CA. 1850]). *Courtesy of the Cuban Heritage Collection, Otto G. Richter Library, University of Miami, Coral Gables, Florida.*

sea stores. Mr Burke has tried several physicians here and receiving no benefit from their prescriptions has discarded them all and put himself under the care of a Spanish or French doctor who has great celebrity & who confines him to a milk diet notwithstanding his appetite which would prompt him to eat everything, he has been upon this regimen for twenty days and complains still that the milk oppresses him. Eliza Sullivan advises his trying the Castilian powders recommended her by Dr Physic, which boiled with the milk removes the qualities which affect an invalid unpleasantly; it rather improves the taste of the milk. Eliza found it very useful.

After my visit to Mr. Burke I went to see Mrs Cunningham who had just recovered from quite an ill turn. She was upon the bed and appeared glad to see me I staid with her an hour. The greatest allay to my pleasure since I came here has been my vicinity to so many sick persons. There are no less than three in the house who may very probably never leave it again. One is Mr Burke who has not left his room for some time, another a young man from New Orleans (Mr Henry) who cannot certainly live more than a week or two & the third Mr Farrel of Cincinnati who is here with his wife and seems rapidly declining. Mr Henry I am told is an exceedingly interesting young man and has come without either friend or nurse to take care of him. Mrs Howard has appointed old Dick to be his attendant but he must of course want many comforts & feel extremely lonely. I have made up my mind to one thing in the short time I have passed in the Island that no one should come here who is not strong enough to do every thing for himself without some friend or a well tried servant; it is impossible to command here, as with us, the services necessary in sickness. I am told the best nurses to be hired are Creoles at four dollars a day and these women are so convinced that they know more than the physician that they altogether disregard his directions. We have also, besides these very sick individuals, sundry gentlemen who are some getting better & some hoping to do so. All these are directing their steps towards the country, it is only those too far gone to move who remain in the city. I began to feel that nobody got well here until this solution of my doubts in consequence of my seeing so many around was given. I am anxious to get away from Mrs Howards on this account alone. It is very depressing to be constantly reminded by a cough on one side or the other that you are in the vicinity of the dying.

Mr Merrick is here (John Lee's former partner) and looks dreadfully ill but considers himself recovering; he has been subjected to a variety of unfortunate circumstances. After his first attack he resided in England and almost immediately after rupturing a blood vessel he was forced, on account of business, to sit for three months, from four o'clock in the morng until eleven at night, at his desk writing, one of his clerks being absent & the other unfaithful and not finding any one to supply their places, during this time he was constantly spitting blood & after wards was exposed to be wet through two or three times & at length became so ill that in going from Manchester to Liverpool, it was necessary to burn ether in the carriage to keep him alive. He passed last winter in Jamaica where he recovered his health in a great measure, he was there surrounded by friends, having taken most excellent letters from England and enjoyed himself highly. Eliza Sullivan who saw him at the eastward in the summer says that he seemed almost well although obliged to take care of himself and he came to New York in the fall intending to sail again for Jamaica but hearing a fatal sickness raged there he waited three weeks in dreadful weather for a vessel to New Orleans & when he reached there the ice was upon the shrouds of the ship. Here he remained twenty days eighteen of which he was confined to his room and at length came to Cuba greatly reduced. If any thing will restore him the climate of this island must.

After dinner today we took two volantes one Mrs Howard's & the other Mr Tennant's (an English gentleman who resides here and who offered his to Mr Sullivan) and took a drive into the country. Eliza the Miss Searss' & myself. Every thing struck us as most peculiar. The Paseo (a beautiful part of the city bordered on each side with trees & flowering shrubs, the orange bearing blossoms and fruit, the palm the cocoa the almond which grows singularly; a leafless stem to the height of eight or ten feet with horizontal branches spreading out much in the form of an umbrella, the plantain banana and many others with whose names I am unacquainted) first excited our admiration. We passed some of the troops with dresses all of white without a speck of dirt ornamented with green shoulder pieces & black caps with gilt bands. We passed through the gate of the city & etiquette then allowed us to put down the piece of broadcloth which screens the front of the volant & to breathe more freely the delicious air. It is not fashionable here to ride with your face exposed in the city except on Sunday evegs on the paseo, or other holy days. We were quite charmed with the scenery on all sides of us and rode to the sea shore a distance of about three miles from the City. We saw quantities of the prickly pear running wild over the ground & rocks & in endeavoring to pluck some flowers which grew among it I pierced my feet with thorns.

All along the road we were regaled with the sight of ladies, or women, walking dressed most fancifully not one without her crown of tortoise shell. These combs which are set on one side the head have the appearance of weighing at least a pound but, I am told, are exceedingly light for their size, the fashion has prevailed about three years. All the windows were filled with females blacks & whites. It is the ambition of the Spaniards to have as many slaves about the doors as possible and the opulent keep a great many simply for show. In the city every body is busy but after leaving the gates no one was employed except the drovers on the road. I saw, it is true, one tailors shop where the men were at work & passed a room in which two or three women were sewing. The Spanish women all grow exceedingly fat in consequence no doubt of the complete state of indolence in which they exist. Their hands are universally soft & delicate. The windows of all the houses we passed were very large & to the ground not glazed but protected by slats or bars of wood (in the city some of the handsomest houses have iron gratings).

<drawing>

Here and there a young man leant against the bars talking to the fair damsel within. All the furniture, of course, and every thing that goes on in these rooms upon the street are visible from without. In most of the houses we passed today there was little except the chairs and tables or perhaps a pair of French vases and a French clock, sofas, indeed, in all.

Many of the cottages on the road were thatched with dried palm leaves presenting quite a rural appearance. On one I observed a cactus (the nightly blooming cereus) trained against the side. This vine so prized with us finds a home in this island and is extremely common in the woods. We saw on one side the road a large pit or room dug out of the rock but whether a lime pit or a place where they get the coco with which the floors and buildings are made we had no one to tell us. From my description Mr Lowell supposed it to be an excavation for baths which are in contemplation. At all events, the negroes moving about on the ledges of red earth in the distance had quite an imposing effect and in my imagination bore no unapt resemblance to the infernal regions. We passed also a blacksmiths forge cut out of the rock which had a pretty effect. Coming home we stopped our volantes for a moment at the Campos Santos, the

Catholic burying ground. We did not alight and could only see the enclosure in front which is tastefully ornamented with trees and flowers. Several carriages stood in front of the gate one covered with black cloth fringed with black the calesero & other servants dressed in black. This was the herse. It is customary to dress the body in its usual costume & with face uncovered expose it in passing along the streets.

Among other beautiful flowers in the garden I noticed the double oleander. The leaf precisely like the single one which stood so many winters in one corner of Mother's parlour but the flower infinitely more beautiful, double of the finest shade of pink with a perfume somewhat resembling vanilla. We entered the City through another gate from that we passed going out, and riding along a square in which was a jet d'eau (water coming out of the mouths of dolphins and other figures) we came upon the paseo, the fashionable drive. Here we saw ladies, in their volantes, looking more like ladies, than any we had yet met. Those who are really genteel are never to be seen but in a carriage, and rarely leave the house during the day.

This evening after tea Mrs Cleveland and Mrs Moreland called upon us; the former lady who sat next me talked upon a variety of topics; she spoke of the fever here and said, with care it was rarely serious, neglect and delay occasion the fatal cases; it is necessary to administer remedies instantly or the case may become hopeless. The most common subjects are young captains of vessels and other men who are excessively imprudent & expose themselves thoughtlessly. She observed that she herself had had similar fevers in the United States, that the yellow fever was not peculiar but that the principal difference between an attack here & there consisted in the effect upon the constitution; Here the strength remains debilitated for weeks and weeks. We talked about Spanish houses Mrs Cleveland says some are extremely magnificent. They are built, many of them, large enough to accommodate all the children of the family after marriage. The Spaniards visit a great deal among themselves but never invite strangers Mrs Cleveland said that a native lady of distinction with whom she was much acquainted & who had been sometime in the states said to her "if you come to see me & my friends happen to be here they will talk with you and will consider you afterwards at liberty to come & visit them. but I cannot according to our customs introduce you. that is to say, I must not make you formerly known to each other by saying this is Mrs. Cleveland &c." The greater part of the Spanish ladies do nothing but play upon the piano or harp, dance draw and dress. They never touch a needle and their minds are wholly uncultivated. This is not the case with all, but with most; some, like the daughters of the Marquis Ramos, father of Mrs Hernandez, are much cultivated and occupy themselves constantly as our ladies do at the north; the Marquis lost his wife early and took a French governess for his children who was a fine woman and has brought them up with great judgment. Mrs Cleveland says in all her walks & rides she never but once saw a lady employed and the occasion was one sunday morning when she saw a lady sitting in the window sewing upon a blue muslin dress for the evening's Paseo.

Mrs Cleveland is a pleasant well informed woman, said to have a tinge of blue. Her husband is American consul here; they have three sons. The eldest studied civil engineering and, not getting along as rapidly as he wished, determined to join the Poles;[5] he wrote to inform his parents of his intention who sent him a letter expressive of their wish that he should remain at home but before their package reached Baltimore, where he resided, he had already sailed, in company with a Spanish officer interested in the same cause; before his voyage was over Warsaw was taken and they now suppose he will travel in Europe & return peaceably to pursue his profession. Another son is in France and the third, the brilliant Horace, in Havana. He fell from a building some time ago & many think injured his brain. He seems a good natured well intentioned youth. Mrs Morland asked Eliza Sullivan and myself to take tea there tomorrow.

Friday This afternoon I walked with Mr. Lowell to Madame Ruillet's to see Mrs Cunningham who had gone to ride; here we met Mr Sullivan who was leaving his card upon the table and I desired him to add our names; he accompanied us in a stroll upon the gouvernor's square where we admired the beautiful flowers. the gardener who was trimming shrubs in one of the little enclosures gave me a very pretty scarlet flower which he called Mer Pacifica and is known in English as the South Sea rose. Mr Sullivan too, kindly infringed the laws for my sake and plucked a few roses. The Intendant's house occupies most of one side of the square and is a more imposing building in its exterior than the gouvernor's which also fronts upon the garden. Opposite the Intendant's we stopped to admire a pretty little temple white with stone or marble pillars & enclosed with a high fence the yard ornamented with flowers. This temple is erected upon the spot where mass is said to have been first celebrated. It stands upon the place formerly occupied by the tree under which the religious service was performed. Mr Morland told us that Columbus never came to this Island; he touched at St Iago de Cuba but did not land. His bones are here in the Cathedral. Eliza Sullivan rode this afternoon with Mrs Hernandez and the Miss Sears dined at Dr Osgood's and returned only in season to go to Mrs Morlands where Eliza had procured them an invitation. Indeed Cordelia preferred passing the eveg with Mrs Osgood and did not accompany us. We changed our dress entirely expecting a little party but found no company excepting a Mr Sargent who, I believe, is attached to the commercial house. We had quite an agreeable visit & came home ready to go to bed.

Saturday. Mrs Osgood sent Eliza Sullivan & myself a message yesterday, by the young ladies, saying she regretted extremely her in ability to call upon us, but in consequence of a quarrel with Mrs Howard, our landlady, she could not come to the house; she wished us to accompany her this morng to the church of San Domingo to hear the funeral oration of a count who has recently died & whose remains were carried to the grave with great pomp a week since. He has left an immense sum of money, five or six millions, some of which he has bequeathed to the king, and having given something to this church it could do no less than bestow a puff upon his generosity. To one nephew he left three millions. To his steward an hundred thousand, to the Stewards wife fifty thousand, &c&. Mrs Osgood sent her volante for the girls. Eliza & I took Mrs Howards. and all repaired to Dr. O's house where we found a young man by the name of Manly & Dr. Shaler nephew of the Consul. Mrs Osgood is the most *chatty*, vain disagreeable old thing I ever saw. Her house is pleasantly situated looking out upon the water. She had a straw carpet, the only carpet of any sort I have seen in Havana. she carried us into her bed room a small apartment leading from the parlour quite tastefully fitted up, where she arrayed Harriet & Cordelia in white lace mantillas, it being impossible to go to church unveiled. Our black dresses were very proper for the occasion as every lady wears black to church. Mrs Osgood said she had given up the bedroom she usually occupied to a slave who was sick and who she feared would otherwise suffer from neglect.

We found the church arranged for the ceremony. A sarcophagus was fitted up in front of the alter covered with black velvet & bugles, with a deep black fringe. The sword & gold headed cane of the deceased were crossed and a gold key suspended above to indicate his having filled the office of high chamberlain; a cap with green feather & a yellow robe or cloak above these were, as Mrs Osgood informed us badges of his being protector of the Physicians. Various other marks of distinction I did not understand. The coat of arms beautifully painted was placed in a conspicuous situation. All the altars were lighted and a vast deal of ceremony or as it seemed to me mummery was displayed. The priests who were richly dressed officiated with great apparent unconcern indeed most seemed to consider it a good joke. Eliza observed one young frier blow out a long candle in jest which had been just lighted by a brother. The officiating priests were dressed in linen cambrick robes flounced with deep lace with cuffs of Brussels & an outer tunic or cloak of red velvet striped with gold lace. The college of physicians occupied seats prepared for them on one side the church and were dressed in black silk robes with lace collars and black velvet caps with four peaks, between each of which hung a tassel of some bright color, blue & white the most common, in the centre of the cap rose a bunch of flowers formed of silk; upon the whole they were very pretty. On the opposite side were placed officers & various dignitaries pointed out to us by Mrs Osgood who kept a continual chatter in my ear which was unfortunately next her. Every other moment she congratulated me upon having been so fortunate as to have come with her as she could always command the best place and was so great a favorite with every body. I confess I was at a loss to conceive why.

The Priest who delivered the oration is considered a great orator; it was in Spanish, of course, unintelligible to all our party. He used a vast deal of action and succeeded in throwing himself into a complete persperation. He occasionally took his pocket handkerchief from a bag in his sleeve which had a curious effect. It hung from the elbow and was only visible when he raised his arm. Mrs Osgood informed me that this fashion originated the expression of "laughing in the sleeve." The handkerchief had a mourning border. The priest wore black gloves outside of which glittered a ring on one finger which, my neighbour told me was probably a legacy from the deceased. He commenced his eulogy with looking towards the Sarcophagas which he addressed for some minutes in an animated manner. Then turning he apostrophised the people of Havana. At one period of the discourse he clapped on his cap, composed of black velvet ornamented with blue & white tassels & blue & white flowers. I was told he laid much stress upon the Counts having declared to him in his last moments that he had not a debt in the world. It seems the man who caused all this fuss was the meanest wretch in creation and, although rolling in riches, kept his relations & indeed himself in a state of starvation. We walked round the church after all was over and examined the pictures which Mrs Osgood who is a rigid catholic declared to be very fine but which to my unpractised eye looked like miserable daubs. The music was exceedingly good, one voice in particular was rather remarkable. It was altogether martial instruments. I observed a large organ but it was not touched to day. I am told that the music in all the churches is gay, marches country dances, waltzes &c. St Domingo is by no means considered a fine building here. But from it being the first of the kind I have seen it struck me as imposing. The blacks & whites kneel together promiscuously and although in most there is not the slightest appearance of devotion yet Mrs Osgood seriously observed that she thought the scene before us gave us a more perfect idea of heaven than any which could be imagined. It is a very common thing for ladies upon their knees to be gazing about the church. Mats & low seats are placed by the slaves of each family for the ladies. The gentlemen throw down their pocket handkerchiefs. A few I observed on the bare pavement, but most have more regard to their white trousers. Pocket handkerchiefs with fanciful colored borders are universal here. Even the priests flourish very gay ones.

After leaving the church we returned to Mrs Osgoods where the young ladies dined and where I took a sip of brandy instead of wine: we had some most curious cake being a little of every thing. On our way from the church Mrs Osgood carried us to the gouvernor's private garden to which it seems she has access. It is extremely tasteful & pretty; filled with flowers I observed one pine among the trees and a miserable looking bed of strawberries. At one end of the place is a cockpit round which are ranged the boxes containing the birds. E Sullivan & Mrs Osgood sat in a little pavilion while the rest of us walked on to a fence which enclosed some rare birds, among others the flamingo which is most curious. It is about the size of a goose in its body with a neck as long as a swan having the motion sometimes of a snake a long black beak and slender legs not bigger round than a very small pipe stem a foot and a half long. while sleeping the creature draws up one leg & puts it so completely out of sight that we were almost led to imagine that all three of those we saw had but one. However upon throwing a stone we soon discovered they could produce two. A live aligator was among the curiosities of the garden. From Mrs

Osgood's Eliza & I went to see Mrs Cunningham who seemed very feeble she is thinking of leaving here in the steam boat for Matanzas tomorrow

Sunday. This morning Eliza and myself called to see Mrs Cleveland; she received us very pleasantly. Mr C. was reading when we entered & his wife came from an adjoining room with a book in her hand; they evidently were keeping the Sabbath, a rare occurance, I fancy, in Havana. In this city the day is only marked by the most brilliant balls and the greatest cock fights. Mrs Cleveland talked about the Catholic religion here and said it had lost much of its influence among the Spaniards. The Bishop who has been a very sensible man, although his mind is now enfeebled by age & illness, abolished a great many ceremonies and rendered the worship more simple, but received orders from the King to restore them all and they are now in force without exciting a feeling of devotion either in priests or lay men. Indeed the more respectable parts of the community rarely enter the churches and mass is attended only by the lowest rabble and the blacks. The Priests themselves find it difficult to keep their countenances while officiating. There is no religion here to take the place of the Catholic and no restraining influence of any sort, upon vices which are not punishable by the laws, consequently the state of morals is at its lowest ebb. The Spaniards have not even the philosophy which with the French has become a substitute for religion. Mrs Cleveland said it was difficult to imagine where all this would terminate. The younger members of those families even, who profess the Catholic faith (indeed most *pretend* to do so) pay not the slightest regard to the worship of their fathers and are coming forward utterly reckless.

From Mrs Cleveland's we went to Mrs Morlands and found the good lady asleep in an easy spanish chair precisely like the one I have seen at Judge Putnam's. The house is quite a large and fine one with a good view of the water from the balcony. Mr Morland occupies the largest apartment for his counting room which would open with folding doors into Mrs M's parlour but that they have run a screen across to separate them. We saw a little daughter who was born here & called Clara for an interesting daughter of Mr Fellows who died the day she was to have been married to Mr Coit of New York. She was quite young and took the fever in consequence of being too late in the season in town where she remained because a little sister was ill and needed medical advice. Mr Morland has four daughters in Brookline at the Miss <*illegible*> the eldest sixteen years of age.

Every Sunday eveg the Spanish ladies ride in their volantes upon the Paseo, dressed in their most splendid attire with the top of the carriage thrown back while the gentlemen stroll along on the sidewalk; we intended to have taken Mrs Howard's vehicle as none but private ones are allowed on show evegs and I engaged it this morng but our landlady, who has not the sweetest temper in the world, being in a little pet told me when I wanted it that the volante was broken. I did not believe a word of it but said carelessly it was no matter and as it proved rainy it was in fact of no consequence. Mrs Hernandez made a little party this eveg for Eliza at the Bishops garden, a place of resort a short distance out of the city but on account of the weather Mr Sullivan would not suffer her to go. Don Swett was here, as usual, about a dozen times in the course of the day.

Monday. William Gorham was quite ill this morng. The attack was principally nervous. He has not looked well for several days & I suppose took cold in consequence of sleeping upon the ground floor in a room as damp as a cellar. Dr Shaler paid him a professional visit and carried him off in his volante to Dr Osgood's where he lives. This afternoon we visited Mr Soler y Cubi's establishment. I believe it is called a college the house is immensely large and beautifully situated upon the Paseo it was originally a private dwelling and has been enlarged to admit about 140 scholars, every thing seemed to us in fine order. The classes were in separate rooms each master not having more than ten or twelve boys. We could judge of their proficiency in nothing except music, drawing & writing. All the boys play upon some musical instrument and Mr Cubi said they had as many as ten professors of music. We did not hear the full band some of the best performers being absent. Four of the lads played upon the flute extremely well one upon the piano & two sung one of these last had a most wonderful voice. He was fifteen years of age. His singing more resembled that of a woman than a man. The same boy afterwards recited in Spanish and produced a most extraordinary effect by his expression and gestures. The mother of this child came in while we were in the parlour and he stepped forward and kissed her hand. I believe this is the ordinary mode of salutation from a child to a parent. Some of the crayon drawings were very good and one painting of a collection of scraps most peculiar. I was completely deceived as were the rest of the party. We supposed that actually the medley painted were pasted together. The specimens of penmanship were fine. I am told the Spaniards excel in writing. At this school there are some rewards for those who are the best and one for drawing struck me as particularly calculated to excite ambition in the mind of the pupil. The best scholar at the end of the term has his likeness taken by the master and it is framed & hung in the painting room to be seen by all who visit the establishment. The sleeping apartment is immensely large, each boy has a cot to himself provided with a nice muslin musquito net; the sheets all looked extremely white & of delicate linen. I presumed they were provided by the mothers as some of the pillow cases & sheets were ruffled or embroidered and others were plain. The use of cotton seems hardly known in this island. There is a large basin for bathing into which the water is admitted by pipes and flows off through an opening when it reaches a certain height being thus kept always perfectly clear.

Mr Cubi said he had great difficulties to contend with in getting up the college in consequences of the prejudices of the people, even experiencing opposition in his plan of putting glazed windows in the bedrooms, he succeeded however in his wish and now all acknowledge their utility. From his own room we had a most extensive and delightful view, the city beneath with the surrounding country the Moro & Cabana in the distance. I was so much fatigued by my visit to the school and previous exercise that, although engaged to take tea at Mrs Clevelands, I threw myself on the bed & dropped fast asleep & was only awaked by Mr Lowell's rousing me to enquire if I intended to go. I jumped up accordingly & without changing my dress got into the volante. Eliza & the Miss Searss also went as they were; for we had been so taken in at Mrs Morlands in consequence of expecting a party that we resolved to go this eveg in our usual black silks. We were, however, quite horrified to find Mrs Cleveland in white satin, rather antiquated in shape, to be sure, being exactly like one Mother wore at Elizabeths wedding, and several other ladies in white muslins or linen cambricks. A very pretty English woman Mrs Norman was dressed for a ball short sleeves white kid gloves & white satin shoes the other ladies were Mrs Wade who was recently married. Mrs Tolman from Hamburg, herself an Englishwoman married to a german. Mrs Grosvenor, (a Miss Winchester from Boston) and sundry gentlemen among them Noel Clarke who is brother to Fanny Jackson's friend and who flourished in Boston for a while. All the men with no exceptions except those of our party wore white vests & trousers and looked infinitely the better for their dress. Indeed we were the only black sheep of the party. Mr Lowell Mr Sears & Mr Sullivan are only waiting the tailors pleasure to conform to the fashion of the country. We had a little music this eveg. Mrs Wade played & sung & her husband accompanied her with his voice Mrs Cleveland & Eliza Sullivan played. Three of the ladies present had children in other lands Mrs Norman & Mrs Tolman in England & Mrs Morland in the States besides Mrs Cleveland whose sons are travelling.

Tuesday. Having been favored by the generosity of Dr Robinson with some new quills (mine having disappeared) I hope to be able to write more legibly. This morning Harriet Sears and myself went to some of the shops, with William our servant for interpreter; we were told before we left home that the shopkeepers would ask us twice, perhaps three times as much as they intended to take for their goods; we found the case to be precisely so & we came home much better qualified to make a bargain than we had ever before been. The gentlemen accompanied Mr Shaler, the consul, to see the Gouvernor this morng. He received them very graciously and shewed them a map of the Island of Cuba which is executing under his direction; it is very large & will give the situation of every plantation; there are said to be very good engravers in Havana and it will probably be struck off here after it is sketched. The Gouvernor speaks French but the gentlemen complimented his English so far as to talk with him in that language although his knowledge of it is quite imperfect.

Mr Shaler made us a call this morng and Mr Manly paid the Searss' a visit. He observed a sword cane standing against the wall which belonged to a stranger and remarked that it must not be displayed in the street; the use of a weapon of this kind is prohibited by law under a penalty of five hundred dollars and imprisonment. Mr Manly said he was himself seized by an officer one day while carrying one; he stoutly denied that it was a sword cane while the soldier as firmly protested that it was one. At length he said you may try & see & while the man was pulling at the head he let go the other end & ran & turned a corner & concealed himself in a house until dark.

I had some conversation to day with Mrs Burke about the Rutledge's of Nashville. She has a sister residing in the place and is acquainted with the family. She informed me that Edward Rutledge's shooting himself was attributed by some people in Nashville to his having been rejected by a widow lady there. He told her at the time she refused him that if he ever heard of her marrying another that he would shoot himself and Mrs Burke said she was married & he put his threat in execution. The Rutledges are now going into society after having been two or <*word missing*> years in seclusion. Eliza & I went to [Canchois] this afternoon to make our selection of preserves. She went afterwards in the evening to Mr Hernandes found Madame ill in bed.

Wednesday January 18th This afternoon Cordelia and I went to ride in a volante hired by Mr Sears by the week. He supposed by engaging it in this way it would have all the privileges of a private carriage, but his calesero made no change in his dress and it passed for a common hack as it was. As no respectable females ride without a gentleman in a hired volante we of course attracted universal attention from the gentlemen as we passed along. Not understanding Spanish we could not be edified by the compliments they paid us but soldiers and all made us some civil speech & shook their hands to us. I was half frightened to death, although I did not communicate my fears to Cordelia who seemed greatly amused, but I could not avoid thinking of the situation in which we should be placed should any one go so far as to tell our calesero to stop, neither of us knowing Spanish enough to bid him go on or to explain that we were highly respectable persons. I was quite glad when we were safely landed at Mrs Howards. It is the custom with Spanish gentlemen to pay all ladies some compliment as they pass & it is not meant as it would be with us, for impertinence I do not know if those of the first rank do it & presume not, but it is common with others. But I have no doubt this afternoon we met with peculiar devotion from the questionable situation in which we were placed. We have now a fine moon.

Eliza Sullivan accompanied Mr & Mrs Hernandez to a nunnery where she saw two or three of the vestals through a grate. One of them talked English and was very particular in her enquiries about Eliza it is quite a matter of favor to be admitted, although there is little to be seen when you are once in. Eliza has enjoyed great advantages in consequence of her acquaintance with Mrs Hernandez who is of the first rank and has been devoted to her she invited her to a small party immediately upon her arrival where she had Madame Feron send some other choice musical spirits, and since not a day has passed without some agreeable attention. Mr Derby gave Mr Sullivan a letter of introduction just as he was leaving Charleston & it was fortunate he did so as the letters sent by Mr Walsh one of which was to Mr Hernandez have not yet arrived. The custom of the Spaniards not to invite strangers unless introduced by letter is exemplified in this case for although living at the same house & considered of the same party we have none of us received similar civilities although Mr & Mrs H. have been invited to Dr Warren's in Boston. But perhaps they are not aware that the Searss are neices. Mr Sullivan seems to think they are not very anxious to attend to people from our country because they felt themselves slighted when travelling in the States. Eliza went home with Mrs Hernandez to pass the eveg and heard some good music, while Mr Sears & myself took Mr Tennants volante & Mr Lowell & Cordelia Mr Sears's and went to hear the music upon the square. It was raining a little & we were thus again deprived of the pleasure of seeing the ladies walking in the garden.

Thursday At an early hour this morng Mr Sullivan & Eliza were preparing to commence their journey to Mr Fellows's they had just taken a slight breakfast when Mr Tennant entered to see them off. The equipage consisted of a wretched volante & two horses & a simple mule to convey the baggage; it was necessary for them to be rather crowded as Eliza had her maid servant with her & the carriage though wider than our gigs is hardly broad enough for three, particularly when one is a gentleman. The day promised to be rainy but cleared off and they had quite a pleasant ride. Mr Fellows's is about 24 miles from Havana. Mr Sullivan intends after passing a few days there, to go on to the Marquis Ramos's, father of Mrs Hernandez & from thence to Mrs Juive's after which I hope we shall again meet.

After dinner Mr Paine, who holds the office of interpreter to the gouvernor, called to accompany us to the Casa de Beneficiencia, or House of Mercy an institution which in the first instance was appropriated to the support & education of female orphans by the Governor La Cases[6] in 1795 who was its founder. An accession to its funds has of late years admitted the addition of friendly boys to the beneficiaries. The buildings are in the suburbs of the City several hundred feet long on the main street and as many broad. I saw nothing there very remarkable. We ranged through large & lofty rooms; in the first which we entered was a picture of the procession of children, with the Governor La Cases at their head, which first took possession of the building, after its completion. All the orphans were dressed in a uniform extremely simple in its form & material. There was also a portrait as large as life of the Governor & two or three others of benefactors to the institution, also one or two charts of lands which have been bestowed. In one room was a large class of little girls engaged in needle work superintended by a female who left her pupils and led the way for us up stairs: here we saw the older girls some of them apparently upwards of twenty years of age. They were also engaged in various kinds of embroidery. In the same apartment was a bust or statue (I could not discern which) of the king of Spain covered to protect it from injury, and a portrait of the present Queen who is a benefactress. The superintendant of the establishment showed us some specimens of work which were mostly engaged, but having been told before I went that it was best to purchase something, I had the pleasure of spending eight dollars, for a pocket handkerchief worth perhaps two or three, which liberality I put down directly to the score of charity. The yard is large and paved with stone through which runs a stream of water rendering the air cool and fresh.

The female orphans are endowed upon their marriage with a sum from eight hundred to a thousand dollars and consequently are not obliged to pine in vain for admirers. We enquired of Mr Paine how the gentlemen found opportunity for making themselves agreeable to the ladies, and he said he supposed they became acquainted at the windows; we observed in a large hall two couples sitting upon a sofa conversing, the girls more dressed than those up stairs, & he said they were courting. I believe they are allowed to see each other an hour a day. We visited the part of the establishment appropriated to boys which is entirely distinct from the females. All the lads are orphans and are taught some useful trade upon leaving the house. We saw their eating rooms & sleeping apartment the latter was entirely empty the cots having been removed to a small room adjoining for the day. The gentlemen afterwards visited the lunatic asylum for females adjoining. Mr Paine exerted all his eloquence to induce the Miss Searss & myself to make one of the party but we preferred wandering about a neat little garden filled with flowers in front of the house.

After entirely satisfying our curiosity at the Casa de Beneficiencia we entered our volantes and drove to the Insane hospital where we again waited for the gentlemen who explored the building. The Campos Santos, the Catholic burying ground adjoins this establishment and here we got out & entered the gate which admitted us into a yard neatly & tastefully ornamented with flowers; through an arch we were entered the burying ground. There is a painting and inscription over the gate way. I can give no account of either from my own recollection but upon looking into Abbot find he describes the centre picture as emblematic of death & the consolation a Christian may derive from a look into futurity. On the left hand a widow shrowded in a veil with Hymen's torch reversed in her hand & the dust extinguishing the flame. In the same compartment the widow without her weeds resting her arm upon a circle, the emblem of eternity. On the left is another compartment with a female figure with a cross & bible on the right another female one hand resting on the bible the other on a staff round which a snake is entwined. The inscription on the tablet below the paintings

A la Religion
A la Salud Publica

El Marques de Someruelos	Juan de Espada
Gubernador	Obispo

The burying ground is in very good taste. A stone walk runs through the centre on each side of which are brass headed posts & chains. No monuments are allowed. Slabs only are horizontally inserted. A neat chapel at one end encloses a most beautiful altar. The grass is of the most vivid green and the place is bordered with trees. I saw there the stone which covers the remains of a daughter of Mr Fellows. The Bishop who designed & carried into execution the plan of burying in a grave yard met with the greatest opposition. He was a man of fine sense & judgment, though now much broken, and during part of the time this place was forming, it was necessary to guard the workmen; public opinion was so entirely in favor of interring under churches. It had become almost necessary for the health of the city to make the change but perhaps no other man could have effected it. Certainly none less resolute. Mr Paine invited us to return with him & take a glass of wine at his house which we did not think civil to refuse and we therefore drove to his door where a young man, perhaps a son, handed us out of the volante he could only bow & smile upon us Mr Paine being the only member of the family who speaks English. We were introduced to Madame & three daughters, the latter quite pleasing looking girls but of all the horrors I ever saw Mrs Paine bore the palm, she was arrayed in a flabby looking chintz gown with short sleeves & enveloped in a large crape shawl head & all, either black or some very dark color; after giving us her hand she sunk into an easy chair where she sat coughing during the remainder of our visit. It is difficult to imagine a more awkward position than that in which we were all placed drawn up in two lines not understanding a word said by each other. (Mr P. being engaged with the gentlemen) At length observing a piano Harriet Sears made signs for the eldest daughter to play, which she did very readily & with considerable execution & after hearing two or three pieces we came away quite pleased with having killed a lion.

Friday. Mr Bruce clerk of Scull Story & co. came this morng to take us to the Count O'Farrels palace the family being out of town & he having obtained permission of the Steward. Mrs Burke accompanied me in the volante the young ladies not wishing to go, it is a most splendid establishment the rooms being all painted in water colors with various devices. We ascended a flight of marble steps from the court yard, which is extremely fine, to the gallery paved with different colored marble the railing is of iron beautifully wrought. The rooms are all very lofty & large the drawing room on one side is a splendid apartment communicating with a smaller parlour at each end by folding doors. It is lighted in the eveg by three chandeleers which were covered (as indeed was all the furniture) but which from their size I should suppose were exceedingly costly. Four large mirrors with pier tables one each side of the doors two round mahogany tables with marble tops chairs sofas & paintings completed the furniture of this apartment it did not by any means strike me as very rich The music room contained a grand piano forte & I observed several three cornered tables with marble tops fitted into corners. This is an extremely pretty sort of table; in one of the sleeping rooms the bureaus were arranged in the same way; high wardrobes are more common here than bureaus; I was peculiarly struck with the dining hall which was painted with appropriate emblems fruits vines &c. & the perspective of the landscapes at each end was so go[7] as to increase the appearance of size. The cots were all removed from the chambers; the Spaniards make nothing of sleeping. I have taken the greatest fancy to their cots which are very light & taken away at a minutes warning. In the most magnificent houses you find no beds more costly than these, they are made with holes into which light wooden posts may be inserted to support the musquito nets & are usually unprovided even with matresses. To me the sacking is most comfortable in this climate.

We examined the kitchen a large room where they cook only with charcoal upon small furnaces the best economy of fuel as no more need be used than is necessary. There is a large wash room & every other convenience. We mounted to the top of the house which commands a view of all Havana & the surrounding country. It is flat & might be filled with flowers. Some of the roofs are thus ornamented. In the yard we peeped into the bathing house a large place with conveniences for admitting hot & cold water. Saw the warehouses where sugar is kept & came away. This palace cost with the land 260 thousand dollars that of the brother in the next street 600 thousand and the brother is not so rich as this man but more extravagant. I am told although the other house is largest it is by no means as much more splendid as might be expected from the difference in cost. they are both calculated to hold all the children with their families after marriage. This is a good Spanish fashion.

Saturday Harriet Sears & myself rose early and accompanied by Mr Lowell went to the Cathedral which is open for early mass every morning; it is quite a fine building being paved with marble & near the altar mosaic. It is adorned with many large pictures, whether good or not I am no judge; an altar of marble which a priest, who did the honors, informed us was brought all the way from Rome fronted us on one entrance. On the left of this altar enclosed in the wall are said to be deposited the bones of Columbus. A slab with his portrait in basso relievo is inserted over the spot. This is the object which no traveller can omit in Havana although were it not for the excitement which ought to be produced by viewing the precise place there are many others which greatly resemble it. We observed one lady at confessional. A priest entered one of the mahogany centry boxes for so they seemed & the damsel knelt & put her mouth close to a small window to which he inclined his ear. I could not help thinking with what a light heart she must return home having deposited all the sins she had been committing for a week upon his shoulders. I find myself so unhappy in description that I shall attempt none of the Cathedral. We returned in time for breakfast which Mrs Howard gives us at half past eight. I examined her kitchen to day which is about as large as Papa's bathing room with a brick bench all round to support the pots & kettles which are set on grates over charcoal. She has also an oven; of course we do not see such a thing as roast meat but the cooking in general is very good, French most of the dishes, indeed her cook is a French boy.

Mrs Howard has the smartest little African, only two months since from the coast of Guinea he is not more than nine or ten years old and has acquired considerable Spanish and is constantly gaining English. He seems never to sleep for he is up the last in the house & if you rise with the earliest dawn he is to be seen scouring or sweeping. He already sets the table and tends as well as the Steward. Some of the slaves are complete drones and a little girl purchased at the same time with Francisca cannot be prevailed upon to move beyond a snail's pace. The manner in which the servants sleep surprised me extremely, one night on coming home I observed Lorette the chambermaid lying upon the stone steps with her baby on her arm its head on the stairs and around were several other negroes all lying upon the stones. I believe they are provided with a blanket and cold nights cover themselves with it but this evening they were without pillow or covering of any sort.

Sunday January 22d There is nothing to mark Sunday here especially with strangers. The citizens of Havana amuse themselves with cockfights. We found the volante engaged to Mrs [Barrow] a lady from Nashville but as the eveg proved rainy did not regret the Paseo. Mrs Howards carriage is quite a pretty one of the sort. Although I have hardly become sufficiently accustomed to the volante not to think it the most awkward vehicle it is generally acknowledged, however, that one of any other construction would not answer for the streets of Havana or the roads in the country. The carriage is swung very low & the wheels are extremely high & wide apart which prevents its upsetting continually.

The Calesero rides the horse which is at considerable distance from the carriage the shafts being long. The Calesero strikes a stranger as a most extraordinary piece of composition immersed in his boots which nearly reach his waist when seated. They are tight to the knees & from there expand. They come half way up the thigh when standing; the rest of the costume in private volantes consists of white trousers short jackets in livery, some very pretty scarlet & other colors striped & ornamented with gold lace & a cap or hat similarly ornamented. In rainy weather the Calesero envelopes himself in a great coat & huge straw hat in which he bids defiance to the storm. The hacks have all square tops like our old or new? fashioned chaises but many private carriages have the bellows top which may be thrown back. Some have a most beautiful fringe all round the front & all are ornamented with one more or less showy. A screen of cloth buttons to the top; it is thought necessary to keep this always up in the city except upon the Paseo on holy days. The ladies can, however, peep out each side.

<light sketches on overleaf>

Monday, 23d Sunday is the usual day for the steam boat to go to Matanzas & it returns in the middle of the week, but in consequence of bad weather there has been a delay and we shall not go until tomorrow. I have been engaged in packing today one of the disagreeables which falls to a travellers lot. I have never yet learned why it need take so long but find it always a most tedious affair after remaining a fortnight stationary. I received a letter of introduction by Miss Bumstead of Boston (from Dr Jackson) who has come to Cuba with Mr Henry Hubbard for her health. She arrived to day & this eveg I called at Mrs Morelands where she is staying, but found she had gone to bed having been up since two in the morng. I was sorry not to see her as we shall leave Havana early in the morning. Mr & Mrs Grosvenor, Mr Sargent Mr Hubbard & two Mr D'Wolfs were there. After my return I went in to see Mrs Burke and sat some time conversing with her. Mr Metcalf called to bid us farewell, he is a friend of Mr Lowells with whom he became acquainted last year, from his appearance one would suppose him in a confirmed consumption and he is much troubled with lung complaints but has saved his life for the last seven years by passing his winters in a southern latitude. His family reside in New York but as early as September or October he always sails for Cuba & does not go home earlier than June. For four years he has been to this Island and previously was in some other of the West Indies or in New Orleans. He says he finds the climate of Havana the best for him. Matanzas is too bracing. Mr Metcalf is a portrait painter &, from the specimens I have seen, I should judge him to be one of the most successful on the stage. I went one day with Mr Sullivan, Eliza & Mr Sears to his painting room & we were all much struck with his pictures. He has taken all the great characters in Havana. He was kind enough to say he would endeavour to procure me some of the native flower seeds in which attempt I hope for the sake of my friends he may be successful. It is, however, no easy matter as there is no shop where they can be procured. The seeds sold in the stores are in general those imported from the north.

I did not attempt to go to bed until every one else in the house was quiet and just as I was stepping into my little cot was alarmed by the most violent shrieks & knocking & breaking of glass in the court yard. The first idea excited in my mind by these sounds, as usual in Cuba when any thing out of the way happens at night, was that of insurrection, and I could not help feeling how defenceless we were without even a pistol to make a show of resistance & I was half inclined to go to Mr Sears's door & beg the loan of one of his. "Cool reflection" however came to my aid & the sounds continuing I was convinced they came from some one in distress below. We opened our door which is upon the gallery & found Mrs Howard just peeping out, she screamed to Dick & a host of negroes lying in the yard, to know the occasion of the uproar & he told her it proceeded from a crazy boy, or, as I understood from his broken English, from one who had the night mare & slept in the barbers room adjoining among a parcel of bottles & becoming frightened in his sleep he got up & in the dark made dreadful havoc among the bottles & knocked against the door which with his howling were the sounds we heard. For a short time I was much alarmed but fortunately was soon relieved from apprehension and shall now retire to rest with the gloomy prospect of being obliged to rise before day light to be ready for the boat.

Tuesday, 24th. We (Mr Sears's family & ourselves) left Mrs Howards at ½ past six after having partaken of a cup of chocolate prepared for us. The steam boat was built in New York and cost eighty thousand dollars which is said to have been much more than its worth. It was more expensive in consequence of the owner's being unwilling to trust entirely to the discretion of the steam boat company, but chose to send an agent of his own to superintend the building. It was completed at first without a single berth, but as people are usually sick on board two have been added. The cabin is constructed with wooden shutters all round which may be closed in bad weather, but which today were thrown back to admit the refreshing air. There is a wide bench all round and, as a lady occupied one berth & little George the other, I established myself upon it to get rid of uncomfortable sensations from which I am never free when sitting up at sea. We found on board a Spaniard & wife (the deputy collector) and a Spanish lady who was sick all the passage. I believe her husband was also on board. I will describe Mrs Collector's dress as it is a pretty fair specimen of that worn by ladies on ordinary occasions. A thin bask muslin with short sleeves & pattern embroidered in cruels round the top of the hem, a wrought handkerchief on the neck & an embroidered one also in the hand. A watch long gold earrings, large comb curved in points, diamond rings blue satin shoes, wrought stockings & a blue canton crape shawl worked in colors, sufficiently large to be worn as veil. She was a good natured looking dame of about 40 apparently, but the women here grow old so early she might be much less. The other lady's costume I did not see, except her gown, which was of thin muslin with bright yellow figures all over it. A black dame also looked very fine. I felt quite a curiosity to see a Spanish dinner but was too sick to rise & look at the table. I observed some of the dishes in passing & they all seemed to be dressed with eggs & oil & salad.

After dinner a man on board took a guitar & amused us for an hour with playing & singing occasionally another voice would join in. Some of the songs occasioned a great deal of merriment among the listeners. I, of course, could not apprehend the wit. The sail out of the harbour was fine the view as I have already said most beautiful. The Moro castle stands upon a most commanding situation and adds greatly to the splendour of the scene. We arrived at Mrs Harpers in Matanzas about five o'clock. I am extremely glad that in sailing for Cuba we determined to come to Havana, the harbour is so much more beautiful than that of Matanzas. The latter has nothing to render it peculiarly striking. For some distance from the shore it is too short to admit any thing of greater depth than a small boat and we accordingly came to land in one. Mr Bailey accompanied us to the shore.

<drawing on overleaf>

Mrs Harpers is a wooden, ordinary looking house but pleasantly situated and always commanding a fine breeze. She pays eight hundred dollars a year and is thinking of removing to one in the neighbourhood at two thousand. Mr Lowell dissuades her from the change thinking she will lose money by it: she has a good many stationary gentlemen boarders who are equally well satisfied where they are and her transient lodgers are only for a few months in the winter season. Hers is the only boarding house for Americans in Matanzas. Thermometer 86° at noon.

Wednesday. Rain a norther which is here greatly dreaded it is the theme of discourse as a strong east wind is with us. I amused myself looking out the window at the horses which were continually passing, all with their tails braided & turned up. Such a thing is never seen in a volante as a horse whose tail is not tied back to the harness or knotted up in some way, nor often in any other situation in Havana or Matanzas. In the coun-

The entrance to Matanzas. From José María de Andueza, Isla de Cuba, pintoresca, histórica, politica, literaria, mercantil é industrial (Madrid: Boix, 1841). *Courtesy of the Cuban Heritage Collection, Otto G. Richter Library, University of Miami, Coral Gables, Florida.*

try you sometimes see a gentleman riding & the animal is at liberty to brush off the flies. I presume the custom was established to save the rider from being immersed in red mud. Every thing is brought into town on horses or mules. It is quite curious to see a long string of them passing with corn stalks which are used as fodder, the animal is nearly concealed the head & tail alone being visible. Vegetables and many other things are carried in seroons a sort of straw saddle bag which goes over the animal's back the rider sits in the middle & it is large enough to hang down each side. Molasses is brought in small kegs three or four tied on the back of the horse & twenty or thirty in a string the head of one tied to the tail of another. Two hundred pounds are said to be a load for a horse. The oxen here are small and scrubby in appearance but considered much stronger than ours perhaps they may be enabled to draw more in consequence of the way in which they are harnessed the yoke instead of going over the neck as in the States is placed behind the horns and the creature pulls with his head a string passes through the nose. Every part of a Spanish harness (except that belonging to a gentleman) is most clumsy & shabby. The saddles made of straw are certainly the most enormous things I ever saw, & have, it is probable, been unchanged in fashion since the country was settled, they seem enough in themselves for a load.

<drawing>

A man in this country is poor indeed who does not own his horse. The common class of men wear a strait long sword called machéte in the use of which they are very expert. They give a blow in drawing it out which gives a severe gash to an enemy unused to the weapon, & unprepared for attack. The negroes have a large chopping knife which bears the same name with which they cut plantains and weeds for their pigs it is a sort of half circle in shape, something likening my idea of a scimitar. George was cruelly bitten last night by musquitoes and in consequence of this affliction & feeling still a little weak he is quite fretful and pronounces a most emphatic *no* whenever any gentleman takes sufficient notice to ask him to come & sit in the lap. I never, in the heat of summer at home was so much annoyed by the musquitos as within the last night or two.

Thursday This afternoon we sent for two volantes & Mr Sears & the girls Mr Lowell George and myself took a short drive to the fort which is pleasantly situated upon the sea shore the weather still continues unfavorable, yet we enjoyed our ride. The carriages are all so low as to trouble the gentlemen when they wear their hats; my husband took his off we passed the barracks returning and received the compliment of a civil stare from Officers & soldiers. The travelling even in the streets is excessively rough & it is incredible how easily you are carried by a skillful Calesero over ruts and holes which we should consider in America as perfectly breakneck; the carriage is swung so near the ground as hardly to be shaken in the least degree. Mrs Harper says she was one day riding with Mrs Macomb in the same direction in which we went and they met a procession carrying the host to a criminal who was to be executed the next day & to whom it was thought necessary to give extreme unction. The ladies supposed it would be sufficient to kneel in the volante but this was not allowed and they were forced to get out & kneel on the pavement. This looks as if the Catholic religion were more respected in Matanzas than in Havana where the host is permitted to pass in the street without the slightest acknowledgment from passers by. Mrs Harper thinks however the Priests were thus rigorous in this case merely for the sake of shewing their power & that in fact there is a great falling off in observances of religion. She says she remembers to have seen frequently, on great occasions the principal men in the place walking bareheaded in the procession in the middle of a hot summer's day, and a white Calesero driving two fat jolly priests who were comfortably riding in a volante.

27th Friday The norther and rain still continue; this house which is expressly constructed to afford a constant draft is by no means comfortable in such weather. The windows & doors on one side, when closed would leave us in utter darkness & on the opposite Venetian blinds. If this, however, is the most uncomfortable air that blows it is not extraordinary that so few windows are glazed. The Spaniards are extremely afraid of cold and when there is what we should term a light breeze only, you see in passing along the streets most of the shutters barred. In all the houses in which I have been it is almost impossible to get out of the draft and the Spaniards are said to dread one very much. I cannot, if that be the case, imagine why all their habitations are so constructed.

The gentlemen dined with Mr Grace to day a most fiery, disagreeable looking little body. He is the head of the firm with which they do business. His wife is in the country and he is keeping bachelors hall. Mrs Harper's butcher last night stabbed a man in a quarrel and being lodged in prison she is obliged to employ another; this is the second assassination within a week or two I had frequently heard before I came here, that any one who witnessed an affray or saw a man murdered in the streets did the best he could to get out of the way as soon as possible for fear of imprisonment. The fact I believe is this that any responsible man, Mr Grace or Spaulding, for instance, would find no difficulty in procuring bail and would not be confined here more than in other places upon giving his word to appear at the trial but those who are less known are subject to the same confinement as the prisoner and hence arises the difficulty of bringing a criminal to justice. The bystanders are afraid to acknowledge that they have seen the deed done lest their liberty should be taken from them.

Saturday January 28th I received a letter from Mrs Sage this morning inviting us to make her a visit. After dinner shopped with Dr Robinson and Harriet Sears and after our return we took two volantes and rode into the country. Little George enjoyed the drive as much as any of us. We went through rows of beautiful green trees with vines & flowers running over them to the bay where from a hill we had a beautiful view of Matanzas and the neighbouring hills. Mr Sears attempted a sketch in Harriets pocket book. W. Gorham has not been well for a few days. I think he will convalesce when we get into the country. Cordelia was indisposed this eveg and I read to her after she went to bed.

To day we heard more about the insurrection in Jamaica the news of which reached us a fortnight since. It seems the blacks have driven back the soldiers and there is every prospect of their ultimately obtaining possession of the Island. There has been very little bloodshed, none except where there was resistance. Mr Merrick who spent last winter in Jamaica attributes all to the influence of Missionaries some of whom are bad men & who have frequent opportunities of exerting their power over the blacks as they have liberty to go to church Saturday eveg and Sunday. It seems altogether impossible that so well organized a plan should have originated with the negroes & there is little doubt whites are at the bottom of it.

Mr Lowell's friend Griswold called here this morng. He was administrator upon Mr James D'Wolfs estate, the Mt Hope, and is now slowly recovering from injuries received about two months since. He was aroused by a slight noise in the next room about two o'clock in the morng, and thinking it might proceed from rats or something of the sort he got up to investigate matters when he received a blow and was suddenly seized he resisted for five minutes but was at length overpowered and probably left for dead. The unknown enemy, for it was in the dark, having attempted to strangle him & imagined he had succeeded in the attempt. He did not come to his senses until five or six o'clock when he was surprised to see a negro girl standing by his side crying he was so free from pain that at first he could not imagine the cause of her tears & thought she must be ill & was going to call for the medicine chest when upon attempting to move he found he was hurt & then remembered the affray.

There are various conjectures respecting the affair, it would seem to have been a well organized matter & could not have taken place unless more than one had been engaged; in the first place the doors must have been left unlocked by some one inside and the dogs tied as they are very ferocious upon this estate & always seize a negro if he is out at night. Mr Griswold said if the villain had been a moment later he should have had his sword in his hand as he never went out without it & it was only two or three feet from him. He is a [at] present trying to make some arrangement with the D'Wolfs and Govr Collins (part owner of the Mt Hope & brother in law to James D'Wolf) who refuse even to pay his expenses. It is the most abominable meanness on their part. His demand is a thousand dollars besides his expenses. He has lost his time & is perhaps disabled for life from making his living; his back was much injured. He has considerable hold over the D'Wolfs for the law in this country is so long & subtle in its operations, that it would eat up the whole estate before the case was settled and as his life was attempted there he has a right to demand investigation &, although he does not choose to say how much he knows, it is thought by many that he has very good reasons to know the individual and might bring proofs of his guilt. This investigation is what they most wish to avoid, and I consequently hope he will make them pay handsomely. Although the place never produced a better crop than last year & Griswold has amply done his duty there yet these men are adding to his misfortune by trying to injure his character, all in their power. They insinuate that it could never have happened unless he had been too severe to the negroes so now, he asserts there had been no correction for some time. One story is that in his struggle he left the marks of his fingers upon the negro's throat and that they were perfectly visible the next day but perhaps this is not true as he does not himself say what he knows.

Mr Macomb was talking today, at table, about sugar cane and observed that the kind which was sold in the streets for eating was not so large as that from which the sugar is made the former "the Creole," is never much taller than the sticks we see while the latter called Otaheitan grows to the height of eighteen or twenty feet!!! Mr Lowell took little George to the sea side this morng and had him dipped he was excessively terrified, his father said he would have gone into a fit if he had been plunged two or three times more.

29th

Sunday I accompanied Mr Lowell & Mr Sears to church to hear Mass in which I was disappointed for the priest was at such a distance that allthough, I presume, he uttered words yet to me and to the greater part of the congregation a profound stillness appeared to reign. I suppose I must have scandalized every body for I stood during the whole service. It was a most peculiar sight, ladies & and gentlemen kneeling & sitting alternately as a little bell rung without any other visible cause for their change of posture. There were a good many females present all with black gowns & various colored shoes & all veiled. I saw one black woman near the altar who seemed really to be absorbed in devotion. The ladies all knelt upon mats carried by their servants.

We walked round the church, after the ceremonies were over, which is a simple common looking sort of building enough We examined the pictures which are ordinary and stopped in front of a curtain, which was down, feeling some curiosity to know what was behind. A gentleman approached and drawing it displayed a carved representation of our savior upon the cross with three female figures beneath one probably meant for the virgin and all three dressed most fancifully. The individual who did the honors of the picture seemed greatly amused and kept pointing to the figures and jabbering in Spanish & laughing immoderately. I presume he was a Catholic or he would not have been at Mass and cannot account for his apparent want of reverence. He walked with us as we came from the door & kept by our side until we came to a gate of entrance to the Cockpit where he bid us farewell giving a pretty fair sample of the manners of the place which admit of a man's going directly from the church door to partake in this disgusting amusement. It is said that many ladies are not ashamed to be seen betting upon the different birds.

We rode after dinner to a sugar estate near town belonging to a Marquisa there are a good many buildings on the place being parts of a mill which has been abandoned. Here we had a pretty water view. George was again dipped and is getting over his terrors he seems already revived by the salt water. Thermometer 79 at noon. Shops open to day.

Monday I shopped with Cordelia this morng. It is the most vexatious thing for a foreigner to attempt to make purchases in Cuba. The shop-keepers always ask twice as much as they are willing to take in the hope of gulling the strangers; the first time I went out I was rather amused, but now it only vexes me, and I have once or twice given their price for small articles, rather than be at the trouble of beating them down.

This afternoon Mrs Harper accompanied us in a ride to a garden near town owned by a man she called Don Lewis. Here we saw quite a variety of flowers of which he was very stingy. We returned by way of the bay and had a pleasant ride. The gentlemen of the house having kindly procured invitations for us to a ball given at the theatre, we prepared to go after our return. The dance is given in honor of some general who is here to whom the governor wishes to be civil. We were seated in a box where we had a most excellent view of the dancers who occupied the pit. The benches being moveable it affords an extremely good dancing hall. It is the custom for any who wish it to sit in the boxes even the dancers when fatigued frequently do so. I was glad to have an opportunity of seeing the beauty & fashion of Matanzas. The theatre is a pretty building tastefully fitted up; one of the scenes on this occasion formed the background to the orchestra which was very good. The dancing consisted of country dances & waltzes alternately the former admitting the waltz into its figure. The girls, some of whom, were very pretty universally danced well and in perfect time and the gentlemen far excel ours moving as if the [they] were used waltzing & liked it. The ladies generally were not richly dressed. I saw one diamond necklace but most were arrayed in simple costumes with nothing in particular to mark the nation, the first glace [glance] at them made me feel as if I were in a Boston party of two or three years back the sleeves hardly reaching the present fashion in magnitude the heads were dressed principally in bows made over frames with feathers or flowers & very large combs placed on one side. The gentlemen & their partners do not talk much together when dancing they move as if engaged with the occupation, but when they do speak it is in an easy manner. After the music ceases the girls retire to seats placed round the room & gentlemen occupy the middle of the room as in our parties.

The children in Spanish families are left much with the blacks but as soon as a girl is grown up her Mother is afraid to have her out of her sight she is never, when it can be helped, left to her own discretion. Mrs Sage was at a party one eveg and an acquaintance of hers told her she would be greatly obliged if she would look after her daughter as she herself was obliged to go away. Mrs Sage said, certainly, supposing the lady was going home & was quite surprised to see her returning in a quarter of an hour when she thanked her for her kindness in looking after the young lady. It seems altogether preposterous in a country where the morals are said to be in a most degraded state that such attention is paid to forms. There did not seem to me any restraint in the manners of the young ladies. I was quite shocked to observe one deliberately spit upon the floor and understood such incidents are by no means uncommon. The girls all looked much older than they actually were. One who was pointed out to me as sixteen looked at least six and twenty. The Spanish women many of them cover their faces with a sort of paste which gives them a white appearance in the eveg but which injures the complexion and after once using it they do not find it easy to discontinue the practise. They as well as the men use a great deal of oil upon their hair. No refreshments were offered this eveg but I believe there is a bar at the theatre to which gentlemen can go. The women here, I believe, think it vulgar to eat in public we returned home at 11 o'clock much pleased with our evening.

Tuesday. This morng Cordelia and myself with Thomas (Mr Sears's servant) behind took a walk to a high hill which overlooks the town & has a view of the harbour & shipping, and sat down under a tree to rest; here we sat talking until warned by Thomas that two men approached, and always dreading a Spaniard, unless in the city with a gentleman, we jumped up to descend the hill; we did not readily find the path and as the men had nearly reached us I thought it best to face about & look unconcerned when they bowed & pointed out the road to us. When about half way down we were assailed by a lady whom I had seen the night before at the ball who talked to us very fast & kept pointing to a neighboring house; finding she could not make us divine what she was saying she began to scream to a child who was at some distance to come to her as interpreter. The little black thing who was lame at length began to move in the most leisurely manner & upon reaching us said her mistress wished to know if we had come to hire the house. Being strangers she supposed we had. We explained that we were simply taking a walk, upon which she begged pardon for detaining us & withdrew.

We then proceeded and not far from home stopped at the open gate of a courtyard to admire the beautiful flowers that were arranged around the sides and in small stone enclosures in the centre of the place all the plaster being painted a pure white, the floor also white. While we stood lost in a maze two ladies approached and made signs for us to enter which we did accordingly and after shewing us all the shrubs & desiring a young gentleman there to cut flowers for us, they invited us into the parlour; their hands, which they offered us, were very small and delicate, one I saw the night before at the ball. They talked as fast as they could run on, and when they found they could not make us understand they laughed and seemed to consider it a great joke. We were not wanting in words and talked away in English which was as unintelligible to them as their Spanish to us. By pointing to the eyes of a little child & other signs I made the mother understand I thought it pretty which greatly pleased her. They shook hands when we came away & as far as we could understand asked us to come again the next day. Mr & Mrs Cunningham arrived this afternoon from Mrs Sage's in her volante which they wish us to take tomorrow to go to Santa Ana but we prefer being independent in our travels. Mrs Cunningham looks a good deal better she has enjoyed her visit much. This eveg we went to the theatre to see a Spanish play Carlos y Carolina which was so well performed that I could understand the pantomime after getting a clue to the story. The part of a porter was particularly good. A new singer made her appearance.

Wednesday. This evening we have been to a masquerade ball given at the theatre. It was got up in a hurry and said not to have been as brilliant as such affairs frequently are here. Mrs Harper accompanied us and we sat in the second row of boxes which is considered the best situation for seeing. None of the very young ladies wore masks and they were generally better dressed than at the other ball. The dancing was the same. When we first entered the company had not assembled only a few characters were perambulating the room. One, an old man riding picaback on an old woman was a most absurd ridiculous figure and did not occasion much amusement I understand he has been at two or three masquerades before. The greater part of those who were dressed in fanciful costumes did not come in until the middle of the evening when they mingled in the dances with the rest. I could not judge of many because the language in which they spoke was unintelligible to me. Some came round into the boxes and Mrs Harper talked in Spanish with them. One man addressed Dr Robinson in English but he could not discover if he were an acquaintance. A young man who personated a French portrait painter was said to perform his part admirably and I was highly amused by a party of blacks who executed the Creole dance in grand style. There was an excellent Calesero. These last characters are always well personated here as every one is so familiar with the originals that it is impossible to mistake. The masquers are obliged to show their faces as they enter to the officer at the door and they usually after puzzling the company all the eveg do so before they go home but this is optional. A short time since the wife of the Governor of Matanzas played him a trick at one of these balls; she pretended illness & declined going & he accordingly went without her. He had been there only a short time when we has accosted by a lady who in a disguised voice told him about his most private affairs & censured his conduct most unmercifully as well as that of the Officers of his staff. She was so extremely piquant and severe that he ordered an officer to follow her as she went out & oblige her to unmask when who should it prove to be but his wife.

Coming home we saw a building on fire at a distance and heard a most dismal bell; but little sensation was caused by the disaster and I imagine the house (or whatever it was) was suffered quietly to burn to the ground.

Friday Feby 2d[8] Mr Sears and his daughters left town to take up their abode at Don Carlos Smith's in Canarioca [Camarioca]. We have engaged lodgings on a neighbouring plantation in the same township, Don Juan Smith's, where we expect to go after having made our visit at Mr Sage's. George has derived such benefit from sea bathing that I feel in no hurry to discontinue it but we shall probably leave on Sunday. More strangers are coming & Mrs Harper's house will not long be theirs. This lady is a Philadelphian by birth and was married at the age of fifteen & went to New Orleans to live where I believe she was in good society but being unfortunate in business Mr Harper moved to this Island where after his death his wife was left entirely destitute with several children. She opened a boarding house and some of the gentlemen now with her were among the first boarders & have always befriended her. She is said to have amassed eighteen or twenty thousand dollars. Some of her children are dead One daughter a girl of fifteen or sixteen is at school in Philadelphia, another is married to a planter by the name of Bartlett who has a fine estate near Mr Sage's but who is extremely rough in his manners and has quarrelled with his Mother in law & will not suffer his wife to see her. Mrs Harper has a son Tom at school in the country who is the theme of her discourse. He is about eight years old. She is a woman of a good deal of acquirement & speaks fluently the French & Spanish besides English. She talks to her negroes altogether in French.

Sunday. Having sent our luggage by the boat we set forth in a volante & three horses (that is Lorenza baby & my self) Mr Lowell on horseback, for Sage's. The ride was altogether quite comfortable although some parts of the road are unimaginable to a person who has never been out of the United States and looking forward it seems an utter impossibility that the vehicle should avoid upsetting, thanks, however, to the inventer of volantes & a skillful Calesero we descended & ascended forked rivers and scaled rocks with very little shaking. The distance is about two or three & twenty miles. I say *about* for in this country no two persons agree on the subject of distances. Each judges by the length of time he is upon the road which of course depends, in a slight degree, upon the speed of his horse. We left Matanzas at eight o'clock and reached Mr Sage's at one. Hepsy was in the bath when we arrived but soon came out & welcomed us.

The Santa Ana is a most beautiful plantation in Lumidero. The whole place is in a high state of cultivation and here I have seen the handsomest palms which have yet greeted my sight in the island. Mr Sage's house is beautifully located upon a hill commanding a very picturesque view of the estate & surrounding country. On one side at the base are his secederos [secaderos] or Coffee dryers; his out buildings of various description, & the boheas [bohíos]. In front, the slope is finely wooded, but not so as to interfere with the view, & a large sand box tree faces the house standing on an elevation of stone work which has a very pretty effect; the garden is kept in good order, and here one sees every species of tree plant & shrub that Cuba produces; both Mr & Mrs Sage are fond of cultivating them. The house is a handsome one story building of stone work with a wide piazza in front & opening upon the garden behind a large hall runs nearly through & opens into a smaller back room with wide folding doors appearing like one apartment extending the width of the house, when open.

A coffee plantation in the Vuelta Abajo region, Cuba. From Francisco Pérez de la Riva, EL CAFÉ: HISTORIA DE SU CULTIVO Y EXPLOTACIÓN EN CUBA (HAVANA: J. MONTERO, 1944). *Courtesy of the Cuban Heritage Collection, Otto G. Richter Library, University of Miami, Coral Gables, Florida.*

On each side are the bed rooms two of which were appropriated to ourselves & the baby, a small room back is used as an eating room. This is adorned with some of Mrs Sage's paintings.

Hepsy seems very contented though placing great happiness in the idea of going home next spring to stay a year; she says she passed the first years of her abode here quite pleasantly but was made unfit for the place by going home upon a visit, she occupies herself all the time being obliged to do all her own sewing, to visit the sick negroes & to superintend every domestic arrangement. She knows a great deal about the place every tree upon it & all the variety of interests. She has acquired sufficient knowledge of Spanish to converse fluently which is necessary to live here with comfort. It is excessively awkward to be always obliged to employ an interpreter.

Sunday has so little to distinguish it in this country that I was about to take out my work after dinner when reminded by Hepsy of the day of the week. She says that most of the Americans who reside here fall sufficiently into the fashion of the country to dance on Sunday, she, however, has never done so. In the eveg we went out to see the negroes dance which is a most peculiar exhibition. Formerly, they were allowed to have this recreation Saturday aft & Sunday but since the insurrection Mr Sage has forbidden their dancing at any time except before sundown Sunday.

Monday. Mr Sage having two volantes he took Mr Lowell in one, while I accompanied Hepsy in the other and we rode to one or two neighbouring estates. We stopped at the sugar plantation of Mr Hernandez and I was introduced to several ladies, two or three of whom spoke a broken sort of English. We walked over the building where the sugar is made. It is perfectly marvelous to see how the negroes who skim the syrup can avoid scalding themselves and every one in their vicinity. It is as hot as fire can make it & is thrown up without any apparent caution; but I presume habit gives a slight of hand which renders the operation harmless; it is said the blacks are never scalded in this way. Occasionally one drowns himself in a fit of despair or temper in the boiling liquid. Those who feed the mill with cane frequently injure their hands very severely between the rollers.

Mrs Hernandez has the remains of considerable beauty but has grown fat as all Spanish women do. She can never pull her stocking above the ankle in consequence of the size of her limbs. She carried us into her garden and Mrs Sage admiring the size of her cabbage heads, this eveg a present of several have arrived. You cannot praise any thing belonging to a Spaniard without running the chance of having it offered to you. From this place we drove to the Ontario plantation partly owned by Mr Sage & in part by his brother in law Mr Webster who resides upon it. We were very kindly received by the family who invited us to come again; having arranged a riding party for the afternoon we returned home. Mr Webster & his eldest daughter coming to the Santa Ana to dine that they might accompany us. I felt rather unwilling to make my first attempt in horsemanship before spectators who have no idea of timidity but was overruled in every objection I made & we accordingly set forth after dinner & had an extremely pleasant excursion to a high hill two or three miles from the house where we had a commanding & beautiful view on all sides. On one the hills of Camarioca where we are going bounded the view.

Our road lay in part through the wood where I was much struck with the variety & beauty of the glossy leaves which surrounded us. The most luxuriant vines were hanging in festoons from the trees. I saw a great abundance of the passion flower seeds but none in bloom I am told some of the varieties in Cuba are extremely beautiful. The cactus runs wild. I had a very easy horse and enjoyed my ride.

This eveg Mrs Sage told me about the insurrection which took place a few years since just after she had gone home on a visit. It commenced on a neighboring plantation & Mr Sage's negroes were concerned as indeed were almost all for miles round. It is probable both Sage & Hepsy would have been murdered had they not been absent. It began on the estate of Mr Armitage himself, his wife & three sons & I don't know how many more were killed. They were extremely indulgent to their blacks & had not the least suspicion of danger. The Spaniards soon put a stop to the affair nine of Mr Sage's slaves were killed in the struggle & one shot. The slaves said after killing Mrs Armitage that it would go against them for they had killed a woman. Mr Sage shuts all the blacks out of the house at night, indeed, the house itself is a sort of castle & in his bed room he keep [keeps] two or three pairs of pistols, guns & swords. Every body rides armed. I have even persuaded my husband to purchase a sword. Mr S. has most noisy dogs and they do not suffer a negro to approach the house without giving alarm on this estate they are all very well clothed Mr Sage flogs the little ones if he finds them naked near the house Some of the dogs here are very savage. Griswold in speaking of his said he had one which would frequently leave him & follow his mayoral off into the woods and yet one day when the man came in suddenly & was about to take the keys from their place the dog jumped up and bit his hand so badly that it was feared it might be necessary to amputate; this he did because the Mayoral was going to take the keys himself instead of asking Griswold as he usually did.

Tuesday Having been persuaded to stay another day, we accompanied Mr & Mrs Sage in a drive to Mr Chapeau's plantation partly owned by Mr Howland of New York. The avenue is superb double rows of palm all of the same size and resembling pillars with carved capitals. The trunk of the palm when transplanted is large at the base and rather diminishes in size towards the top, it looks as Mr Abbot justly observes as if formed by a turning lathe and is white like a tree which has been washed with lime. Just under the branches is a plain green strip which encloses the palm cabbage I have been told that there are never more than twelve leaves (or branches) on the tree at a time, when a new one comes out the old falls off. But having myself counted fifteen I am inclined to believe it a Spanish fable. As some however on this tree looked in a dying condition perhaps they were preparing for departure. I had heard so much of the exceeding beauty of the Palm that I must confess myself rather disappointed, particularly in those which grow without cultivation in the woods & which are frequently irregular in their surface & have a bulge half way up the trunk which is a great blemish; I am beginning to acquire a taste for them. Mr Chapeau's avenue is perfectly strait with a wide close shaven walk of grass in the centre and on each side a carriage road of red earth bordered with palms between which are varieties of the South Sea rose. The house is small of wood but extremely neat Mrs Chapeau gave us very nice bread & butter & delicious preserves. Here I saw a preserve new to me made from a plant called "sorrel" & which resembles the currant jelly in taste.

Wednesday. We rose at day break and found Mrs Sage ready to give us a cup of coffee little George was quite sick in the night but has recovered. After a sufficient delay on the part of our Calesero we found ourselves on our way to Camarioca. The road was generally pretty good but in a few places almost impassible. Our volante dashed through one mud hole which half covered the horses but they worked their way out. I gave the baby to Mr Lowell going up one *perpendicular* hill & Lorenza & I walked up lest the horses should fail on the way. Part of the road was quite rocky and

I received a severe blow in the eye from a stone thrown up by the horses feet, at first the pain was so severe that I feared the light was forever extinguished but upon closing the other discovered to my entire satisfaction that I could see with it. The blood began to trickle down & Lorenza to grieve, but I was so well pleased to retain the sight of my eye that I disregarded altogether the blemish to its beauty.

In passing through the Savannas we saw the fan palm which never grows to any great height & which makes a very pretty fan We arrived at Camarioca before dinner where we are tolerably well accommodated upon the St Juan estate formerly owned by Mr John Smith. He now resides on it in consequence of a law of the Island which prevents the possibility of creditors turning a man off a sugar estate, and although he was in jail two or three years in Hartford his family resided here & were allowed twelve hundred dollars a year for their support. Mr Smith superintends the coffee part of the establishment but as the whole estate is called a sugar plantation he avails himself of the laws although he has no control over the other part Mr Wilson another of the former owners takes care of it on account of James D'Wolf. Mr Smith involved himself very much by endorsing for Genl D'Wolf. Dr Robinson & W. Gorham have been here some days.

Wednesday. Mr Sears & daughters called, they are quite pleasantly situated at Don Carlos's.

Feby 16th Thermometer 82°. It has not varied much from this since we came here

13th[9] There has been so little variety in life here that I have kept no regular journal We rise about seven & sometimes ride before breakfast which meal takes place at nine or later. A cup of coffee before. The morng I spend working or writing and generally ride after dinner. We dine between three & four consequently there is no time after our return except to stroll a little upon the secadéros or coffee dryers in front of the house. In the eveg cards. This morng Mr Lowell & Dr Robinson went over to Mr Sage's the former had business respecting Mr Griswold. The latter when on to Mr Jenckes's. This eveg I accompanied Mrs Smith & W. Gorham to Miss Bodin's she had called upon me a few days since. Just as I was riding into the yard little George began to scream and on coming in I found something was the matter with his arm; it seems in coming up the steps Lorenza had hold of his left hand and was not aware that he pulled more upon it than usual, but he suddenly cried out & said "hand hand." I found it gave him extreme pain to have the arm moved in the least and feared he had put it out. No physician was nearer than Limoral seven or eight miles off and we sent down to the sugar estate to desire Mrs Wilson who is experienced in illness to come up. Mrs Charles Smith & Mr Sears happened to be there & all came up together. They examined the arm & did not think it dislocated but still advised my sending for the Physician which I shall do before I go to bed expecting to see him early in the morng George is unable to move the arm in the slightest degree himself & screams if his position is changed.

14th[10] Monday George passed a comfortable night. When he wished to turn Lorenza held his arm while I moved him. He was free from pain this morng but still suffered if his limb were moved. Dr Beattie arrived before breakfast & pronounced it only a severe sprain & orderd 6 leeches I could procure however only three which I applied and he experienced such relief as to be able to run about & make use of his arm this afternoon. I think his shoulder has been sprained for some time slightly, or weak in some way for when we were in Matanzas Lorenza told me one morng that he had sometimes cried out when she lifted him suddenly & something seemed the matter with his left shoulder. I hope this sprain will be the termination of the trouble.

Tuesday George has quite recovered the use of his arm and my only fear now is lest he should meet with another accident to which it is probable he will for some time be liable. Mr Lowell & Dr Robinson returned from Mr Sage's yesterday morng before Dr Beattie left here. They had a pleasant ride Miss Bumstead was there. Mrs Sage sent me kind messages. I find that there is not that strong feeling of hospitality now among the planters that formerly existed. No visitors are asked who do not bring strong letters of recommendation. This backwardness which has only been in force for a year or two no doubt arises from the ingratitude which has frequently been displayed by those who have been treated with the utmost kindness. Mr Sage mentioned to us an instance of a gentleman who desired a friend of his to ask him for letters to his Mayoral one winter when he was at home. This gentleman was coming to Cuba for his health and Mr Sage, although not personally acquainted gave him letters desiring that he should be treated with every attention, the house opened for him & that he might ride any horses he preferred in the stable. He came to Cuba staid five months upon the Santa Ana & returned to Boston without even thanking Mr Sage who had in the mean time returned & did not even call to tell Mrs Sage, who was at her mother's, how her husband was. The man selected the finest horse in the stable and killed him by hard riding.

Mr Sage observed this was but one instance among an hundred which had disgusted planters with the practice of receiving all strangers. It is fortunate that now there are several willing to take boarders. Mr Macomb who has a fine sugar estate and an expensive house & who formerly entertained a great deal of company went to the States a year or two since & says he was continually passing people who took no notice of him or his wife who had staid in his house for weeks perhaps. Sometimes indeed he was asked to call, but rarely more. Of course he does not now feel the same desire to see foreigners.

In returning from a visit to Lorenza this eveg Isabella, Miss Sears's woman, met with a singular adventure. She was accompanied by two of Mrs Smiths children, Robert & Leocadia, they had just reached the edge of the wood when they were overtaken by a Spaniard who dismounted and seizing Isabella round the waist attempted to place her in the saddle. She resisted but finding he still continued to hold her & to talk away in Spanish, she began to scream vehemently in which she was seconded by Robert. The little girl, in the mean while ran home and was so frightened as, at first, to be unable to speak. The man upon hearing Isabella scream so lustily dropped her & rode off. So much for Spanish gallantry!

The Monteros are a desperate set and handle the machéte with great adroitness they are said always to treat ladies with politeness and perhaps this individual thought Isabella had no objection to take a ride Mr Smith was telling us about a common Spanish ball he attended where they roasted a pig whole & cut it with the knives they always carry & eat fried plantains as an accompanyment.

17th[11] Thermometer 83°.

18th[12] Thermometer 82°. Rode to see a beautiful tree described by Mr Abbott, certainly a fine tree. Not very high but the foliage extremely thick the shape at top of a cabbage, leaves resembling the pear in shape. Had to leap logs & ditches in the expedition.

Saturday Feby 25th Mr Lowell Mrs Sarah Smith and myself spent today at Don Carlos's where we had a very good dinner. We rode home before dark Mrs Smith staid the night. we walked over the premises which are very pretty in the neighbourhood of the house. Mr S. is erecting a mill for grinding sugar cane and has thought of turning his coffee estate into a sugar plantation. We visited the portrero for pigs an important part of every estate. All the pigs raised here, that I have seen, are black. Mrs Smith says the native race are light colored. They range at large in a field and look much more happy than when stived up. All the negroes rear pigs and make money by selling them to the Spaniards. Almost every black upon this estate is worth at least an ounce. Guinea hens are common here and are esteemed quite as much as our fowls, to me they are inferior; the wild are preferred to the tame. They are always shot & usually wiled away from the house in which case they run home when wounded but if fired at near the house they run into the coffee and are lost.

Sunday. This morning I saw Mr Smith deliver the weeks rations to his slaves. They were ranged in rows the men standing together & the women & children a little way off. Four mackerel were placed in a pile and there were as many piles as men & women. After being counted each stepped forward and took his fishes and marched off with them in one hand & in the other he took a bundle of fodder for his pigs. Each of the children had one. This is the luxury allowed them their food besides during the week consists principally of plantains & some corn. When plantains are scarce corn is substituted & so the reverse. The slaves here are apparently happy though worse clothed than upon any estate Mr Lowell has seen; their rags hardly hold together. They should have had their new wardrobe last Christmas, but the poverty of the land prevented. Most of the little ones are naked.

After the rations had been distributed W. Gorham & I walked round to the boheas [bohíos] to see the cooking. We found some already seated on the floor with a mess of pounded corn & soup flavored with wild tomatos which are about as big as a gooseberry & boiled plantains; they have not learned the use of forks & entirely prescribe to the old opinion that fingers do more execution. Their mess looked savoury enough, but their manner of eating from a calabash, seated in the dirt, was most disgusting.

W. Gorham purchased a horse for two ounces yesterday ($34). My husband took a ride on him this morng. I walked to the sugar house this afternoon on the lower part of the estate to give Lorenza, who accompanied us an opportunity of seeing the process of extracting the juice of the cane. In this mill two negroes are employed one to put the cane between the rollers & the other takes it out on the other side. Don Carlos has erected a mill which saves the labor of one slave by causing the cane to drop after passing through. The oxen who turn the mill are guided by blacks and constantly goaded the poor creatures seemed perfectly in despair. We afterwards called at Mrs Wilsons where Mr Seaver & Mr Lawrence are staying. We went on the roof of the house which has a very pretty view of Camarioca river. We brought home some flowers & leaves to press. I saw one tree entirely leafless in the garden & was told it was a plum which bears & ripens its fruit before a leaf appears. It is very brittle & a branch snaps, on taking hold of it, like a dead stick.

Tuesday. W. Gorham set off this morng at an early hour for Limoral where he is attracted by a ball which is to take place this evening. Mr Smith, Mr Kinkannon & Mr Lawrence accompanied him. Mr Seaver dined with us. Thermometer 86 at half past four in the afternoon

Wednesday The house has been quite a hospital today. Mrs Smith, the old lady who has been indisposed a day or two has not risen from her bed. Dr Robinson has hardly sat up at all and Lorenza has suffered from one of her sick headachs. Dr Robinson has not recovered from the fatigue of his ride to Mr Jenks's and indeed it has probably done away all the good effects he had derived from this climate. He is now laboring under some complaint brought on by too great exertion I do not know what. It is astonishing to see the imprudence of all the invalids who come here for their health they expose themselves to hot suns & night dews, which are exceedingly heavy; & to every sort of fatigue. It is only those whose cases are hopeless who are disposed to be tolerably careful. Mr & Mrs Fales & their daughter Mrs Monroe spent the day with us. They are neighbours & friends of Mrs Smith. Thermometer 82.

W. Gorham returned without Mr Smith.

Thursday. We received on invitation early this morng to breakfast with Mrs Wilson & meet Miss Bumstead who arrived last eveg from Limoral. We accordingly (Frank, W. Gorham & myself,) rode to the sugar estate about nine o'clock and found assembled there the Searss' with their Mrs Smith, Mr Hubbard & Miss Bumstead, Mr Seaver & Mr Lawrence. Miss B. is a most robust young lady looking the very reverse of an invalid. She says she had suffered from a pain in her side & cough for a year or more & was quite in different to every thing. Now she rides every day, making nothing of ten or twenty miles, takes long walks, which she had been unable to do & subjects herself to all sorts of exposures without the least inconvenience; she seems delighted with Cuba and enjoys all the time. This climate is almost a certain cure for those whose lungs are slightly attacked & who would grow worse if they remained at home, but with those whose complaints are fixed it rather accelerates the disease. The difficulty is in knowing who are too ill to come, for many are brought here apparently incurable & recover but I have seen several this winter who would have been more comfortable at home, and no one much out of health ought to think of coming to Cuba without some friend to take care of him.

We had a very nice breakfast at Mrs Wilson's at 11 o'clock, it might have been dignified with the title of dinner for we had some most substantial fare, roast turkey, oysters, made dishes of variòus kinds omelet besides apple pies, plantains, funche, cakes, tea & coffee. The Sears party went home soon after breakfast to pack and after sitting a short time with Miss Bumstead & Mrs Wilson I returned here. Mrs W. urged us to stay to dinner & I half consented but having engaged to go to Don Carlos's in the afternoon concluded to come home & see little George who always most joyously welcomes us. Not feeling well after dinner I suffered Mrs Smith & the gentlemen to go to Don Carlos's without me. They spent the evening there & had quite a pleasant time waltzing & playing whist. Miss Bumstead & company[13] Miss Fales & brother were there. Mr Wilson being as usual rather excited made his wife go home before the rest. Almost every man past the middle age of life in this part of the country (foreigners I mean, for the Spaniards are temperate) is addicted to the bottle and almost every individual is in debt. I never heard in any other place of so many bankrupts. It is the rarest thing for a man to possess his estate free & unembarrassed.

Friday. This morng before breakfast Mr Lowell & I rode to Don Carlos's to see the party off. They had just finished breakfast when we arrived and were arrayed for the journey. Two volantes, most wretched looking vehicles with three horses each stood in the yard & two other horses one with a seroon for baggage & the other for Thomas were standing in the yard.

Mr Packard, a friend of Mr Sears, who has an estate seven or eight miles off, was also there. Cordelia seemed to regret her departure very much, she has gained in health every day since she came to Camarioca. Harriet is more homesick and hails with joy any change which is preparatory to going home. She is not fond of travelling and being perfectly well has no inducement to make her wish to be away from home. I regret very much that they must go but hope we may meet again before reaching home. Mr Sears has purchased a very fine mare to take home for ten ounces which is esteemed an enormous price for a mare here as they are not prized like horses. If she gets home uninjured I do not believe he will be sorry for his bargain.

This eveg Mrs Wilson, Mr Griswold Miss Bumstead & the gentlemen of the party called in leaving about eight o'clock Mr Hubbards horse reared & threw him off & fell upon him he asserted that he was not at all hurt & insisted upon walking home. He selected a gay horse though advised against it and Mrs Wilson insinuated was unwilling to do any thing which gave him the appearance of old age.

Saturday. Letters from home by Mr Rollins which were very welcome Mr Griswold dined here. Walked to the sugar estate in the afternoon with Mr Lowell & Mrs Smith found the ladies had gone to walk & joined them. We ascended a hill near the house to the hut of a Spanish Montero who received us courteously & brought us out some dusty chairs & showed us some pretty blue headed pigeons & described in a most animated manner in Spanish to Mrs Wilson the manner in which they were caught. They are of a most beautiful dove or fawn color with blue heads & a blue fan under the throat edged with white. These Monteros are a wild looking desperate race living in small huts not better than the negro boheas [bohíos] and surrounded by dogs, they all own at least one horse they are great thieves.[14]

From the top of the hill there is a very fine view. We brought home some leaves to press, which were very pretty. Mr Hubbard said he was a little stiff, but not otherwise incommoded by the turn over he had last night. Played whist this eveg.

Sunday, March 4th. We had a slight shower this morng but the weather cleared & though cool it has been very pleasant I wrote several letters home. This afternoon we rode to the town of Ciguapa; it consists of two or three houses & shops, and an old church looking precisely like a little barn. The road lies through quite a forest of Palm trees. These trees look well rising one above another on the side of a hill. The dogs which are barking in every direction and the loose horses anoy me in riding. On our return we found Mr Seaver, Miss Bumstead & Mrs Wilson here, the two former are going to Matanzas tomorrow. They intend to go on horseback. A new moon. Thermometer 77° at a quarter before nine in the eveg.

Monday. Mr Hubbard, Miss Bumstead, Mr Seaver & Mr Lawrence left Mrs Wilson's at an early hour in the morng for Matanzas. Mrs Wilson called here in the evening. Thermometer 80°.

Tuesday. To day we have had a norther and some showers. Miss Fales came to spend the day and in the afternoon Mrs Charles Smith & Mrs Wilson called. We accompanied them back to the sugar estate where we found the Misses Wales, who had come from Limoral in the morng. The brother who is out of health seems to me but little better. He has a hectic flush upon his cheek & his voice is quite husky; his cough has rather lessened. He thinks he was injured by going first to New Orleans where the weather was very severe & it is highly probable if he had sailed for Cuba his fate might have been different, for at present there seems to me little chance of his recovery. Six weeks earlier in this climate perhaps might have saved him.

I begin to tire of Camarioca in consequence of having had my feelings shocked within the last day or two by two or three unpleasant events. Yesterday while sitting at work I heard the lash going with great violence and was told by Mr Smith that it was the Mayoral on the sugar estate whipping negroes. This gave me an immediate distaste to the place and this morng there was a story that a negro had been torn to pieces by the dogs set on him by this man. The exact truth of the story, I presume, we have not learned but it is certain the man was killed by dogs & buried yesterday. The sugar estate is now nominally under the care of Wilson who was originally fourth owner but like our landlord lives here now without possessing any of the property; he is all the time under the influence of liquor and takes no care of the place. He appointed this mayoral who is a brutal wretch & winks at his misdemeanors. It is hinted that he is too much in the Spaniards power in consequence of some tricks of which he has been guilty to be willing to turn him off. If they are not careful the negroes will some time take their revenge upon both. The slaves upon this estate are miserably clothed, they should have had a new suit last christmas but their masters have not yet afforded them one their rags are dropping off them. On this part, the coffee part, of the plantation they seem tolerably happy & I should think were not over worked. There is but little discipline or order of any sort. Mr Smith's second son is administrator & is young and likes better to go to Matanzas upon a frolick than to stay at home & see to the slaves. He is paid five hundred dollars a year for his services. the eldest son, husband of Mrs Sarah, has a small portrero; or farm, which he manages. He does not live at home.

The blacks on the sugar estate are the most ferocious looking set of beings I ever saw & it would not surprise me at any moment if they were roused to vengeance, they are worked unmercifully and most cruelly treated. I believe it is much more difficult upon a sugar than upon a coffee plantation not to over work the negroes, there is so much to be done when the sugar is making. Within a very short time one has hung & another scalded himself to death. It is the custom to burn the bodies of those who commit suicide to deter the rest from a similar act for the blacks have an expectation of meeting their friends in the next world and they imagine if the body is burnt that it is dispersed to the winds & cannot unite again & get to heaven. They have a fashion of putting money into the mouth of a dead negro to pay his way to heaven. One of our slaves came home & said that a little black child who lay dead had his mouth so filled with half bits that it could not be shut. It astonishes me that there are plantains enough to supply such a number of negroes with food for after cutting the fruit the tree is destroyed. They usually cut the tree down to get at the fruit & the shoots which surround it spring up in its place it takes a year for the tree to arrive at perfection It is a rare thing to see a very old negro. I observed one at Mrs Charles Smiths who looked upwards of seventy. She had the charge of the young children & seemed to possess quite a faculty in stilling them. She is so old she has lost her memory & has returned to her native African dialect having forgotten her more recently acquired Spanish.

1832
Wednesday March 7th This being the last day but one we are to spend in Camarioca, Mr Lowell, Mrs Smith & myself mounted after dinner to make some take leave calls we rode to Don Carlos Smith's and my horse proving very hard Mrs S proposed my exchanging him for one of hers which I was very glad to do. We sat some time and after looking at a fine mare purchased by Mr Sears we proceeded to Miss Bodens. Mr Sears gave ten ounces for the mare which is said to be a remarkably fine animal. This is considered an enormous price as horses are much more highly valued here; they frequently sell for twenty ounces. On our way to Miss Boden's we passed two or three bulls which were tied on one side a little off the road. It is very common to see them in this way, one seemed to be quite furious & kept continually bellowing & pawing the ground & trying to break his rope. I did not fancy passing him particularly, but supposing there was no danger rode on. We made one visit at Miss Boden's and returning passed several more of these animals one of whom sprung towards us but did not break his rope. This made me feel a little queer & on approaching the animal who first startled me we found him directly a cross the path we were to take conducting in a most furious manner; this was more than my philosophy could encounter & I at length prevailed upon Frank to ride back to a house we had just passed where Mrs Smith was acquainted, and the woman who lived there sent out some negroes to tie the creature after which he suffered us to pass with only bowing & scraping. I do not find that these animals do any mischief in this country & the other day I passed through a field in which there were four, but this was apparently so enraged, he excited my fear.

Thursday. Miss Anita Boden came to spend the day with her younger sister I was much engaged packing in the morng. In the afternoon we had a visit from Mrs Charles Smith & daughter Mr & Mrs Wilson, Mr Griswold & a Mr Amy. William Gorham was thrown from his horse (a colt of Mr Smith's) in attempting to mount him at Don Carlos's & sprained his wrist slightly & cut his hand he does not seem much injured but is disabled from riding to town with us tomorrow on horseback; fortunately Walter Scott's last novel has arrived tonight so that he will have something to occupy him when we are gone. We played cards this eveg.

Friday. Left Camarioca about 8 o'clock having been detained by the carelessness of the man who sent us horses for our baggage; they came without seroons and we were forced to send far & wide to borrow them Dr Robinson accompanied us to town. We had two volantes with three horses each & five other horses for luggage. The day was rainy but we were not much incommoded by it & when not actually showering we enjoyed our ride the more in consequence of its being overcast. I was delighted with the view descending the Canama hill we stopped at the small inn at the foot and were delayed some time by the transportation of our baggage & horses over the ferry. The view was most beautiful of the opposite shores. Little George did not fancy going over in the launch I believe he thought he was to be dipped in the water. We arrived at Mrs Harpers about dinner time the house full to overflowing. Our rooms were already engaged. I was fatigued with the ride & lay on the bed until tea time. Mr Hubbard & Miss Bumstead are here. The Sullivans gone to Mrs Sage's.

Saturday I have loitered so much to day that I consider the time lost. Some new gentlemen arrived this afternoon in a vessel from Havana they were out two or three days the weather very rough. Mr Storey, Mr McLean, Mr W. Rollins &c. Recd letters from home with the news that Eliza's wedding was to take place on the 12th of this month. Mr Knight called he is going tomorrow to Havana on horseback & Miss Bumstead had prevailed upon Mr Hubbard to accompany him a distance of 60 miles, but has been dissuaded by the gentlemen here from undertaking the journey. She is a most adventurous young lady, Mr Newton is quite devoted to her.

Sunday. Nothing extraordinary today except another letter from Mother.

Monday 12th Mr Taylor having kindly offered us his horses Mr Lowell & myself accompanied by Mr Newton & Miss Bumstead took a ride of four miles to the Combra a most magnificent view. our design was to arrive just at sunset to see the deep lights & shades which add much to the beauty of the scene but although we got there in season we loitered a little too long in a garden on top of the hill & the sun had sank too low when we left there. You look down from a great height upon a valley of palms & sugar estates. The hills opposite are peculiarly and beautifully formed and you have a fine view of the Pan of Matanzas. Our ride to town was quite pleasant although the moon had not risen sufficiently high to give us a <*words missing*> the city which lay below. After tea Mrs Harper accompanied us to Mrs Grace's where we made a short call; the house is quite comfortable & the floor the prettiest I have seen in Matanzas being composed of marble tiles alternately black & white. Mr McLean a gentlemanly man from Alexandria sung to us most delightfully after our return. Wrote to Eliza & Mother.

Tuesday. Mrs Cook & son came into town this morng to be ready for the steam boat tomorrow. Mrs Harper's house is full to overflowing. It is small & she has contemplated taking a fine one on the opposite side of the street, the only three story house in Matanzas, but the rent is two thousand dollars and she is advised against taking it. This eveg Mr McLean again sung to us. Jacob who accompanied Mr Rollins to Cuba called to take letters. Mr W. Rollins accompanied some gentlemen into the country this morng. The thermometer today has stood at 86°.

Wednesday. This morng a little after six we were ready to set out for Mrs Jenckes's plantation. A volante with three horses was appropriated to myself, the baby and Lorenza. Mr Lowell preferred horseback; we found the roads rather heavy but the calesero was skillful and the country through which we passed quite romantic. We stopped about two leagues short of St Cyrilo to breakfast at quite a fine inn. The hall was large & handsome & we were well attended. We walked into the garden & a pretty Spanish girl gave us some flowers & pomegranites; two girls under twenty were sitting smoking & sewing in the courtyard. We arrived at Mrs Jenckes's before eleven o'clock and I was sufficiently fatigued to lay on the bed until dinner time. Mrs J. has her sister Mrs Noyes & daughter staying with her. I was delighted with the avenue the first quarter of a mile being shaded with bamboo trees which are beautiful to my eye, & the rest with orange trees. A porters lodge was placed inside the gate. The house is plain & was not originally intended for the mansion house but for the Mayoral but upon calculating the expense of finishing the buildings which were projected & finding the amount would be sixty thousand dollars Mr Jenckes resolved to occupy this house which was already built & put his money into the estate in a way more profitable. The coffee mill is rather too near the house for comfort as the dust is troublesome in the season when it is in operation; the secaderos come quite up to the piazza. It is a very large & fine estate in extremely good order. About 150 negroes. Twenty new blacks have just arrived recently brought from Africa. They yet speak no English, they are not put to work but are under the process of fattening. Mrs Jenckes says that in about a month they will be quite hearty; they seem well pleased with their situation, and upon arriving said fino, fino, & they wished to stop. they were all dressed in blue checked pantaloons & shirts & having been recently christened had their names pasted on their shoulders. It is necessary to make Christians of them as soon as they arrive or the owner cannot claim them. All the young creoles too must be baptised Most of the boys who have just landed are troubled with weak eyes.

Mrs Jenckes is a remarkably fine looking old lady, about sixty five or six years of age. She has a high smooth forehead and good features. She dresses in a plain lawn cap with a delicate lace border & white lawn gown she wears a black lace veil which is sometimes on her shoulders & sometimes drawn over her cap. Her manners are extremely cordial & dignified & one feels at home at once.

<end of first volume>

<pencil drawing of magnolia on first page of second volume>

1832

March 15th Thursday. This morning I had a better opportunity of looking about the place than yesterday, having in some degree, slept away my fatigue. The house is situated rather low with hills on all sides; the boheas [bohíos] in a semicircle on one side have a very comfortable appearance; a small house is appropriated to the children too small to work and there you may see from ten to twenty little creatures enjoying themselves under the charge of an experienced negress. I was invited to look at a pair of twins a few days old, the drollest little creatures imaginable and a rare sight among the blacks. Some buildings, the stables &c occupy the centre of the yard; the volante house, coffee mill, Mayorals rooms, &c. being attached to the house. Opposite the back piazza is the hospital, a building indispensable on all large plantations; underneath which are store rooms, ironing room and kitchen. On the other side the house the coffee dryers extend a long distance giving the idea of large crops. At the further end, up the hill, is the hen house, quite a large building. Mrs Jenckes says she sends to her son an hundred eggs every week; the fowls are examined each morning and those which are going to lay kept confined until after dinner when they are suffered to roam at large. Two pigeon houses stand in front of the hen establishment and the flock is immense; indeed we have found plenty every where, Mr Sage I believe has two or three thousand. The large bell which is rung at stated intervals stands on one side; near the house is a small kitchen garden and, at some distance one filled with flowers.

To day the weather clouded early and we had a violent hail storm; the second only since Mrs Jenckes came here, a period of upwards of twenty six years, some of the stones were nearly as large as pigeons eggs and the ground was literally covered, negroes were running in every direction collecting them and having filled a large bowl brought it to Mrs Jenckes. The Mayoral put one into his mouth but instantly spit it out as if he were scalded; he insisted upon one or two of the little blacks doing the same but they seemed equally alarmed; it was altogether quite an amusing spectacle. The wind was high but it is not supposed much damage was done to the young coffee. They are just now in the act of fanning; the coffee is passed through three mills, to get rid of the hulls and dust, and is then picked over by hand. I mounted the stairs to day and found the women seated each side a long table busily employed in performing the operation, they sing all the time the same tune by which they dance; indeed they seem to have but one. It is very monotonous, but I like to hear it, as it has a happy contented sound. The slaves here are well fed and taken care of; they all look hearty. Mrs Jenckes says they have fresh meat every day and plenty of plantains and funche. She seems rather tired of the life she leads here but does not like to live at Matanzas and is unwilling to reside at the north because her son, an only child, resides in this country; he is a man of wealth and intelligence, she seems wrapped up in him and his children. He married a Spanish lady of whom Mrs Jenckes speaks very highly & who seems to satisfy her in all respects. This eveg Miss Noyes sung to us. The thermometer 72° in the house, colder than any weather we have experienced 69° has been the lowest.

Friday. This afternoon, the weather having cleared away, the volante was ordered and Mrs Noyes, little George and myself stepped in. Mr Lowell Miss N. and her brother accompanied us on horseback to a neighbouring plantation.

The family were in Havana but the Mayoral did the honors in very good style. There is a fine view from the piazza of the house. The garden quite pretty we brought away a collection of flowers and fruit. George has become tired of riding, and was continually saying "home home". Mrs Jenckes has been extremely kind to him and takes the place of his Grandmother in loading him with good things. Lorenza says she is a "beautiful lady".

Saturday. The sky was again overcast this morning, but the weatherwise saying it would not rain Mrs Jenckes ordered the volante after dinner and setting forth in the same cavalcade as yesterday we rode to the estate of Don Manuel Garcia about six miles distance. Mrs Jenckes's avenue is certainly very pretty, it is a mile in length and the last quarter is bordered with bamboo trees which meeting over head have much the appearance of gothic arches; the gateway is in very good taste and the porter who inhabits a lodge just inside is extremely prompt in opening it. Don Manuel Garcia and his wife have been intimate friends of Mrs Jenckes ever since she came upon her estate; the day after she was established there they rode up to dine and ever since they have been very sociable: she calls them the best people in the world. The plantation is in fine order and from the extent of the secaderos I should judge extensive but we did not ride over it. From the top of the dryers you have a most magnificent view. We found a volante at the door as we rode up which brought the Mother of La Senora Garcia & two or three neices from Havana. They talked Spanish as fast as possible and Mr Noyes acted as interpreter; they carried us into the garden and presented us each with a boquet, it is quite amusing to observe those they select as most precious; the marigold, poppy and all our gaudy garden flowers and they seem to consider those we most prize and which with us inhabit the greenhouse as quite beneath notice. Our ride home was very pleasant.

Sunday The volante having arrived for us last night, at two o'clock we set off for Matanzas; in some places the road was quite heavy, and bad, as all the roads are throughout the island; a vast deal of limestone is mixed with the red soil and it would be easy to make them fine but the government is not sufficiently energetic to do so. Mrs Harper was expecting us. Miss Bumstead had left the day before for the country accompanied by Mr Hubbard and Mr Newton, her devoted admirer. The young lady has occasioned a great sensation here. The gentlemen in the house are very attentive, Mr Newton particularly and I do not well see how she can reject him, but young ladies know how to manage such matters, and none better than Miss Bumstead; She came from Havana in the boat with a Spanish officer with whom she had no acquaintance and who played upon the guitar and eyed her very hard, it seems the idea of her being a great fortune is very general here, and one morng a letter was delivered to her by one of the negroes which she returned unopened, the officer had endeavored before to bribe the servant to give it, but he refused in fear of displeasing his mistress; the offer, however, of half an ounce was irresistible. A night or two after Miss B. was sitting with two or three gentlemen when a letter was brought in addressed to Mrs Harper; as it was handed in by two soldiers, she, fearing that she had got into difficulty handed it to Mr Taylor to open. When it proved only an envelope to a letter to Miss Bumstead, she broke the seal and soon discovered it was a proposal, written in French, from this same officer, referring to her Father &c &c. She immediately closed it saying no answer was necessary and the next day returned it in a blank envelope.

Since our return from St. Cyrilo Mrs Harper has shewn us a letter received from the man written in a most piquant style; he says he was informed Miss Bumstead had made public his proposal and he was surprised Mrs Harper had not advised her better; that it was the fashion in this country to return an answer of some sort, either yes or no, to such a letter, and that if Miss B. did not wish to do so she should, at least, have sent his back unopened; but he supposed she was carried away by curiosity, a frailty common to human nature. He added that he considered it very unfortunate Miss B. did not join the qualities of heart & education to her extreme beauty and said he now saw clearly the misfortune he was preparing himself. All this was written in French and well touched off. Miss Bumstead seems to have been quite a firebrand in the house. My Bayley rallied the Consul about her the other eveg and the conversation at table which took place, ended in their giving each other the lie, and the difference is not yet adjusted.

Monday. Captn Shubrick, of the United States ship Vincennes, with some of his officers dined here and a Mr & Mrs Harrison & children, who are going to Jamaica to reside. Mr H. is appointed American Consul there; in the afternoon I went to ride with Mrs Harrison & Virginia the little girl. Capt Shubrick invited us on board tomorrow morng at eleven o'clock.

Tuesday We recd a note this morng from Captn Shubrick post-poning our our[15] visit to the Vincennes until tomorrow, on account of the wind, and shortly after, were informed by a young midshipman that the boats had come for us. We did not feel at liberty to go, after the note, supposing they had come by mistake and accordingly sent them back. I went with Mr Lowell to dine at Mr Grace's with no company but Mr Rollins & Mr Story, who are staying there. We had an excellent dinner. I returned before night and went with Mrs Harper to call upon young Mrs Jenckes, daughter in law to the lady with whom we staid; she received us graciously & shewed me her children. A picture of Doña Serafina hung in the room, a fine likeness. Mrs Jenckes was arrayed in a thin white muslin embroidered with short sleeves, and a colored handkerchief on her neck. When we came back to the house we found Capt Shubrick & Lieutenant Ingle who said the note we received this morng was not to have been delivered and came through some mistake, this we regretted extremely, as the ship was prepared to receive us.

Wednesday This morng at eleven o'clock we rode to the wharf stepped into the boat in waiting and had a delightful pull to the Vincennes; there the officers were ready to welcome us on deck and Mrs Harrison in the cabin. We were carried all over the ship and I never saw any place in such perfect order; after exploring every part of the ship we mounted the upper deck and sat some time listening to the band which is very good; two of the young midshipmen waltzed with Virginia. We had a pretty collation and Mrs Harrison begging me to stay to dinner I consented, but afterwards regretted I did so, as it made the day rather too long. Mrs Harper went home to receive the company from the steam boat which was expected but did not come. At Sunset we rowed to the fort where we landed, Mr & Mrs Harrison & Capt Shubrick accompanying us, from thence we walked home and in the eveg went upon Gov's square to hear the music. Extremely hot.

Thursday Mrs Harper having purchased a new house I went this morning to see it, she will probably find it much more convenient than the other which is small and out of repair; this is one recently vacated by a French woman who has taken Spaniards as boarders. She happened to find it troublesome to pay her debts one day, and was obliged to run away from her creditors, leaving house, furniture & every thing in its usual order. Mr & Mrs Brimmer arrived in the steam boat before dinner from Havana Mrs

H. has been obliged to give them apartments in her new house. Mrs B. lay on my bed until tea time, her health has improved. In the eveg, after her departure, we walked with Mrs Harper, Mr Taylor & Mr McLean to a crockery store and then round the square, stopping in front of a coffee house where the gentlemen ordered some ices. The crockery establishments are arranged here with the greatest taste and exhibit the articles to advantage. I do not know that the shops possess a greater variety than ours but the fashion of displaying every thing, makes them look much more shewy; Mrs Harper, having made considerable purchases, the merchant invited her to take a contra which is allowed in such cases, this is some article she fancies which is thrown into the bargain; she helped herself to a small pitcher and he then insisted upon my doing the same, although I had bought nothing. I resisted some time but Mr McLean took a pitcher also for me, a very pretty pink one which I transferred to Mrs Harper.

Friday. Mr Sullivan and Eliza returned from Santa Ana while we were at dinner. E. has not gained since I first saw her at Havana, or rather she has lost what she gained in the mountains at Mrs Jouve's, she was caught in a violent shower going from there to Reserva and that in addition to riding forty miles in one day made it necessary for her to lay by a week and she still suffers from the effects of exposure; she makes friends wherever she goes and is a general favorite. In the eveg we sat talking until nine o'clock at which time I commenced a letter to Mrs Jenckes.

Saturday. My last day in Matanzas! I spent the greater part of the morng with Eliza, hearing her experiences in the west. In the afternoon called with Mrs Harper upon Mrs Grace, and afterwards went to a neighboring house to see a fine view of the city and environs altogether quite striking. Sat talking, in the eveg with Mrs Brimmer, Eliza, &c. Thermometer 81°.

Sunday 25th We left Matanzas at half past six in the morng in the steam boat, several of the gentlemen made an exertion to get up and see us off. The day has been fine, but I was sufficiently seasick to lay in my birth all the way. I left Matanzas almost with regret for it was with the prospect of never again seeing the place and in it I have passed many pleasant hours. We found Mr Sears and the girls at Mrs Howard's and the house full, but in consequence of the politeness of some gentlemen who turned themselves out of their room for me we were accommodated.

Mr Knight called in the eveg, we rode on the Paseo. There was a great show of Quiterines & volantes, some of the gentlemen counted one hundred and fifty; some of these carriages are as handsome as splendid painting & high varnish & gilt can make so awkward a vehicle. The top of the quiterine is thrown back and is usually occupied by three ladies, the prettiest in front, all dressed in their best attire. It is the great ambition of a Spanish family to keep an equipage and to appear to advantage on the Paseo and frequently every thing else is sacrificed to this luxury. Occasionally, on the Paseo, you will observe a Don seated, in solitaire, in his quiterine, but generally the men stand in rows on each side and exchange bows & smiles with the dames as they ride along. Frequently a brother & sister, Husband & wife or Father & daughter are together. The ladies make great use of their fans flirting them at the gentlemen of their acquaintance as they pass; it is said they have a language of the fan as well as of flowers the last they employ on many occasions. Their significations are very different from any we ever use as emblems and I am entirely ignorant of them. The dinner tables of the opulent are always ornamented with flowers, and if a gentleman send any nice thing to a lady from his side of the table, he always adds a little wreath. A belle at table is distinguished by frequent favors of this sort, and may be seen with her plate surrounded by half a dozen others from which she tastes a bit and sends them away. As a mark of particular attention the gentlemen will take something peculiarly nice from their own plates & send it to her. At a Spanish dinner it is considered a rudeness if you do not taste of every thing offered, and frequently have your plate changed fifteen or sixteen times.

Monday. At home all the morning; in the afternoon accompanied the girls to shops, and afterwards in a ride to Principi hill four miles from town, from which we had a fine view of the city and surrounding country. The ocean seems almost to surround you. Mr Shaler & Mr Swett called. I wrote a letter to E. Sullivan.

Wednesday. We went this morning to Mr Metcalfs room to see a picture he has recently painted of Mr Fellowes; it is considered very fine as indeed are all, I have seen, of his productions. Mr Swett called before dinner to ask us to go to the botanic garden at five o'clock saying that Mr Knight would meet us there if possible, but at all events, he was himself so well acquainted with Mr Sagra, the gentleman who has charge of the place, we should require no other escort, he also told us Mr Knight would send his volante. Accordingly at five o'clock, Mr Sears, the girls, W. Gorham and ourselves set forth for the garden & at the gate were joined by Don Guillermo, who was running up stairs to find Mr Sagra, when he was stopped and informed he was in the garden. He consequently went forward to the spot where Mr S. was superintending some men & returned, saying he would come in a moment; we walked leisurely all round the garden, but still no host appeared and at length Mr Swett attacked him again, we, in the meantime were glad to sneak out of the gate into our volantes, where we hid our diminished heads. Don William soon appeared to say that Madame Sagra was preparing to come down I replied, we were sorry to give her so much trouble, and rode off, provoked at having trusted ourselves to the guidance of such a hairbrained youth. The only way we could account for the man's rudeness, for he is generally very civil, was that Mr Sagra having been frequently bored by W. S. did not care to interrupt his labors for any company introduced by him, & probably did not understand we came from Mr Knight.

We rode from the garden to Principi hill where we enjoyed the magnificent view. The city looks small for the number of its inhabitants (one hundred and thirty thousand) but the suberbs are very extensive. They contain fifty thousand inhabitants, the city eighty. Mr Cleveland and son called in the eveg & said Mrs C. was too much indisposed to see me. Mr Knight also came in & enquired how we were pleased with our visit to the garden &c. He expressed his regret. He was obliged, by business, to forego the pleasure of accompanying us and said he hoped we did not need him as interpreter. I replied we did not see Mr Sagra who seemed particularly occupied, but made no further explanation. Mr Swett must do that. Mr Knight afterwards went with us to Mrs Morelands, where we found Mrs Cook and son, and one or two others, and on our return shewed us some shops. Thermometer in the middle of the day 84°.

Thursday Mr Knight having sent us word in the morning that Madame Feron would give a concert in the evening, I prepared to go, but after dressing, found that in consequence of the bad weather, it was postponed; they always are influenced here, in these matters, by the clouds. Mr Burke has been a little better to day, it is not probable he will live more than a few weeks. Mr Sears with bag & baggage, went on board the Felicia for New Orleans after dinner, but the whole concern were driven back to pass the night by contrary winds. Mr Knight called this eveg. I wrote a letter to Elizabeth.

Friday. The Sears's went off before I was awake. Mr Burke has been very ill to day. Mr Swett called, he brought me some lace of the Daguilla tree mentioned by Mr Abbott. It is, even here, rather rare and considered quite a curiosity; it is found on the mountains in the western part of the island; the part which bears resemblance to lace, is the inner bark which, when wet, can be pulled out very thin. The weather has been rainy, showers coming up in a most sudden manner. I employed my self this morng in copying a print of the market square lent me by Mr Metcalf.

Saturday. Windy & rainy. Mr Knight called in the eveg. We heard of the arrival of the Hermosa Habanara, the vessel in which we intend going to New Orleans. This afternoon I walked with Mr Lowell and W Gorham upon Governor's square which has vastly improved since our last visit, vegetation is much more luxurient and many new flowers in bloom; we afterwards stopped at Mrs Cunningham's; she returned from the country this morng and considers herself better in all respects excepting her cough, which remains the same; she has been riding on horseback and deriving benefit from the exercise. She looks extremely ill and is rather impatient to get away from here dreading the coming heat.

April 1, 1832
Sunday Mr Lowell and myself attended three churches this morning The Cathedral, St Domingo and St Philip. The last, I judged from the number of volantes at the door to be the most fashionable; it has a very shewy gilt altar but no ornaments of peculiar beauty. Two of the priests, I noticed, had black beards. The Cathedral is the handsomest building and is filled with paintings, the walls, ceilings &c. the spot where are placed the bones of Columbus is, of course, the most interesting in the church. A very handsome marble slab is inserted in the wall. A head of Columbus in bas relief behind this. his remains are enclosed in two silver urns.

We dined at Mr Morelands today with Mr Shaler, the consul, two Mr

Grays and another gentleman I did not know, while there we saw from the window the steam boat arrive. Mr Hubbard and Miss Bumstead came in her, the vessel in which they are to sail for Mobile has been waiting for them. Mr H. came in during dinner and Mrs Moreland accompanied me back to Mrs Morelands to see Miss Bumstead. We found her sitting with Mr Carter & Mr Metcalf. She seemed quite unwilling to quit Havana. Mr Knight's volante came to take her to the vessel and Mr Shaler &c to take leave. She has reason to be flattered by the attentions she has received. Genl Parker is to go in the same ship; he is to me by no means an agreeable old man, being altogether too talkative & inquisitive he lost his wife about a year since and has children. He was adjutant general of the united states and now resides in Philadelphia. He has more general gossip than almost any person I ever saw and to me renders himself peculiarly unpleasant by his prying disposition. Mr and Mrs Cunningham also went with them, in the present state of Mrs C's health I should think the experiment of so long a journey rather hazardous.

We have had bells ringing and guns firing all day in consequence of the birth of a princess; many of the balconies of the houses are hung with red damask, the Intendants and others in the square with red & yellow, striped, like the Spanish flag. This evening we walked on the square, there being music and a feeble attempt at illumination. The Intendants house looked quite prettily, lamps being arranged with taste, but nothing could be more miserable than the attempt at display upon the Governor's. He does everything meanly and had on this occasion hung out only a few candles in glass lanterns. I am told, that on some occasions the illuminations here are most splendid equalling any in the European cities. I sat up late packing my trunk for the country tomorrow. Mr Burke is very ill, his poor little wife greatly distressed.

Monday. This morning Mr Lowell waked me at an early hour, but I was so entirely weary I could not rise in season to get off before seven; at that hour we were all packed into two volantes, Mr L. Lorenza and George in one, and William Gorham and myself in another two horses in each and the owner of the carriages accompanied us as guide leaving Havana in good spirit for Mr Fellowes's; the roads are much better than any we have yet travelled, in this we were agreeably disappointed having been told they were miserable and finding them such an improvement upon those the other side of Matanzas we felt extremely fortunate. The scenery along the road is very pretty and constantly varied. We passed some fine houses and one or two pretty villages; that of St Antonio near Reserva is quite a little city. It contains a good looking church, indeed we have seen two in our ride today. We stopped to breakfast at a dirty inn and were wretchedly served in all respects except the luxury of silver forks which we hardly expected to see (they are by no means common in Cuba) and upon a table cloth too much soiled to be looked upon with composure.

We arrived at Reserva an hour or two before dinner, a most splendid place. We were received at the door by Mr Fellowes and Mrs Williams, his sister, who resides here with her daughter. I lay down before dinner and upon coming out of my room was introduced to Miss Matilda a very pretty girl of sixteen or seventeen; she is tall, finely formed and most graceful in her motions. Soft blue eyes, a pretty nose, and coral lips, her hair is of a glossy dark brown her complexion fair as a lily, and not generally tinged with the rose, but slightest exertion brings a beautiful color into her cheek, and in conversation she is seldom quite pale. She plays with execution and taste upon the harp and always rises with a bloom. Her hand is perfect and she has the foot of a fairy. She is very ladylike and although diffident has not the slightest mauvaise honte. She was educated in Philadelphia where she resided ten years. I have not seen so attractive a girl for a long while. Pauline, the elder daughter, is confined to her room by indisposition and Miss Williams absent in a Spanish family where she has gone to perfect herself in the language. Mr Fellowes has three little girls, the eldest six and the younger two years of age, they are rather pretty children. Young Warren, of Boston, is, at present, staying here.

Mr Fellowes has three estates, all in a high state of cultivation. Reserva, Fundador & Pequeña Cabaña. He rents a fourth called Silencio which is also a beautiful plantation. He resides upon the Reserva, the house being best. The avenue is strait, as upon all those I have visited, and a quarter of a mile in length, bordered on each side with palms, behind which stand other trees of thicker foliage forming quite a grove; among the trees coffee is planted. It seems to me they shade the coffee more in this part of the island than upon the estates we have before visited. The plantains which are every where placed among them, are much nearer together. We sat down to the dinner table at half past four, and in the eveg listened to Matilda's harp. She took lessons for six years and seems quite at home at the instrument. At ten we had a little supper upon the piazza.

Tuesday. This morng after my cup of coffee I accompanied Matilda in a drive round the estates. The contrast of the red earth with the brilliant green of the trees and shrubs is most beautiful and there is not a stone in the avenues to interrupt the smooth, easy motion of the carriage. It is complete luxury riding in a volante upon roads as level as a carpet. There is the greatest possible variety upon in the avenues, one of palms a third of a mile in length upon the Pequeña particularly excited my admiration; the trees are all of great height and beauty and you can hardly divest yourself of the idea that you are riding between columns of some splendid order of architecture. There is a fine guaderia of mangoes, impervious to the sun at noon day; one of bamboo trees; beautiful to my eye; one at Fundador of Cocoa nut, and, in short every variety. I like the cocoa nut much and although not considered beautiful as the palm yet in some respects I prefer it; the trunk is not so strait nor the bark so smooth, but the foliage is thicker and the leaf itself handsomer although it does not bend in so graceful a curve

After riding upon the estates some time and passing the portrero which has much the appearance of my idea of an English park, we stopped at the billiard room at Fundador, where I took my first lesson of Mr Warren; Mr Lowell and Mr Fellowes came in the other volante and the rest of the gentlemen on horseback. Mr Fellowes formerly resided at Fundador and the family now prefer the plantation, but the house is inferior to that of Reserva. We returned to breakfast about ten o'clock. The house is built with a wide piazza before and behind into both of which opens a bed room on each side. a hall runs through the centre opening into the piazzas and at each end are bed rooms, the walls, as in most houses in this country are painted in landscapes and other figures, the floors of composition with the most brilliant polish. Mrs Williams told me this was obtained by constant washing, they are passed over with a sponge twice a day. When the floor is completed it is rubbed down very smooth, after which nothing more is necessary than the frequent use of water; one inconvenience usually attends these floors, when not constantly washed, which is the dust, which may at any moment be swept off, occasioned by the friction of the feet. In the back piazza is swung a hammock in which Mr Fellowes every day takes his siesta, it is made of small twine netted together and is very comfortable. Hammocks of this sort are quite common among the Spaniards. In front of the house is a little patene of flowers and behind a grass plat beyond which are the secaderos on the right of which is a house containing offices and on the left the kitchen, coffee mills &c. Mr F. prides himself upon the neatness of his estates and the little stone walks leading through the grass to the different buildings are all brightly polished. After breakfast we sat sewing and talking until time to dress for dinner and in the afternoon again rode round the plantations.

Mr Fellowes is subject to epileptic fits which attack him without warning and which are extremely violent. Mrs Williams told me it was sometimes several hours before he recovered from their effects; his face turns quite purple and his features convulse; he once fell on the stone floor and hurt his head so badly as to confine him to his room for two months; he is extremely nervous and a single game of chess excites him extremely. This eveg we played whist and again at ten o'clock were summoned to supper.

Wednesday. Mrs Williams accompanied us in one ride to Fundador before breakfast, and we explored the house which is falling to decay. It is not so comfortable a residence as Reserva although the family vastly prefer the estate the avenue to the front door of cocoa nuts is long and beautiful, here too is a little circle of flowers before the house. Mr Fellowes has 406 hundred negroes in all. The house servants are very good and Mrs Williams expressed her surprise at hearing of the wretched set upon the other estates I had visited, she said she considered the good servants one of the greatest advantages of living upon the island. Of course they require a steady hand and superintendance but when once you have established your authority but little discipline is necessary. Matilda and the gentlemen played billiards, and at a reasonable hour we returned to Reserva to a good breakfast. Young Cook who has been here for a day or two left us before dinner.

<pencil sketch of house on next page followed by blank overleaf>

Mr Cook and his Mother are at present staying at Mr D'Wolfs from whence they intend going to Mrs James's. I know of no one who has had finer advantages for seeing the country than Mrs Cook. She does not seem satisfied with the climate, but I am convinced the difficulty is in her own constitution which is very feeble. She complains of the damp mornings and evenings and at the same time exposes herself very imprudently; from what I have seen of her I should judge she would not have lived at home, and here she has been very comfortable though to all appearance her complaints are deeply seated. Mr Sears also does not seem inclined to give the air its due, he took an unfortunate cold at Camarioca in consequence of admitting the morning fog too early into his bed room and sleeping with it pouring up from the valley upon him and this cold nearly cost him a pleurisy fever, and not liking proper remedies, he had hardly recovered from its effects when he left the island. This might have occurred in any other place as well as here; he had a slight return of the disease at Reserva and derived immediate relief from putting his feet, at night into a tap of hot water in which were orange leaves and at the same time drinking the lemon grass tea which threw him into a perspiration which lasted a long time. I am not aware whether or not the lemon grass is known with us, it has a strong flavor of lemon and is much used by the negroes <*word missing*> a tea, in cases where we should give balm tea. it must be much pleasanter to the taste.

After dinner I rode with Mrs Williams, and our evening was again spent in hearing music and talking, Miss Pauline, who has been confined to her room since we came, made her appearance just before night, she is not so pretty as Matilda being shorter and her features less regular. She has an unfortunate defect in her eye occasioned by some complaint in it, when a child, and which suffered in consequence of being bathed in the waters of Madinga; her voice too has a natural hoarseness which is painful to the ear. She is however, upon the whole, an attractive girl and is said to be very well educated and extremely amiable. She played to me on the piano. The family seem to cherish with great fondness the memory of the daughter (Clara) who died two years since, she must have been very lovely, every one mentions her with regret. Mrs Williams told me she was devoted to her Father and probably her life was sacrificed to her unwillingness to leave him; she remained in Havana after the sickly season and fell a victim to the fever; she died on the day fixed for her marriage. Mr Fellowes has a daughter married in New Orleans to Mr Saul, brother of the young man who died at Reserva this winter. Eliza Sullivan says the thermometer was a low as 60° when she was here.

Thursday, April 5th We rose early, with the intention of departing for Havana, and found all the family assembled except Mr Fellowes, who was much indisposed yesterday, and did not make his appearance this morng until we were setting off when he stepped out of his room to bid us good bye. After partaking of a good breakfast we bade adieu to Reserva, having experienced during our short visit the greatest degree of kindness from the family. The girls, naturally, find their residence upon the plantation very dull; it is a very small portion of the year which brings them visitors and the remainder of the time their life is entirely monotonous and they are confined exclusively to their own resources. Mrs Williams says they are very cheerful and contented, but still long to return to the States where so many years of their youth have been passed. Mr Fellowes has, himself, a strong desire to go there again, but his embarrassments are such he would find it difficult to procure the means to defray the expenses of such an expedition, as he cannot, of course, go without all his family; he is allowed by his creditors six thousand dollars besides a living upon his estates but this sum is not sufficient to meet the demand that would be made upon his purse. The crops from his plantations must be so great, it seems almost incredible that in the course of a few years the debts should not be liquidated. In case of the death of Mr Fellowes, the property would, probably, become the prey of lawyers who would make an immediate attack and in a great measure it would fritter away under their kind investigations. The Spanish laws are said to be perfect as any in the known world, but it is in the administration of them that the defect exists, there is a continued series of iniquitous proceedings, and woe to the poor wretch who appeals to justice; he had better make any compromise to avoid litigation. I presume the family would fare less well, should Mr Fellowes die, than if his wife were living (for (the Spanish nation and Spanish laws being the most gallant in the world) the wife is always provided for, even where the children would be disregarded.

We enjoyed the first part of our ride highly; the sky being overcast, we were able to put down the screen and look abroad with freedom; it soon, however, began to rain, and, much to our discomfort, we were forced to button up the cloth, and content ourselves with peeping out each side. I had a more distinct view of the village of St Antonio than in going to Reserva, being now fully awake and free from fatigue; it is a watering place of considerable size three miles from Reserva and is said to contain 12,000 inhabitants. On the main street is a very good looking church and a number of well filled, well arranged shops. I have been much struck, to day, with the cotton tree of which there are several on the road; it is to me a most beautiful object the large, long, smooth, leafless trunk with the thick, bright foliage in a mass at the top, frequently all on one side, though sometimes extending like an umbrella form to my fancy one of the most magnificent of forest trees. Although an admirer of many of the best India trees, I do not think in general they rival those of our woods. With the exception perhaps of the Palm, which is peculiar, I know of none so striking as our elm or oak.

When about half way to town, we stopped at a small hut thatched with Guava (or Palm) to change horses; the rain poured in torrents and my first impulse was to remain ensconced behind the screen of the volante, but thinking there might be something worth seeing within, I braved the elements and soon found myself under a shed with dogs, horses, men and boys most lovingly grouped. I entered what I presume was the drawing room of the Montero and was seated by the side of a poor old nag, driven by stress of weather to seek the same shelter The sleeping apartments communicated with this room, one of which I explored finding a motley assemblage of moveables. We passed many farms where vegetables are raised for market. It is curious to observe the peculiar manner in which the produce is carried in; the poor fowls are universally tied by the legs and conveyed alive with their heads hanging down at the side of the mule, of course, in such a climate they must be sold living, and all the produce is put upon the back of the animal in seroons or tied on in some other way.

The practice of cock fighting is common throughout the island and it is not considered disgraceful for even the priests to engage in the amusement. Mr Sullivan was told (in passing through a village one Sunday where they were regaling themselves in this way) by a gentleman that he had just bet and lost four dollars on a bird in honor of his Padre (the creature belonging to him). These priests lead a gay life in every respect. The ball which William Gorham attended at Limoral was given by the Padre of the place in honor of the consecration of a burying ground. The occasions selected for such festivities would seem rather extraordinary to us. Mrs Jenckes told me of a gentleman who had given a ball every year for the last twenty on the anniversary of the death of his wife.

The suberbs of the city are very extensive, covering more ground, I should suppose, than the city itself. They present a most busy appearance, being filled with shops where all sorts of trades are prosecuted. We arrived at Mrs Howard's before dinner finding Mr Carter standing at the Court yard door. We were received cordially up stairs by our friends who expressed their pleasure at seeing us again, and (marvellous to relate!)

Mrs Howard condescended to remember her promises sufficiently to allow us to take the rooms we had left; which wonderful effort of memory I think we may attribute to her having had no application for them. The steam boat did not arrive, to day, as we expected; it is very cautious not to leave if there be the least appearance of dull weather.

<one-half page left blank>

Friday, April 6th While we were setting at dinner Mr McLean and Dr Robinson entered bringing the pleasing intelligence that Mr Sullivan and Eliza were on their way from the steam boat; they soon made their appearance, Eliza looking much better than when I parted from her at Matanzas, she says she gained every day while there, and I have made up my mind that of all the spots I have visited on the island none possesses a purer air than this place, there is a vast difference, perceptible to the strongest lungs in going from Havana and to some the change is too great and the climate altogether too bracing. I should not hesitate to remain there, were I again obliged to come to Cuba, did I find any difficulty in procuring accommodations in the country; and with many the air has a more beneficial effect than that upon the plantations. Eliza says, if she were to come here another winter she should endeavour to obtain lodgings at San Antonio, the village I have mentioned near Reserva, where she has understood very good ones may be procured; the place has the advantage of a pleasant neighbourhood and the roads extremely good.

This morning I went to some shops with Mrs Burke, and purchased two or three shewy pocket handkerchiefs with colored borders. There is no article of dress that the Spanish ladies (generally so fond of gay attire) consider so indispensable, except perhaps the immense comb, the shops are filled with the greatest variety, some superbly embroidered, and I have understood two ounces are sometimes given for one. I heard of a gentleman who gave an ounce (17 dollars) for having one folded; it was done up, I believe, in the form of a basket and intended as a present. Even the men are very nice in this respect and you see them flourishing every possible color; some are figured all over. During dinner to day, Mr Knight sent to ascertain if we would like to attend the concert this eveg, and, having no other engagement, we resolved to go While dressing I was informed that Mrs Cleveland and Hepsy Sage were in the parlour. Mr & Mrs Sage came over land to Havana, and found the roads so extremely bad, they sent their volante back and are to return by water; in one place nine horses did not succeed in extricating them from the mud. I am told, during the rainy season, the roads are almost impassible; horses are continually swamped and no lady ever thinks of undertaking a journey in the summer. Most Spanish families, who can afford a house in town, come to Havana in May and return to the country in October; this would seem with us, reversing the proper order of things, but here, where a perpetual summer reigns, it is the only arrangement for those unwilling to be confined altogether, for six months, to their plantations.

I have been frequently told by residents, that there is as much difference in seasons here, with respect to beauty of scenery & vegetation as in our northern latitudes. To a casual observer the remark seems almost idle, but upon noticing how many trees in the woods are quite leafless at this season I can well believe the summer to be much more beautiful; the colors are constantly freshened by the rains and there are also the greatest variety of wild flowers, forming arbours in the woods, of which we now see nothing. The forest trees, too, are most magnificent when in blossom. I have been rather surprised to find so few pretty wild flowers but understand their number and variety are countless in their season.

Mr Sage has been much troubled with asthma, since he came here, which he attributes to the air of Havana, he is less subject to it at Santa Ana, though it sometimes attacks him there; he invariably suffers when he comes to town and has now been forced to sit up every night. The air of the north operates most favorably with him, he feels nothing of his complaint from the moment he leaves Cuba. The asthma is a disease of this country.

Mr Sage & Hepsy concluded to accompany us to the concert and Mr Knight and his friend Mr P. (a very genteel young man, native of Old Spain, but who speaks English perfectly) having sent their volantes and Mr Lowell having procured another for Mr S. we all set off. Mr Knight handed me down stairs and desired Mr Lowell to get in with me, but he refused, desiring Mr K. to take the seat saying he would himself ride with Mr P. Mr Knight strenuously refused the honor intended him, but was at length obliged, by my husbands urgency, to take the place, much to his discomfort. I, who saw through his reason for objecting all along, was greatly amused, for I have been here hardly long enough to feel shocked at violating any of the customs of the country and, it seems, this eveg we have infringed one thought all important. It is considered extremely indecorous for a lady to be accompanied by any gentleman except her husband Father or brother and Mr K. felt it as much as his reputation was worth to go with me; he said, however, it was of less consequence in the eveg as we should not probably be recognized, but that nothing would induce him to ride on the Paseo or, in short, any where in the day time with a lady. I was sorry to see the poor man disconcerted although, I must do him the justice to say, he behaved very much like a gentleman on the occasion, and turned it off as easily as any one could and it must have been a matter of some importance to him as he has resided long enough in Cuba to feel almost like a native.

It is well for a stranger, visiting this island, to ascertain, before she comes, some of the customs here which are deemed most important otherwise she will be very apt, innocently, to make great mistakes and, as it is certainly the most scandalous place I ever heard of these mistakes are to be avoided, if possible. One of the things impossible to do here, without exciting great remark is riding in a hired carriage and as strangers cannot be expected to own one their situation is embarrassing I find we occasioned much wonder by doing so when we first arrived and, at that time, although we knew it to be unfashionable we did it, thinking as we should go away and be forgotten, it was of little importance, but since I have understood the reason it is never done by respectable people I regret we were so imprudent as to go two or three times, without a gentleman, in a hack. It seems in Cuba, none but women of the lowest and most profligate character ever get into them, and they are, in consequence, banned for all others. I do not object to riding in them with my husband, but should never again go unattended. We usually in Matanzas had a private carriage and, since Mr Knights return, have always had his in Havana. When here before we generally had Mrs Howard's and should never have taken any other, had I been as wise then as now. A person who comes for the winter, and intends residing in the city should bring a volante or Quiterine, the latter has a bellows top resembling our gigs and is the more stylish vehicle of the two. I have applied the term volante to both, indiscriminately, but the Spaniards made the distinction.

The concert was at the Diorama, a small theatre outside the gate of the City; the building rather pretty, but badly lighted and not crowded with company as we anticipated; many of the boxes being empty, the pit, however, was quite full. Madame Feron (the attraction this eveg) is not so fashionable this year as the last; she then carried away five thousand dollars and in consequence of her success was too high in her demands this season and could make no arrangement with the managers of the large theatre & could give no concerts as they had command of the band and took care to secure it whenever she advertised. She has, accordingly, been singing in small private parties waiting until lent when she can engage the band. Her singing did not please me much, her voice is softer than I expected but, to my taste, she is too scientific and her style too ornamented; she does not touch the feelings, but perhaps my judgment may have been influenced by the music she selected which was Italian, with which I was unacquainted. Sagara a famous violinist also performed, and another of almost equal celebrity; also a man of some note, upon the violincello The ladies in the house were dressed much as usual, flowers in the head, of course. We experienced some difficulty in disentangling our volantes from the mass of others but, this labour achieved, we reached home unscathed after the concert.

Saturday. We dined today at Mrs Clevelands, Mr Sullivan & Eliza, Mr & Mrs Sage, who are staying there, and Mr & Mrs Wade and the Consul Shaler who reside in the same house. The last pays Mr Cleveland half his salary (the whole being <*blank space*>) and thus enjoys the privilege of returning home every year, if he please, he is a most forbidding looking personage and extremely uninteresting in conversation, but, I am told, is generally respected by all those with whom he transacts business His cold, positive way renders him less agreeable to ladies. Mrs Cleveland's two sons were also at table. One of them (Horace) who has the air & appearance of being younger than he is (being about nineteen) is to sail for Boston in a day or two with the intention of entering a store, and the other, the adventurous youth who sometime since commenced an expedition against the Poles, but was diverted from his part by the taking of Warsaw. He is rather fierce in his appearance. Mrs Cleveland is a reading lady and has written some tracts, which have been published, and I know not what beside; she has treated us with great kindness. The house is badly situated, being, on one side, close upon the custom house, and upon the other, facing the back part of a Spanish mansion the balconies of which, are constantly filled with the black servants of the establishment. Being attracted to the window by a fray in the street between two negro girls, I had an opportunity of seeing this fairer portion of the creation, and found them all adorned with their high combs and flowers in their wool.

Mr Knight called in after dinner; he brought his volante for Mr Sullivan & Eliza to make a visit to Madame de Suzane, a daughter of the Marquis Ramos, who was married in church a week since. She became acquainted with her husband, who is a French officer, eight years since, in Old Spain, where she was residing with her sister Mrs Hernandez, and formed an engagement with him. Hernandez, who for some reason, did not fancy the match, wrote to the Marquis respecting it and received his commands to forbid Monsr de Suzane the house and to bring Josefita immediately home, he had no serious cause of objection, except his being a foreigner. He is said to be a man of family, fortune & very gentlemanly manners. The measures pursued occasioned, of course, a coolness between Hernandez & himself and has caused a vast deal of unhappiness in the family. Josefita, being a girl of much principle, refused to marry without her Father's consent, or during his life, but has every six months, written a few lines to M de Suzane, expressing her constancy of feeling, although she could not be his. She has devoted herself to the comfort of her Father who is very infirm and exceedingly petulent, but for the last year she has been subjected to a great deal of persecution, partly through the intrigues of Hernandez and his wife who are said to be influenced by interested motives in wishing to keep Josefita unmarried; by their representations, the Marquis believes M. de S. to be merely an adventurer and Mr Knight says that Josefita had no choice but marrying without her Father's consent or a convent; she consequently permitted her lover to come to Cuba, Upon his arrival he sent a letter to the Marquis which was returned, unopened, after which he made use of legal measures. She was taken by order of the Captn General, from her Fathers house and put in deposit at [Mr Charletains] and from thence came to town to be married.[16] Mr Knight, an old friend of the family wrote to the Marquis but received a harsh answer and the letters of Josefita, her husband, & the French Consul were returned with seal unbroken

After our return from Mrs C's Mr McLean and other gentlemen called Mr McLean & Mr Taylor also in the morng.

Sunday. This morning early Mr Sullivan Eliza and ourselves made an attempt to hear the military mass, but missed the hour and were again disappointed, I understand the whole service is performed by the band, the congregation kneel at a particular roll of the drum and all is transacted without a word from the priest. I regret to have lost the sight, which must be very curious; we afterwards looked in at St Philips.

After dinner we took Mr Knights volante and Hepsy Sage Eliza and myself drove in it to Cubi's school, Mr Sage and Mr Sullivan followed in another. Hepsy was desirous to visit the establishment because a son of Mrs Webster (the sister of Mr S.) has just been sent there and she wished to carry home some account of the place. Mr Cubi, who had heard we were coming, appeared with his great eyes beaming, and his embroidered shirt, to receive us; to me he is a most disagreeable looking object, and from what I can learn of the College there may be more show than substance; it is said the morals of the boys are very defective. I could not but grieve that such a fine boy as Frederick Webster seems to be, should be sent to a place which as yet is at least but an experiment. We again explored the house which has undergone considerable change since our last visit, the dormitories being greatly enlarged and the refectory finished. Mr Cubi says they have a watch of two or three constantly at night walking the sleeping apartment to guard against fire and to give immediate alarm in case of disturbance. We went to the top of the house which has a noble view of the city and harbour.

At the fashionable hour, about half past five, we commenced our drive upon the Paseo. There were some beautiful carriages in the course, some highly painted, varnished and gilt, most were quiterines. We passed the eveg at Mrs Morelands with Mr & Mrs Wade & one or two others and returned home early quite fatigued with our labors.

Monday Shopped with Eliza in the morning and received a call from Mr Knight. After dinner Mr Sullivan Eliza Mr Lowell & myself walked to Mrs Cleveland's where we were joined by Mr & Mrs Sage and stepping into a boat at the wharf close by, we crossed the bay to the town of Guanabacoa, or rather, we landed at Regla and rode up the hill to the first place. Upon reaching the landing the gentlemen engaged three miserable looking volantes which however safely carried us over the ground; the view as we ascended and looked back is very fine and I regret not being able to copy a print of Mr Metcalfs taken from this side the bay.

We drove to a place of Mr Drake's occupied by Mr Macleay commissioner for the slaves, an Englishman by birth. He is appointed with two others (Spaniards one, or both) to judge all the slaveships captured and brought in, and has a salary of from twelve to fifteen hundred pounds and a house provided by government, that which he occupied & which is a country seat of Mr Drake who now resides in Spain, is a delightful spot. The house is a palace, almost in its size and arrangement and possesses from its balconies and roof a most extensive and varied view. The garden immediately below is small but arranged with taste and filled with flowers, some quite rare.

Mr Macleay is a naturalist and amused us with a variety of curiosities; after culling for us, his choicest flowers, he carried us into an enclosure where he showed us a pair of pet deer, a pair of pet cranes, whose principal beauty consisted in their delicate dove color, a pet crocodile, indeed the heads of *three* were visible in the stagnant pool they inhabited, a most knowing looking owl, several different sorts of birds, a small ungainly animal, a native, called <*blank space*>, barking and ferocious bull dogs &c &c &c. There I saw the most splendid tea rose that has ever blessed my vision; this plant grows to great size and beauty in the gardens here. Our damask and other common roses are more prized because more rare. Mr Sage is a friend of Mr Macleay's and has been staying recently two or three days in this beautiful spot with his wife; he told Mr M. that he should bring us & this morng despatched a note to say we were coming, consequently, we were expected.

When fatigued with our wanderings we entered the house and were conducted all over its apartments. At the request of Mr Sage our host carried us into his own sanctum where his friend declared he kept "confusions holyday". And indeed the expression seemed most appropriate for every thing around bore the careless air of the retirement of a virtuoso. Here lay a petrified shell fish there a microscope beneath which some poor wretch of a fly or spider occupied that uneasy position, the point of a pin, the victim, however, happily released from the sufferings of life. Around were strowed [strewn] books, pamphlets, drawings and indescribable instruments of every form. The walls lived with rare volumes. Mr Macleay shewed us some engravings of various insects taken from drawings of his own, and also a collection of these little creatures fastened by small pins to boards which were nicely fitted into a large box to send abroad. Some of the butterflies were most beautiful, and many of the small bugs shone like gems. I, of course, could make no comparison between these natives of Cuba and a collection of our own insects being nothing of an Entomologist. It is a study which must become extremely interesting and offers a never ending fund to those curious in such matters. We observed a bow gun, the string of which was very hard to draw and which Mr Macleay gave us evidence would send its arrow with great force; he says he frequently employs it in shooting small birds; he displayed a most beautiful humming bird shot the day before, in the garden, the breast of which in the sun shone like a ruby and another which bore the emeralds hue; they formed side by side a brilliant contrast; one was of a species new to himself and he seemed to enjoy the acquisition exceedingly.

After partaking of some refreshments, we bade adieu to Mr Macleay and his curiosities and entered some volantes which Mr Sage had procured as an improvement upon those which brought us up, but which seemed to me little better. We had a delightful drive to the boat which we entered just as the sun was setting. The bay was smiling in beauty and the line of shipping drawn up on one side, or rather sail boats of larger size with their canvas drawn tight to the mast reminded me of pictures I have seen of Venice. We landed about dark, Mr Sage having been helmsman and steered us very adroitly between two large ships which as we approached seemed too closely united to admit us. In the evening Mr McLean called.

Tuesday. Having been informed some days since, that we were to go on board the Hermosa Habanera, the brig destined to convey us to New Orleans, this afternoon, we made preparations for sailing, indeed, yesterday my packing was completed and I have felt a lady of leisure since. This morning I took out some prints lent me by Mr Metcalf & for a short time occupied myself in copying one of them feeling almost certain we should not go until tomorrow but being suddenly informed that we must go this aftn I laid them aside, and although the order was afterwards declared to be a mistake I determined not again to attempt the sketch and tied up the roll to be returned to Mr M. Mr McLean & Mr Taylor called this afternoon and amused themselves by discussing Miss Bumstead. In the eveg we received visits from Mr McLean, Capt Armstrong & Mr Duke of the Porpoise, and Mr Knight. I should mention also a visit before tea from Monsieur & Madame de Suzane to Eliza. I was pleased with Josefita's appearance although she possesses no pretentions but fine eyes & hair to good looks; her story has so interested me in her that I presume I was in some degree influenced in my judgments of her person; her husband is tall & genteel in appearance; they are to sail immediately for New York and from thence will take a packet to France; perhaps they may visit Boston. Eliza gave them a letter to Mr. Ticknor. W. Swett insists upon going in the same ship, whether he does or not remains to be proved.

Wednesday, April 11th Mr McLean & Mr Taylor called this morning and again spoke of Miss Bumstead who has been subject of a vast deal of conversation wherever she has shewn her face. She is one of those indepandant young ladies who care not for remark, and unfortunately for her reputation this is the most scandalous place in the world. We gave up all idea of sailing today in consequence of unfavorable wind but were suddenly told, while at dinner, that we must be on board at four o'clock and accordingly made ourselves ready. Mr McLean came up to go with us. We found Mr Taylor on the wharf and Mr Metcalf, who dined at Mrs Howards, Mr Duke has kindly ordered his boat to take us to the vessel which was without the Moro. The swell was slight, but I was glad to leave the boat, fearing I might be forced to say that seasickness had already established his rights. The harbour looked most beautifully and I was almost sorry to learn for the first time in passing the Moro which added so greatly to the enchantment of the scene, contained in its dungeons, prisoners who had not seen the light perhaps for twenty years. We found on board our fellow passengers Mr & Mrs Grosvenor, Mr Winchester & Dr Robinson. W. Gorham came up just as we were about to sail in a boat by himself, breathless with fear, having spent his last bit & all his baggage on board. There was some difficulty in finding him, he having left home not expecting to go today. Mr Clarke was also on board to see us off. The gentlemen made bets respecting our fate. Mr McLean saying we should be out of sight of the Moro at sunrise tomorrow & Mr Duke being of an opposite opinion. Mr Duke & Mr Clarke also shook hands over a bet.

Mr D. is grandson to Judge Marshall and seems a very intelligent, gentlemanly young man, he is Lieutenant on board the Porpoise. Those of our naval officers who are disposed to make the most of their opportunities enjoy greater advantages for acquiring general information than almost any other class of men. The rank they hold admits them into the situations they most desire. This young man has visited almost every inhabited spot on the face of the earth and is uncommonly entertaining in his descriptions. He was at Mistolonghi when Lord Byron died and says the account we have had of the grief of the Greeks on the occasion is incorrect. The event made very little impression.[17] Lord B. had exhausted his fortune and had become a complete victim to intemperance. Mr Duke told Eliza S. that in Lyria he had an interview with a Captn of banditti who had acquired great influence over the minds of his men. This man told him that originally he was a Kentuckian and that in the course of his fortunes he had arrived at the station he occupied. He was a remarkably athletic striking looking man. Mr Burke & wife on board the Aurora this morning. I was seasick immediately after the gentlemen left us and shall now retire to my birth. Apparently we have a dead calm.

Thursday There was so little motion this morng I could hardly believe we were getting along at all. We were, however, out of sight of the Moro at sunrise; which way seems a doubt almost, but I believe we are right. We have had little or no wind all day but the Captn says, at this rate we may get to New Orleans in nine days; twenty-nine seem more probable to me. The deck is bordered with boxes put up for the occasion filled with oranges, 60 000, on top of which was spread my matress and there I lay all day. This eveg we had the finest sunset I have witnessed since we came to Cuba. The clouds were most peculiar and constantly varying and the sea unruffled. Our latitude to day has been 24°3′.
The latitude of Havana is 23°9.

Friday Almost a dead calm this morning and intensely hot. The Captn said we should have a breeze after dinner, and so it proved Just as the gentlemen descended into the infernal regions, we were favored with quite a brisk gale. I lay, again, all day upon top of the oranges among which the gentlemen have begun to make inroads, doing little but muse. The Sun went down in beauty though his setting was less brilliant than last night.

Saturday A fine breeze this morning but, unfortunately, the wrong way. Although we have gone 90 miles since noon yesterday, we have made but 28 on our course. But little motion in the vessel, yet still enough to disable me from sitting up. This evening the moon shone in unclouded splendour. We agreed she is more brilliant in these latitudes than at the north. This fact I have heretofore doubted, although it has often been asserted in my presence since I came to Cuba. Mr Grosvenor says it is a subject upon which there can be no doubt for there is much greater facility in

taking lunar observations here than in more northern climes. Perhaps the Moon herself may not be clearer or brighter but there is a brilliant halo around her we do not see with us. Mrs Rotch told Eliza Sullivan that in coming from Santa Cruz to Cuba she saw distinctly, without a glass, the satellites of Jupiter. Dr Robinson was quite poetical this eveg in his quotations
Latitude 24′38′.

Sunday 15th I rose earlier than any preceding day and again occupied my elevated position on deck. Captain <*blank space*> thinks we have made a third of the passage, though there is little appearance of motion. This is the first of the holy days and we have been pleasantly exercising ourselves in considering that we might have seen them through and have still arrived as early in New Orleans as we shall now probably, at the rate we go. The weather has been warm and the sun set most splendidly I hardly ever witnessed a more magnificent spectacle; the moon rose in clouds but still beautiful; she was full last night. My husband, for the two last nights, has swung his hammock under the boom, on deck and has passed the hours much more agreeably A Pelican, an unusual visitor so far from land, has been in sight, and a sail has hovered on the horizon almost ever since we left Havana
Latitude 25°10′

Monday. Tremendous rocking last night, and have been unable to leave my birth all day. Little George has also suffered a little from sea sickness and Mrs Grosvenor confined to her state room. My husband says we have rather gone backwards than forwards, a consoling idea.
Latitude 26°38′

Tuesday The weather has been pleasant all day but the wind directly ahead, and at one moment we were making directly for Havana. This morning we were cheered by the visit of two small birds who have hovered about us all day and this afternoon the little blue swallow died. A shark has also played about the vessel defying all the attempts of the sailors to take him by the harpoon or gun until an hour or two before dark, when they pulled him up. He was small, weighing about 200 pounds, evidently a young fish; he had but two rows of teeth in each jaw, and when full grown they have three. The front, sharp ones, possess a joint which enables them to lay back. The color is a slate, very different from my idea of the creature; a fin on the back as well as each side, and the mouth underneath. The shark has great tenacity of life and after being cut to pieces and his back bone taken out, this bit a sailor who put his finger in his mouth!

The sun set most singularly. The moon made her appearance about nine o'clock. At the rate or *no* rate at which we proceed, she will not last us to New Orleans.
Latitude 26°59′

Wednesday. To day has been little varied. I rose late but enjoyed the fine air on deck when once there. The wind ahead but the weather pleasant. One of the sailors fished up, in a bucket a curious looking sun fish, the centre of a golden hue surrounded by a line of blue and feelers of the same color composed of a gelatinous sort of substance which was destroyed by a touch. The whole resembled the Chrysanthemum. The captain said he had seen them as large as half a bushel; this we put into a tumbler & it varied its form by folding down its feelers. It was destroyed by being put into fresh water. George was again a little sea sick.

Thursday. Considerable wind this morning and sufficiently the right way to carry us on five knots an hour; it subsided, however, and we again became almost stationary. The sun set clearly and had a peculiar appearance more resembling a globe of fire than a flat circle, as usual; it was unadorned with clouds but the atmosphere was tinged with the softest shades of pink and purple. We have changed our course a little, to my great delight. We amused ourselves this eveg with "What is my thought like" &c Latitude 28°32′.

Friday I again mounted my station upon deck we hardly have any motion our progress is so extremely slow. The Captain says this is the first voyage he has taken in these latitudes without being obliged to lash his tables. This eveg has been very damp. We feel a rawness in the air unknown in Cuba.
Latitude 28°46′

Saturday. We were cheered early this morning by hearing we had taken a pilot on board but as it has been almost a dead calm the greater part of the day, and we are still sixty miles from the Balise[18] there seems little prospect of our arriving at present. These pilots are paid in proportion to the size of the vessel, for a brig like ours about $20 for each day and for each day he is detained on board two dollars in addition. This afternoon we have amused ourselves with spying what we have supposed to be whales, sporting at a distance I have been able to sit up almost all day. Latitude 29 the latitude of the Balise.

Sunday, April 22d A dead calm, not motion enough to give a shadow of an excuse for being sick. I consequently sat up all day. It is quite discouraging to be so long getting in, although the weather has uniformly been too pleasant to allow us to complain. We are almost entirely out of provisions, and it is to be hoped, on that account, may soon get in. For forty eight hours we have been within forty miles of the Balise.

Monday The water early this morning was extremely thick, and upon trying it, there was an evident difference in taste between that upon the surface and that lower down, the one being salt, and the other hardly brackish. We had early a tolerable wind in our favor and but for the current, which was against us, should have arrived at the Balise in good season. Large logs of wood, roots of trees and stumps with small knots of cane have been floating around us since yesterday giving sufficient evidence of approach to the "Father of Waters," the surface of the water is literally black with them and in front of us in every direction large mud banks, resembling, in many instances, rocks, have been formed by a collection of this drift wood, some green with vegetation; the pilot informed us that a great part of these had been formed within a few months. They present a most dreary appearance. The light house as we approached varied the scene agreeably; it is said to be taken care of by a clergyman who came there as missionary and kept a school for the children of the sailors and fishermen, but not finding this occupation sufficiently lucrative he obtained the privilege of lighting the beacon. The capt says that in the month of Novr all these shores are frequented by thousands of wild geese.

About twelve o'clock we perceived the steam boat "Shark" approaching to take us in tow, a pleasant circumstance for we had feared delay. Vessels of larger size always take steam, and indeed it would often be impossible in consequence of the mud banks as well as the strong current for them to get up to the city without. Some of the small Spanish vessels are unwilling to incur the expense and are not unfrequently as long in going from the Balise to New Orleans a distance of an hundred and ten miles as in performing the voyage from Havana. The Shark had been out several days watching for those who might need her assistance. She presented in her approach a truly imposing figure. She swept majestically round us and receiving a rope thrown by our sailors attached us to her stern and as one of the sailors remarked, "we had wind enough". The change of motion was quite cheering after so sluggish a passage and we could not but acknowledge the mighty power of steam. The obstructions to navigation here are so constantly varying the pilots are forced to be extremely vigilent.

After depositing us at the bar, the self-willed steam boat left us without power of opposition to flourish off in pursuit of a brig behind and in the course of time (during the interval we amused ourselves with the misfortune of a schooner which attempted to pass without assistance and which had the felicity of being fixed fast in the mud) she swept back again with the brig aurora under one wing and two schooners attached by cables behind & seizing us with her unocupied wing she made us fast and we all proceeded in perfect harmony. We were so closely united as to be able to pass across the steamer into the other vessel and accordingly paid a visit to Mrs Burke who seemed greatly delighted to be so near her home. Mr B, though very ill, has borne the voyage better than was anticipated.

The Captain of the Shark, gave us in a true Kentucky style, a cordial invitation to come on board whenever we wished, at the same time throwing himself back in his chair with his long arms across the table and his feet extended half the length of the room. We availed ourselves of his politeness and ascended the stairs to the cabin which is built upon the upper deck and had a clean cheerful aspect; the sight of white paint again is most agreeable. Behind the cabin is an open space where we placed our chairs about sunset and had real enjoyment in the scene although there was little but grass and a few trees to interest. The engine in this boat is below the cabin on the first deck a much better arrangement than that of old times. The heat has annoyed us a little and the noise and jar are tremendous: we can hardly expect to sleep tonight.

The little town of Balise is hardly worth mentioning being merely the abode of pilots and fishermen. The houses look comfortable and some of them have piazzas. It is considerably below high water mark and a nar-

"A Planter's House and Sugar Plantation on the Mississippi River." From GLEASON'S PICTORIAL DRAWING-ROOM COMPANION, *vol. 4 (1853): 304. Courtesy of the Massachusetts Historical Society.*

row dyke alone preserves it from inundation. The water is now twenty feet higher than in the fall in consequence of freshets. Mr Burke sleeps on deck tonight.

Tuesday I rose early with the hope of seeing everything, but found upon reaching the deck we had passed a fine sugar estate. Mr Lowell says the mansion house and out buildings were superior to any he saw in Cuba. We had heard from persons who had been frequently up the river, such unfavorable accounts of the face of the country that we have felt to day nothing but agreeable surprise; there has been much to interest and I have been unwilling to leave the deck a moment. The banks have presented a variety of pleasing objects, and I consider we are peculiarly fortunate in sailing up while the river is so high as we are able to look down upon plantations and cottages which must be entirely out of sight at low water mark. I can well conceive how dreary must be the trip when the river is not full.

I was much struck with the hackberry or American Poplar which at the entrance is the most common tree, the green is most vivid and contrasted with the dark grey Spanish moss which hangs in festoons from the branches, and which I had never before seen, is beautiful; this moss is extremely abundant as far up as New Orleans; in some places it has usurped the place of the natural foliage. We feel among old friends, now that we see thatched and shingled cottages and chimneys too to which our eye for the last three months has been entirely unaccustomed. Most of the small farmhouses have piazzas and present a picturesque appearance. It seems to me every where more regard is paid to the ornamental than in New England, where it is a very rare thing to see any thing like taste in the establishments of the lower orders. The Aligators greatly disappointed me; we saw today but three and those were small, I expected to have found the shores lined with them but like all the horrors of the Mississippi their numbers were greatly exaggerated. Perhaps the noise of the steam boat may have had some effect in keeping them out of sight. We have suffered much less from mosquitoes than we were led to apprehend and as to gallinippers I have not seen one. I have seen today some beautiful weeping willows the most so of any I ever beheld, and the multiflora rose too, running over the cottages and in some instances covering the whole front. The Palmetto is common here. In Charleston I am told all the wharves are made of it, being the only wood which is not attacked by the worms. Our native trees have also blessed our eyes the oak, button wood &c. The Gum tree is extremely handsome in every respect the leaf peculiarly so.

The negroes strike me as better dressed than those we saw in Cuba even those attached to small estates. We find ourselves continually exclaiming with surprise at every thing which indicates our being in our own land. Oxen yoked and horses with short tails, for instance, both unknown in Cuba. The last considered as a disgrace, none but the executioners ever riding upon them there. A horse and chaise winding through the trees attracted all the passengers and we were each trying to make out with the glass all the particulars of the harness &c. It is astonishing how entirely the eye becomes accustomed to strange objects in a short time and ours have become quite at home in the island We have passed meadows covered with the "yellow flower of the forest", and the vegetation every where is most vivid and beautiful. I am told there are plenty of wild deer in these forests, and the farmers, when they want fresh meat, have nothing to do but to take their guns & go into the woods and shoot them.

It was curious to observe the Kentucky boats with flat bottoms built with roof & windows like a house with three oars, one used as a rudder behind and the two others lying each side to assist the current in bringing them down in these arks. They bring their produce of every sort to market and after selling it dispose of the boat itself for lumber. The boatmen then return home in the steamboats; it is a remarkable fact, that before the use of steam these men used to get on board a vessel for New York and return by the way of the North river, Lake Erie &c as the shortest route home. I was pleased to day to see several estates upon which the negro huts had piazzas and were neatly painted, the grounds however, of none of them seemed laid out with the slightest regard to beauty, no avenues of trees nor roads leading over the plantations. A sugar estate, at best is entirely inferior in beauty to one planted with coffee but here where they are quite unadorned they are peculiarly dreary.

Mr Sullivan says some of the scenery we have, to day, passed resembles that of Holland; you are constantly impressed with the danger of inundation being considerably above the houses as we sailed along and only a narrow dyke to keep the flood at bay, each owner is obliged by law to keep the levee in front of his estate in order, and, indeed, common prudence must induce all to be desirous of doing so as a small breach would carry destruction to an immense tract. As we advanced up the river the character of the trees changed, becoming more those of our forests; and we had great pleasure in recognising many old familiar forms. About six miles from New Orleans we came in sight of the battle ground; the house of Genl Parkinson, a very fine establishment; and a mile or two on found ourselves opposite the head quarters of Genl Jackson.[19] The house is pretty and the grounds appeared to be arranged with taste. The yard in front was filled with flowers among which the double oleander, or cypress rose, shone conspicuously The place is now owned and occupied by Mr Montgomery, a man of large fortune. The tree under which the British were buried was also pointed out to us; here too we saw the first coach since our return to the States, it was passing us on the road at the side of the river and exhibited a novel style of *footman*. At least it would be so at the north; that of a black *girl*, who was standing behind gayly dressed in a yellow gown, and black apron fluttering in the wind.

We were not fortunate enough to reach the city before sundown and consequently lost the view of it as we came up. The wharves and streets looked gay with lights, and the bustle and noise about the shipping was quite overpowering French, Spanish and English being jumbled together forming a complete Babel. The gentlemen took a boat and went up to the city to look for lodgings, which they obtained at Bishops new hotel. We could not be accommodated until morning and, indeed, felt no wish to leave the ship before as the night was damp, and we prepared to transfer ourselves, as well as our goods & chattels, to terra firma by day light.[20]

New Orleans. Wednesday, April 25th It is just a fortnight to day since we left Havana, with respect to weather, a most delightful passage. We were gladdened on arrival by letters from home but as pleasures are never unmixed, found room for complaint that they were not of more recent date, and my husband too, experienced disappointment in receiving no newspapers nor more particulars about his business, concerning which he naturally feels anxious and wishes his correspondants to be extremely minute in their information. Charles Elwyn came on board immediately after breakfast and talked with us as fast as possible until we landed, at twelve o'clock. He says the Searss' Mr & Mrs Cunningham, Mr Hubbard Miss Bumstead & suite of old men left in the "Henry Clay" a week since; it is only her second trip and said to be the finest boat on the river. Charles says the girls enjoyed themselves much while here, particularly Harriet who is fond of society. They were out several times, and went to the races and theatre, thus getting rid of the time very agreeably. On the deck of our ship this morng was a most promiscuous assemblage of all nations and I enjoyed, as I always do, the little fuss occasioned by so many contending voices.

At noon we bid farewell to the Hermosa Habanera and drove to Bishops where our first impressions were by no means delightful. Every article, in my room, was clothed with a garment of dust two or three inches thick and in the drawers and about the apartments were various leavings of the last inhabitants. With respect to dust, I was soon disposed to exonerate the landlady for almost immediately after its removal it again asserted its ascendency and this too after my being congratulated by Charles Elwyn upon having arrived just after a rain, because the dust would not annoy me. The clouds pouring in at the window have been quite overwhelming. We are very well suited with our rooms with respect to size and situation and with Lorenza's assistance I doubt not they will be kept in good order. George immediately upon entering the house was attracted by some children playing in the entry and I hope will make himself agreeable to them. The poor child wants young companions. This afternoon Eliza and I took a carriage and went to half a dozen shops and found on our return that we must pay four dollars for going a few squares. Expenses in New Orleans are much the same as in Cuba.

This eveg we have been favored with a long visit from Coffin Sumner, who is in most respects the same unaltered "Coff"; he has, however, added in appearance at least ten years to his age. Mr Sullivan & Eliza, who had never seen him before, were astonished, and insisted he was intoxicated but to me he seemed quite as brilliant as ever. He gave us the pleasing information that he should come and see us every evening while we are in New Orleans.

Thursday Last night we had one of the most severe thunder storms I ever experienced; they are said to be more violent in the Gulf of Mexico than elsewhere. The rain poured in torrents and when I first looked out at the window the streets were quite over flowed and, of course, I anticipated an exemption from dust, but, alas! soon after breakfast I perceived the cloud again rising, and we were soon as much troubled as ever. Bishops house has been opened but a short time and is as full as possible, an hundred and fifty boarders. The arrangements are not yet entirely complete and there is a continual hammering a room being preparing, I believe, for a separate table for ladies. A Mrs Smith who formerly took lodgers herself, is housekeeper, and, it seems to me her department is extremely defective; it is true, however, she has great difficulties to contend with, having but three chambermaids, and only one of them a white girl. The blacks in New Orleans, as indeed every where, are miserable servants without constant superintendance. We dined at the public table which was filled with company, mostly very second rate looking sort of men, probably shopkeepers and other men of business two or three ladies sat, with their husbands, at the bend of the table, it being arranged in form of a horseshoe, and by them we took our places.

Charles Elwyn called this morng and Mr Shepherd after dinner. They both accompanied us to the French theatre where we were quite amused with two or three spirited little plays in one act, and delighted with the band of Tyrolese, or Bavarians, which made its first appearance to night. The music is the softest in the world, four men and one woman. Two of the men played delightfully upon the guitar. Their voices all harmonized finely. One tenor had a most remarkable note in his throat. They sung German words to some of our oldest, most familiar airs. We walked home, being unable to procure a carriage. Mr Shepherd says the French ladies always walk from such places. I unfortunately forgot, in crossing, the little steam of water that runs in all the gutters and immersed my foot & ankle in the limpid element.

May 2d With the exception of one, it has rained every day since we came to New Orleans, and while the torrents are pouring down, the streets are almost impassible for foot passengers. It has been quite an amusement to look out of the window and see the fruitless attempts of people to get from one side walk to the other. The inhabitants say that, although rather earlier than common, they consider the rainy season as commenced. The gentlemen have received calls from Mr Mongomery Genl Porter, Mr Lanfear and Mr Ogden. The ladies of the two last are too much indisposed to call upon us and Mrs Mongomery has probably been prevented by the rain. The same cause has hindered our riding into the country. Mr M. resides upon the estate which formed the head quarters of Genl Jackson and, of course it possesses an attraction independent of its beauty. We heard that his wife intended calling upon us, but in the present state of the roads she could hardly get to town.

The day after we were at the French Theatre we accompanied Mr

Shepherd in a ride on the rail road which leads from the city to Lake Pont Chartrain. The distance is so short, only six miles that they do not make use of steam and being drawn by a stupid animal we did not exceed the rate of five miles and an half.[21] This was my first trip on a rail road of any sort and I consider it gave me a very imperfect idea of one where the carriage is propelled by steam and where you may proceed at the rate of twenty miles an hour. The scenery on either side is low and swampy with here and there a house, mostly places of entertainment to the wayfarer. In consequence of some repair on the road we were forced to get out of our car and walk a distance of a quarter of a mile. Lake Pontchartrain is fifty miles in length and twenty seven wide. The shores are very flat and uninteresting. I think we should have lost a great deal of pleasure had we come to Mobile instead of taking the sail up the Mississippi which was recommended by some persons. We observed the steam boat lying at a little distance, not a very inviting object. A house of entertainment is at the end of the rail way, and a hotel being erected a little back, probably intended for families who wish to remove from the city during the summer. I understand there is not the least danger of fever to the Creoles of the country unless they spend several winters in succession, away from New Orleans. There is hardly as [an] instance known of any native's being attacked by it. The road where the horse treads on the rail way is paved with small shells brought a cross the lake

The city is paved with stones brought from Boston principally and some perhaps from New York. Mr Shephard informed us that the expense of paving one side of a square was about twenty thousand dollars, perhaps one third more than with us. The city is entirely laid out in squares and may be divided into two parts called the upper and lower faubourgs. The lower, the French, has undergone very little alteration for years and presents the appearance of an old town. The language spoken there is French. The houses differ from ours, having projecting roofs, and piazzas, and altogether to my eye is vastly more attractive than the American quarters. The upper faubourg has been built within a few years. We were told that six years since the part of the city in which we resided was a wilderness and now is built in every direction. The American houses are all like those in other cities of the United States, three or four stories high with no attempt at ornament. The shops are shewey much like those of New York, and I could find little new in them. With the Americans all the improvements of the place commence and it is only they who have paved any of the streets; there are but few which are rendered comfortable in this way but they are continually going on in their operations.

On Sunday morning early I accompanied Mr Lowell to the market. That where butchers meat is sold is in a different building from the vegetables. They are both quite long and the stalls very neatly kept but by no means superior to the Philadelphia market. Women mostly were presiding. They looked white, but probably were quadroons. The marketing is universally brought home by black or mulatto girls, and you see hundreds with a basket on each arm. Their style of tying on the bandanna handkerchief & general appearance struck me as much more jaunty & *French* than that of the Spanish negresses. It was quite amusing to hear English and French talked on each side with equal fluency. Fish is sold in the vegetable market and I observed a great number of crabs which the women handled with tongs. Their bite is most tenacious and they seem to be very beligerent in their nature. Pretty bunches of flowers are to be found upon many of the stalls tastefully arranged for sale. Mr Sullivan brought home two splendid magnolias, the only ones in the market. Coming from this place I observed on the levee a great number of pedlars whose wares were displayed to the greatest advantage upon the ground; every sort of article to tempt the negroes, chintzes, jewelry, toys and, in short, fancy goods of every description.

We stepped for a few minutes into the Cathedral where mass was celebrating. It is an ordinary looking place enough, within, although outside it has quite a venerable air. The levee is considered worth seeing in New Orleans, from its extent, here you see vessels of every nation loading & discharging their cargoes. This city is entirely flat and there are no fine public buildings. From the top of Bishops' house we have perhaps the finest view of the place. The river makes an immense bend just at the city which occasioned a great perplexity to the gentlemen with regard to its situation; they had always supposed it to be on the east side and this gives it the effect, in coming up, of being upon the west. By the aid of the map, however, the matter was settled & the east declared victor. I noticed on Sunday that the shops in the French faubourg were open, but all those of the Americans shut. There is very little observance of the sabbath by either. The Theatres are open, and Dr Robinson says he heard a sensible man who keeps a book store remark, that religion was very easy here. No sect was persecuted and any denomination might come; at the same time none is regarded.

Upon the whole my impressions of New Orleans, which were by no means favorable, are not, from what I can see and learn, rendered more agreeable. Morals here must be at their lowest ebb, and I should regret exceedingly any accident which should induce a friend, in whom I was interested, to settle here; it seems almost impossible to resist entirely the contagion of so impure an atmosphere. Of the society here I can form little idea not having been out at all, but have seen enough to feel sure I should never select this as a place of residence. I imagine the French society is the best. The ladies I saw at the theatre were all with their heads dressed à la Chinois and never did I see a body of such unbecoming dresses; diamonds & jewelry in general are much worn here. I observed some most splendid rings. In the second row, which is dedicated to those who [whose] blood does not run pure & uncolored, sat a lady extremely pretty, adorned with gems & her children wore diamond necklaces and earings, little girls of seven and eight. No one quite white ever goes into the second row of boxes nor is any other ever admitted into the first. It is quite impossible, frequently, to detect the drop of color and the lady I mention was fairer than almost any one in the house.

Two or three of our lady fellow boarders have called to see us; but there is little interesting or remarkable in any respect about them. They seem very common sort of people and are all from up the river. Mrs Fearn, Mrs Pleasance &c. The set of boarders here is some what unruly and we have been once or twice very much annoyed at night by young men of riotous disposition returning late and amusing themselves with singing, screaming &c.

Until very lately the French predominated in council in New Orleans and the Americans could not get a majority for making the improvements they wished. I am told the French are now, the young men particularly, desirous of knowing English and of being called Americans; they are generally sent to the north to be educated. The French ladies form a society by themselves and rarely mingle with those of the upper faubourg. In the public ball room there is a line of division between the two nations, one occupying each end of the room.

<three blank pages>

"Louisiana" Steam boat. May 3d Mr Lanfear called before dinner, his wife has been unable to come and see us in consequence of her own indisposition and of the illness of a child. The fates seem altogether to have prohibited our forming any lady acquaintances in New Orleans. Charles Elwyn came in after dinner and accompanied us on board the boat. There was the utmost confusion upon the levee, and it was with the utmost difficulty our coachmen could extricate the carriages from the crowd of drays & wagons, we were literally hemmed in and were a long time in reaching the Louisiana. We felt a desire to visit one of the boats, acknowledged to be first rate, ours being not one of the three or four best, and stopped on our way to look at the Splendid, just arrived. It is a truly splendid establishment. The cabins both ladies & gentlemens are above the boiler and communicate with each other. They are very large and handsomely fitted up. A piazza extends all round forming a very agreeable walk.The Louisiana is formed upon the same plan but is somewhat smaller and has not so great an air of elegance. Mr Lanfear and Mr Shepherd came on board to bid us farewell, and Charles Elwyn staid to tea.

At 35 minutes past eight we left the landing our departure being greeted by the firing of a gun and a shout so tremendous that I actually started from my seat thinking one of our boilers had exploded. The steam as a prelude to setting us in motion sent up the most unearthly hisses and as soon as the overpowering jar commenced I felt as if we were at the mercy of some mighty monster, some leviathan of the deep It seems to me I never was in a boat where the crashing was so powerful. It is impossible to divest oneself for a moment of the idea of danger, particularly with the memory of the Brandywine so vividly impressed. This great boat was coming from Natchez a few weeks since and just above Memphis was discovered to be on fire; some sparks had caught the straw coverings of some carriage wheels which were upon the upper deck, and the alarm was immediately given, out of a hundred and fifty persons sixty were destroyed, mostly burnt to death; there were but two or three females on board and these perished. The Captain asserts that she was completely on fire in two minutes, and that there was no rescue for those who could not swim. But it seems altogether impossible such a mass should go in so short a time and the more natural supposition is, that struck with panic, the officers of the boat did not take all those measures, necessary to save the lives of those on board. The flames spread back towards the ladies cabin, and an attempt was made to turn the boat to shore but she unfortunately stuck on a bank, and the tiller ropes of the rudder being burnt, she could not be guided. Two or three other horrible accidents have occurred within a very short time, another burnt, one run down & another blown up; so that we feel that danger may be around us in a variety of shapes.

The ladies cabin being all engaged, when the gentlemen applied for us, Eliza and myself have staterooms in the gentlemens apartment; before coming on board we regretted this, but since we have seen the crowd among the ladies we are glad to be so snugly arranged. In the ladies cabin the state rooms are double and in one are actually six persons, four women & two children, and the space between the births is not more than I have in mine, where Lorenza occupies one bed & little George and myself another. I have a window looking out upon the guard and here I could sit and write very comfortably, but for the jarring of the boat occasioned by the working of the engine; it is impossible to write legibly and my hand trembles like an old person. I shall persevere however in scribbling as well as I can, although most of the passengers declare it impossible to hold the pen. Eliza has altogether abandoned the attempt.

Our captain is a young man by the name of Maynard, I confess it would be more agreeable to have one more experienced, but perhaps he may be careful as an older man. Since coming on board we have recognized Mr Lowber of Philadelphia who was with us in Matanzas and who called upon us in New Orleans. He is a lawyer of some distinction & one of the first families in the place. We shall find him a very agreeable addition to our party. I have been conversing with him this eveg about the Catholic religion in Cuba and he has told me some curious facts which he gleaned in St Iago. He was present at some religious ceremony where all present had candles and marched in procession round the chapel. He whispered to his next neighbour that he should hardly like to have one offered to himself and had hardly uttered the words when a Priest stepped up & gave him a candle and he was forced to march round with great gravity of demeanor. In commencing mass, the priest sprinkled those kneeling around, with holy water. A boy carried a bucket into which he constantly dipped his whisk or whatever it is called with which he performed the ceremony Mr Lober said he noticed one woman quite absorbed in devotion, upon whom he bestowed a double dose; she started, and the Priest went tittering away; it was evidently done with the design of amusing others. Mr Lober mentioned a shrine of the virgin near St Iago, where people annually go to make vows. It is situated on the top of a steep hill and he heard of a lady who crawled up on her hands & knees while her husband accompanied her holding an umbrella over her head

Friday We stopped last night on account of fog, and I was pleased at this proof of prudence in our captain, some of the boats run through every danger and are of course constantly meeting with accidents. I can now well realize the injury which may be effected by snags, those enormous things, which bear a strong resemblance to some pityless monster peeping out of the water, seeking whom he may devour. The difference between a snag and a planter consists in the one's facing up, & the other down the stream. They are both large trees which have been washed from the banks and in sailing down the river their roots have struck in the mud and become fixed objects to be dreaded by the strongest steamboat. A *sawyer* has its root fixed, but the trunk is constantly sawing up & down; either, is sufficiently terrific. A large tree of this sort frequently pierces through the boat and of course many are sunk in this way; they are now, however constructed with an outer chamber where there is an outlet for the water to pass off and which renders the danger much less. The drifting logs which are constantly coming down the river, and of which now there are more than usual, are another source of trouble, they are continually striking us, and occasionally get into the wheels which they are very liable to break, and the noise they make whirling round is enough to make one feel that destruction is in the path, this, however, is an evil which may be remedied by stopping and is one of the least of the disasters to be dreaded in the Mississippi navigation.

We passed several pretty houses early this morng and the negro huts are, many of them extremely neat being painted and rendered comfortable by little piazzas in front. On this river, however, no regard whatever is paid to ornamenting the plantations, and we frequently pass those of great extent where there is not the slightest attempt at any cultivation except the raising of sugar cane, and the rudest fences divide the fields. This is particularly striking to us who have come from the splendid coffee estates of Cuba where for miles perhaps you may ride on the grounds of a private gentleman which present throughout the cultivation of a garden. The sugar plantations here, now present a peculiarly dreary appearance as the cane has not grown and you cannot imagine that in any state they can be pretty. About ten o'clock we passed Mr Shepherds place, said to be the finest in point of adornment on the river. The house which stands a little back is embowered with trees & was an attractive object with its white pillars peeping through; the white washed negro houses at some distance with a larger one among them, probably for the superintendant. Along the bank is a row of beautiful weeping willows.

This afternoon we have been detained a long time at the estate of Genl Wade Hampton,[22] who has plantations on both sides of the river and is reputed a close man and not particularly kind to his negroes. We went on shore upon one of his estates and entered one of the negro huts, which though a dark looking place had an appearance within of neatness & comfort unknown in Cuba. A large woman was there and though not particularly cordial, set a bench for us, which however we did not occupy. The large open fire place & board floor were very pleasant changes from the bare ground and small flame kindled in the centre of the bohea [bohío]. At the door of one of the huts sat a pleasing looking negress who told us she was under the influence of fever & ague and had been obliged, within a few days, to discontinue work. Mr Sullivan asked her if she had a kind master and was happy. "Oh yes, she replied, a very good master who gives me enough to eat & drink and does not work me too hard and what more does a slave want?" "I suppose you would not be free if you could" said Mr S. "no," said she, "for then I should have to work for my living and now my master supports me." We stepped into the sugar house, but saw nothing there except hogsheads of molasses for which we are stopping.

We have today become acquainted with two or three of our fellow passengers a Mr & Mrs Rogers of Philadelphia and Miss McCauley and a Mr McCoy of New Orleans who is going as far as Natchez for the purpose of accompanying the ladies. Mrs R. is a very pretty woman, daughter of Fairman the celebrated engraver, much younger than her husband who is a man of large fortune. He seems quite gentlemanly. We have also become sociable with Capt Welles who has been recently stationed at Fort Jackson below New Orleans. We find him a very agreeable, amusing companion, nothing escapes his observation which can afford food for merriment. He has been stationed in many different ports but has found none so uncomfortable as this. More so than any in the State of Maine, where they are sufficiently trying. His family have preceded him to Pittsburg where Mrs Welles's father resides. They intend going on to Boston where some of Captn W's family live; he is well acquainted with some Boston families, Mr Rufus Amory's, &c &c; he says that during the year they lived at Fort Jackson Mrs W. never had any company and left home but once. In the time of the freshet they were nearly inundated. The sunset was most beautiful tonight.

Saturday. The day has been clear and very warm. I rose late and was greatly disappointed to learn that we had passed Baton Rouge. I depended upon seeing this place which is very pretty and has a fortification built round a square considered one of the finest in the United States, it is surrounded by columns and the area planted with trees; here the levee ceases. In consequence of the great height of the river we have been the greater part of the time since we entered the Mississippi above the level of the country on the shores and the reflection of its insecurity is quite painful to a stranger. The inhabitants, no doubt from habit, think nothing of living with only this few feet of earth between them and total destruction. The scenery after passing Baton Rouge becomes more wild and mountaneous. The occupation of those who live in the little log huts along these shores is principally that of cutting wood for the steam boats, this they pile close to the shore and it is incredible how soon a large quantity is transferred to the boat. Our deck passengers mostly consisting of Kentucky boatmen who having disposed of their cargo, are returning home, many of them assist in taking it in. Those who engage to be serviceable in this way, of course, pay less passage money. $6 is charged those who do not work. We pay for our voyage from N. Orleans to Louisville $35 each.

We passed this morng, through a short cut, where the river has broken its way making only three miles of what formerly was thirty: it is continually forcing a new course for itself. We stopped at Bayou Sarah a little place where a fleet of Kentucky boats were lying and the steam boat Telegraph was drawn up against the wharf. The houses generally looked new but one or two near the river were completely insulated and looked as if they had floated down the river. A small boat was attached to their doors to convey the inmates to dry land. Bayou Sarah is said to be a place, I fancy the only one on the face of the earth, which you are at liberty to abuse even before its inhabitants; and they do not attempt to defend it from attack, it is so utterly disagreeable. To day we have seen an enormous aligator, the first of any size upon these waters; indeed the only one above New Orleans. I am greatly disappointed in this respect having expected to see the shores lined with them; probably the noise of the steam boat and the frequent attempts to shoot them by deck passengers have frightened them away. I had some conversation today with Captain Welles who gave me some little balls of amalgamated silver from the mines of Mexico.

Sunday May 6th We today came upon bluffs forming an agreeable variety to the flat uniform country through which we have been passing, even here the scenery can by no means be called grand except by comparison. We arrived at Natches about twelve o'clock and landed to visit the town. It is divided into two parts the upper and lower the latter being built along the margin of the river and, at this moment, *all but* inundated, indeed we noticed several buildings standing rather further forward than the rest whose lower floors were covered with water one particularly, a stable with flaming sign which in its present state can afford fit shelter only for aligators. We ascended the hill in a broiling sun, the gentlemen thinking that yellow fever must certainly be manufactoring below. It is a curious fact that even on the top of this steep ascent, this complaint rages in the summer season and it is thought unhealthy. About half-way up, we stopped under a large tree to look at the view; beneath us lay the lower town looking like a place of business and drawn up to the shores were numberless

Mississippi Steamboat, ca. 1839. Merchant's scrip, Mississippi Shipping Company, Natchez, Miss. Fifty cents, December 2, 1839, serial #1624A, Numismatic Collection, Courtesy of the Massachusetts Historical Society.

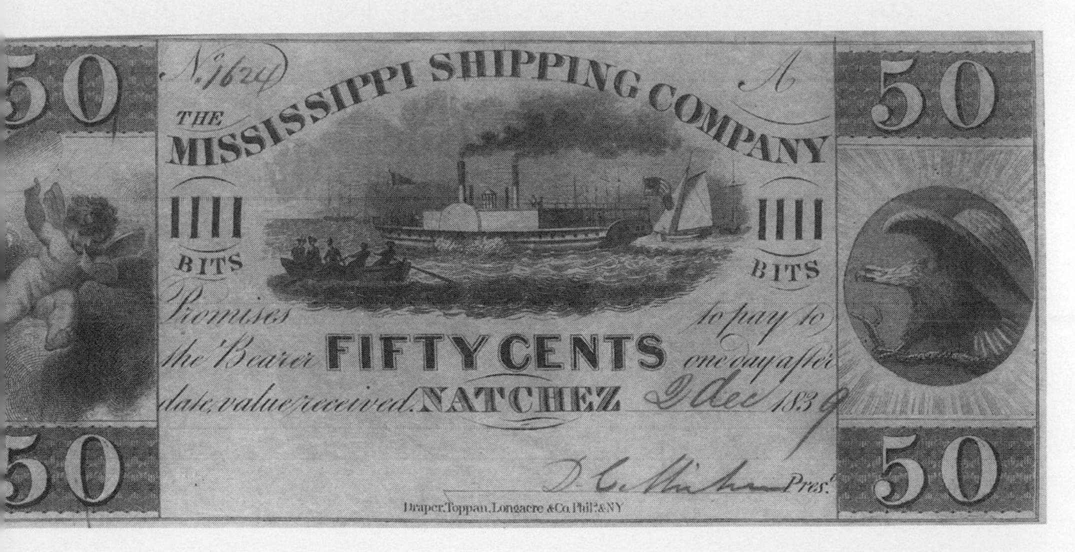

flat bottomed boats; those strange looking arks, filled no doubt with every imaginable article. Some of them are fitted up as stores and carry down the river all that can be wanted by those living along the banks; they are arranged with shelves for books and every possible convenience. The view up and down the river would have been fine but for the muddy color of the Mississippi which to me completely destroys its beauty; it is precisely like the veryest mud puddle that one sees.

The town of Natches possesses nothing very attractive in appearance there are no public buildings of any beauty and the place seemed small; we walked round two or three squares. It being Sunday the streets were entirely quiet, and business as much suspended as in Boston on that day. It is worthy of remark that this is the first place, in which we have been, since leaving home where the Sabbath has been in the least degree regarded. Mr & Mrs Rogers Miss McCauley and Mr McCoy and Capt Welles accompanied us in our walk. This was the place of destination of Mr McCoy and he took leave of us before we descended the hill.

Quite an accession was made to our party by the coming on board of several ladies and gentlemen and there was great tribulation among the gentlemen lest some of them should be forced to relinquish their staterooms or incur the dreaded reputation of want of gallantry but, happily, for their comfort as well as for the character of our captain, no such demand was made upon them, and the ladies were all *comfortably* established on the floor of the cabin. But one rebellious spirit was among them, a woman who made great objection to her quarters and who was at length accommodated in the Captains state room; she came on board with a little boy about four years of age, looking much like his mother, who has virago written upon her countenance. I foresee she will be a firebrand among those who choose to have any thing to say to her. She has already declared that there is not a lady on board "they may think themselves so, but she knows better". As Eliza & I are not in the ladies cabin and have not spoken to the creature, it is to be hoped we may be exceptions to this sweeping charge. Several of the Natches belles and beaux are among the new comers. George has taken a bad cold which makes him dull, it is accompanied by a cough

Monday We have been edified this morning by an account of a declaration made under some of the windows of the ladies cabin and overheard by Mrs Cox a lady from N. Orleans and her daughter Mrs Slocumb; the parties were a gentleman and lady who came on board at Natches yesterday Their conversation was altogether very sentimental and exquisite they compared the scenery upon the Mississippi to that of the Alps, a most apt conclusion; talked of Moore's poetry[23] &c& and the whole was summed up by an offer on the part of the gentleman of his heart and hand and a request that he might have his answer tomorrow this the lady thought too soon. "Ah," said he, "I see how it is, you like to have such a pretty fellow as me dangling after you, and are only flirting with me." She then mentioned Thursday but he declared he could not exist so long in uncertainty, she said perhaps she would give him her decision on Wednesday but he thought Wednesday was an unlucky day & he would try to survive until Thursday and so on & so on. I never saw a swain more beaming with happiness than he is to day so that, I presume, he is not very feaful of his lady's cruelty.

We stopped at Vixburg a pretty place with some good houses on a hill; the ascent is steep and I did not go on shore. We landed a tall Natches lawyer who came on board yesterday and whose pugilistic reputation is quite remarkable; he very recently exhibited his prowess by planting his two fists, one in each eye of the sheriff at the jail who refused to admit a client of his to a prisoner with whom he wished to interview. he is said to be one of the most valorous characters in this part of the country. He has had very little to do with those on board and has remained quiet with the exception of a tremendous walk up & down the room when he was continuously [stopping] & flourishing his handkerchief with the report of a pistol.

George's cold is worse to day. I have been obliged to dress him in his winter clothes. It is almost impossible to be prudent in so uncertain a climate as ours. We went on shore this afternoon while stopping for wood; this we do twice a day, and the delay is usually quite as much as an hour. The captain says he pays from $1.50 to $3 for wood. $2.50 is about the average. He gives much more near New Orleans than higher up. The wood for a trip from N.O. to Louisville costs from ten to twelve hundred dollars.

Tuesday This morning as early as three o'clock I was awaked by a bright light shining into my window, and jumping up I found we were stopping close to a shore where an enormous fire was kindled. The occasion of this was the landing of a Mrs Foster who was put on shore here and whose negroes were keeping the flames alive; they soon lighted another, and the various figures flitting about had quite a pretty effect; Mrs F. had to ride some distance on horseback before she reached her house.

We have been on shore to day in Arkansas territory the weather has been cold and all the morning we were confined to the cabin. When the air is mild, which it has been the greater part of the time, we sit upon the guard and sew or read and observe the country through which we pass, which though low and unvaried possesses an attraction to those who ascend the river the first time. The trees are various but the greater part the cotton tree, which is not remarkably handsome and said not to be valuable nor useful for any one thing, but that of making floors, for which it is handsome; it is never used for fuel.

Captn Welles amuses us very much, he finds food for satire in almost every individual on board, and has waged a deadly warfare with the virago whose child is certainly the most unprepossessing little creature, and insists upon shaking hands with every body an operation by no means agreeable. I commenced Eugene Aram[23] today. George is rather better but still suffering from his cold. Our evenings occupation is usually playing whist, the table E. Sullivan and myself, Mr Lober & Capt Welles, or some other gentleman.

Wednesday Cool, but not so much so as yesterday. This morng a young man by the name of Jacobs who has been ill ever since we came on board, died. He has suffered from liver complaint for three months and was on his way to Virginia to his friends; he was in business in New Orleans, he had no servant and perhaps might have lived, had he been sufficiently prudent. I never should have imagined such an event could take place among so many people, and occasion so little confusion. It was merely accidental that I heard of it, and all was conducted with the utmost propriety; they are accustomed to such things in these boats. I understand that a coffin was made for him this morng and a very good looking head piece with his name & place of residence painted &c and this afternoon when we stopped for wood at St Helena, he was carried on shore and interred in the grave yard. I believe the gentlemen formed a procession but being walking in another direction I did not see it; nor had I a wish to do so. Mr Sullivan and Eliza went into a small house on shore and expressed themselves much pleased with their visit they were welcomed very hospitably by the owner & his family.

Thursday. To day we came upon the Chickesaw bluffs; for Mississippi river, quite bold scenery. We stopped at Memphis, the first town in Tennessee. It is built on a hill and consists of one long street on the river with several shorter running back into the hills. We all went on shore. A disabled steamboat, used as a store, is drawn up to the land & into this we stepped from our own. From the street on top of the hill we had pretty views up and down the river. We entered several shops which seemed to contain a variety of fancy articles. This afternoon we passed the wreck of the Brandywine. It is burnt to the waters edge and only a few black sticks standing up denote that it ever existed; it seems almost incredible, so near shore, that so many should have been lost. An attempt was made to carry the boiler, which was saved, down to Memphis, but some accident happened to the flat bottomed boat which conveyed it and the whole sunk thus destroying the only vestage which might have been rendered useful. We played whist this evening. George is better to day. It is said Memphis & the country adjacent are subject to violent earthquakes.

Friday It rained violently last night and has been cool and damp this morng. I finished Eugene Aram after dinner and transferred the book to Mr Sullivan who was impatiently waiting for the second volume. We passed New Madrid and stopped for wood at a place just cleared; we went on shore being desirous of touching the soil of Missouri, and entered a log hut just erected; here we saw a young girl of eighteen or twenty and one or two younger children; she did not display any great empressment at seeing us and barely answered our questions The room looked neat and there was an appearance of comfort about the bed. Mr Sullivan took up one of several books on the table which proved to be Orlando Furioso,[25] the girl said it belonged to one of her Father's hired hands. I regretted, after I came away, that I did not look at the rest. These books are probably purchased of the Kentucky boatmen who bring them with their other merchandise down the river. Dr Robinson says he was informed that almost every boat on the Mississippi had a copy of Volney's Ruins[26] and Pollock's "Course of Time".[27] The young girl we visited said she found it very pleasant living in this place. On coming out we observed a house adjoining, with a small piazza, where sat several men and beyond, another, which seemed appropriated to the blacks and was probably the kitchen. The bears come down even to the house, and the other day carried off a pig from the door.

While we were engaged with our whist this eveg the Captain came in and invited us to take part in a dance, there being some musicians on board. The tables were accordingly wheeled away and the band ushered in. It consisted of two fiddlers who each knew one tune a jig and although they were different, they took frequent occasion to play together, part of the time sitting at opposite sides of the room. One of these *harmonisers* was the most ludicrous figure, he sat perfectly self satisfied, with his hat drawn down on one side & his black thick hair forming a bush on the other, with one foot drawn up on to the other knee and drawing his bow with an air of entire independance, stopping for nothing hit or miss. Capt Welles amused himself by entering into conversation. The original informed him he was a "*Hoosha*" that is an Indiana man, and the other was a "Kentuck" but said "we don't water our horses at the same brook." We made two attempts at cotillions but were at length quite willing to occupy ourselves with the music or musicians, which were altogether too inspiring to permit us to forget ourselves in dancing. It is a most brilliant night, we have had a fine moon ever since we came on board.

Saturday. About seven this morning, we came in sight of the Ohio river; there is no very perceptible change in the color of the water; the Ohio being rendered turbid by the late freshets. The scene, as we approached its mouth, was very pretty. Directly in front a point of Illinois divided the Cumberland from the Ohio. This spot was beautifully wooded and enlivened by buildings painted white one of which we discovered upon a nearer view to be the "Union Inn." Two or three dwelling houses stood near. I bade adieu to the Mississippi with right good will, having never been able to get rid for the moment of the idea of immediate and pressing danger. There is no situation where the conviction so constantly forces itself upon you. The scenery, throughout, has been extremely monotonous, and upon a second trip would be exceedingly uninteresting to me, indeed I think no small consideration would induce me to take the voyage again, although I am very glad to have seen the Father of waters for myself. I felt at home from the moment of entering the Ohio. The views on either side, even at the entrance, were picturesque. The Kentucky boats drawn up or under the shade of the trees adding greatly to the effect. The water, though of the same muddy color as the Mississippi, is clearer and this alone would make an essential difference. The shores as we advance have become most beautiful, the land rising into hills and the trees of immense size; the log cottages add much to the romance of the scene. A question was started this morng whether love in high life could survive in one of these habitations, Captn Welles thought it altogether impossible but Miss McCauley maintained that it might be kept alive even at the risk of inundation.

We went on shore this afternoon at Smithland or Cumberland River, in Kentucky, quite a pretty place, the houses of logs looking very comfortable in all respects excepting that they can afford no shelter from the rain. We passed some houses which were building and adjoining one a man was erecting his shop which contained a large wheel; not having calculated his apartment for the size of the wheel he was forced to cut a hole in one side and let it come out into the street a little way. A small cottage, with a piazza on the opposite shore looked like a pleasant abode. This eveg we stopped for wood at Golcondi in Illinois but I did not land some of the gentlemen did, however, &. Dr Robinson brought us some leaves as remembrances of the state; he called us just before dark to look at two islands in front of the boat, beautifully formed, and every moment we pass some interesting spot. We walked for the first time this eveg upon the top of the boat and had a noble view from this elevated station. The moon shone brightly tonight and we sat for some time after tea admiring the beauty of the shores. Fires were lighted all along and had a fine effect shining through the trees, I presume they were clearing the land. Mrs Rogers and Miss McCauley sung to us very sweetly; after which we returned to the cabin where we amused ourselves with our customary game of whist. This morng I commenced the corner of a pocket handkerchief[28] I intend working for Catherine. George's cold is very bad.

Sunday May 13 There was such a scrubbing and washing of the guards that it was impossible to go out for nearly the whole morning. We went forward and sat a little while there with Mr Sullivan & Mr Lober but we did not long remain unmolested: a shower came pouring down from the upper deck and we were forced to retire again to our original obscurity in the cabin, where I read aloud to Eliza in in[29] Johnson on climate.[30] I could not hear my own voice but she said she could understand me which was hardly credible. In the afternoon we walked the upper deck from which we acknowledged the scenery to be almost unrivalled, the greatest variety of splendid trees. The constantly changing aspect of the banks the huts mostly of logs (we have seen some frame today) with their inhabitants all standing out to look at us The ravages of the flood are infinitely less in appearance than I anticipated; they are principally exhibited in the immense quantities of drift wood which are piled up in masses on the shores, sometimes at a height of thirty forty or fifty feet from the water. It seems very strange that so few houses are prostrated. One would think the greatest danger they had to apprehend was that of being buried by these logs. Here and there we observe a huge log lodged far up in the branches of a tree and not unfrequently a small boat shewing how high the waters were above their ordinary level. They are said to have risen 66 feet. The consternation of those residing along these shores must have been excessive. Captain Welles says there are three hundred islands between the mouth of the Ohio and Louisville but I think he must be misinformed on the subject there do not seem nearly so many

We are continually passing the flat bottomed Kentucky boats, some with small cabins on deck. Mrs Slocomb a lady on board, says that when she was a child, before steam boats were used upon these rivers, she recollects being three months coming from Louisville to New Orleans in one of these affairs. She left in October and did not arrive until December. They drew up to the shore and lay by every night and always stopped when there was a high wind. These machines are furnished with three enormous oars or paddles, one serving as a rudder and one each side extended like wings; these are sufficient, with the aid of the current, to move them along. Mrs Slocomb says she came down in a double boat, that is two joined together, one part of which was fitted with a carpet and other conveniences. The life on board was of course very monotonous.

This evening we have been introduced to Captn Turnbull of Virginia of the United States corps of engineers; he came on board at Bayou Sarah with two other young men (engineers also) Mrs Barrian & Eastman. They have been suffering every thing from the confinement of the boat, having just come from the most active life. I regret we were not acquainted earlier as Captn Turnbull is uncommonly affable and agreeable. He says it was extremely dull at Bayou Sarah and that these gentlemen took more sketches in a few weeks there than they would in six months at Washington, their desire was such to get away.

This is a rainy, dark evening George's cold is almost gone. He has been in fine spirits to day.

Monday It rained early and we feared we should lose much of the fine view, it afterwards cleared, however, and we were able to be on the guards and admire the magnificent scenery. It had become more rocky & precipitous and in many places was truly grand. The trees are of larger growth than any on the Mississippi and those on the edge of the banks have the same insecurity of appearance shewing all their roots and looking as if the first storm would tear them from their foundation and sending them down the river convert them into snags. The uncertainty of every thing on the Mississippi gave me a feeling of melancholy and I could hardly admire even a beautiful view because, mingled with my admiration came the reflection that a single year might not only convert the fine trees and shrubbery into objects of dread, but that acres of the land itself, on which they stood, might bid adieu to its rightful owner and go to attach itself to some neighbour on the opposite side of the river. We passed New Albany a place famous for repairing steam boats, indeed, many are made here; one is at this moment constructing of immense size, by the owners of the Louisiana, which promises to be one of the finest on the river. It is really curious in passing boats on the river to observe the difference between them, there are hardly to be found two alike; the last is always an improvement on the preceding. (I beg any one who reads this will observe that it is written while the boat is going joggity jog).

We reached Louisville in the afternoon and, our baggage being consigned to a dray, we took a carriage and rode a distance of two miles to the city. We were obliged to land below on account of the falls which are impassible to the steam boat. We left earlier than most of our fellow passengers and hoped to get good accommodations, but after applying at three houses we were received at a fourth Fisher's an establishment recently opened. We were shewn into a drawing room finely situated, having a pretty view of the river and were tolerably suited with our chambers, I was forced to put George and Lorenza into the room with Eliza S. and her woman. Our table was good and we considered ourselves, upon the whole fortunate. Here we have met with a cruel disappointment Dr Robinson came in this eveg and said he had met a brother of Anderson who told him Lars had gone to Washington; he had been out of health some time and went on to consult Dr Physic and is now domesticated in Mr Silsbee's family, where he will probably be until June. My husband has depended so much upon seeing him here that we feel no desire to stay any time in the place which presents few attractions to a stranger. I am told the country in the vicinity is exceedingly pretty and the canal is worth seeing. Master Burke is here and will play tomorrow evening but we shall probably be on our way to Cincinnati

I was not sorry to take my leave of the Louisiana. Our captain was young and had all the imprudence of youth, I did not know until we had left the boat that we took fire almost every day; a place over the boiler was completely charred, and once, Dr. R. says, he saw it burn as much as ten minutes before it was extinguished. Capt Maynard, when spoken to about it, said he considered the danger nothing, because so many men were continually about the place. This sort of reasoning I do not fancy, and a sheet of iron would have remedied the difficulty. With respect to lights, too, there is great carelessness; none but tall candles are used and these are left about in every direction, and with so many musquito nets and other combustibles I wonder we have not been burnt half a dozen times. I have been agreeably disappointed with regard to musquitoes it has not been necessary for me to draw my bar once upon the river; and as to gullinappers [gallinippers] I have not seen one. I feel a strong curiosity to make acquaintance with an individual of the tribe though I should not care to see more. Sand flies too with which we were threatened, have kept out of our reach. Once or twice lately upon stopping for wood just at evening we have been rather annoyed by musquitoes but they have not dared to enter our state rooms. Upon the whole, I do not consider our boat a particularly good one, the fare was indifferent and with respect to noise, there was the confusion of Babel. We had no milk, excepting occasionally, with our tea & coffee an evil easily avoided as we necessarily stop twice a day; and were it once understood as an indispensable with the boats, there would be plenty of cows along the banks of the river. Mr Lowell usually procured milk for George once a day, by going ashore for it himself.

<three blank pages>

Tuesday May 14th[31] I rose too late to see any part of Louisville before breakfast, and immediately after Captain Welles called to say we could be well accommodated in the La Grange, the boat in which Mr Lober & himself were going to Pittsburg. The gentlemen went to the landing to make arrangements and returned saying we were to go at ten o'clock, thus limiting our investigations to a very short period. Eliza and I, having a few articles to purchase, went to some of the principal shops in the main street which seemed to contain every variety of fancy article. Afterwards we accompanied Mr Lowell to look at the devastations of the fire which raged the night before last; thirteen houses were burned and a part of <*word missing*> market building. At the appointed hour we came on board the La Grange Captn <*blank space*> a nice clean looking boat infinitely more to my taste than the Louisiana, where we had the ladies cabin to ourselves. The gentlemen say the motion is greater but I differ on this point and flatter myself that my handwriting bears testimony to the contrary. We found on board our former companions Capt Welles, Mr Lober, Captn Turnbull and his associate engineers. Mr Phillippi a German who we first met in New Orleans, he came from Havana in the "Aurora" with Mr Burke, Dr Robinson and William Gorham

The day has been clear, though windy; the scenery fine and constantly varying; the ravages of the freshet more apparent than before. High in the branches large trees are lodged in some pieces of cane and sticks. We frequently pass houses which bear marks of having been overwhelmed yet still the wonder grows with me that a freshet which could amass such quantities of drift wood and which leaves sufficient evidence of its great height, should have done no more Most of the buildings which must have been under water retain no external marks of the flood We have seen to day some very pretty cottages architecture being in a much more advanced state than in the Mississippi. The sunset clear, a round ball

Captain Turnbull has made himself very agreeable in conversation, speaking of the Kentuckians he gave us a much more favorable impression than we had before received. His own impressions were unfavorable before he went among them and he was surprised to find them so civil, agreeable & hospitable; he was in the state during the time of election and every thing was conducted as peaceably as it would have been elsewhere. Capt T. amused us with a story told by a Kentucky gentleman at a dinner party in Washington; he was asked to try two wines, and after tasting one upon taking the other he said his opinion might be expressed by a little anecdote he would repeat respecting a Kentucky lady who resided back in the woods. One day a wolf coming down to the house, her husband went out to combat him, and they had quite a serious battle. After it was over the lady remarked it was the first fight to which she had ever been witness in which she did not care which beat!

Margaret, Eliza's woman, after having come all the way up the Mississippi and Ohio, declared to day she had never seen a snag. I accordingly took an early opportunity to point one out. Our table is very good. We played whist this eveg.

Wednesday It rained early this morning, but our good genius presided and before we were ready to land at Cincinnati the weather was quite clear. Our chambermaid says that Mrs Cunningham went up in this boat the last trip and was exceedingly ill. She thought she had lost since leaving N. Orleans. I was sorry to find our boat disposed to race with the Magnolia, which sailed directly after us, but we beat and that put an end to the matter. The scenery has again been beautiful. We reached Cincinnati about nine o'clock in the morng and for an hour and a half sat talking with Captn Turnbull and others while our gentlemen were seeking lodgings. They went to Mrs Hamilton's, where they found Sarah Crowninshield & husband, but she could not accommodate us and they finally engaged rooms for us at the Broadway house.

We were delighted with the appearance of the city, as we approached, the fine clean streets and thriving aspect of all about us. The little town of Covington opposite forms a pretty feature in the landscape. Capt Turnbull says that twenty one years since Cincinnati was a military post and contained but a very few houses. Coming up to the city, we passed a fine country establishment owned by a Mr Ludlow a husband of a sister of Louisa Slocum, Louisa's home is in Louisville but Capt T. says she is now in Cincinnati. We found very good chambers at the Broadway house and a good parlour. We were sorry to bid adieu to some of our gentlemen: Mr Lober, Capt Welles and Capt Turnbull, they continue on in the boat, being anxious to get home as soon as possible. We received letters on arriving, which, though of as old a date as the 3d of May, were very acceptable. I wrote to Mother after dinner, and then set off on a walk of discovery with my husband. After leaving our package at the post office, we explored some of the streets and were delighted with those we saw; just before tea I called at Mrs Hamilton's to see Sarah Crowninshield, who looked well and seems to have enjoyed her journey; she represents the Guyandot road as very bad They are, at present, undecided what course to pursue being deterred from going to Lexington by the state of the roads. Mr C. has an inclination to go to St Louis.

We dined at the public table a man, looking very like an imposter, calling himself Count Bretos sat opposite us. He has completely got the blind

"View of Cincinnati, Ohio, from the hill back of Newport Barracks." From GLEASON'S PICTORIAL DRAWING-ROOM COMPANION, *vol.* 4 *(*1853*):* 241. *Courtesy of the Massachusetts Historical Society.*

side of the land lord. We took tea in our own room and were favored with the company of Mr Phillippi, Dr Robinson and W. Gorham. I shall retire early to bed.

Thursday We had an early call after breakfast from John Rogers, Mr James Perkins, and Mr William Greene. A lawyer here, he married Miss Lyman of Northampton and is the gentleman who lost a child in Providence some time since in a most distressing manner. The carriage was going down a steep hill when the door suddenly flew open and the little girl leaning against it, fell out and the wheel went over her. He has but one other, also a girl, remaining.

We were quite provoked to learn the stupidity of our servants last eveg. It seems John Rogers and Mary Jane Derby called and were told we had all gone to the theatre, a most unpardonable mistake. John looks much as ever except perhaps rather more brown, he seems happy and says he is perfectly satisfied with Cincinnati. After the departure of the gentlemen Eliza and I went to the bath and to some shops and from thence to see Ellen Rogers who received us most agreeably and looked as lovely as ever. Mary Jane Derby is with her and very much delighted with the place; she says Ellen is much noticed and that she found, on her arrival, that she had as many warm friends as in Boston. Ellen herself expresses herself happier here than she was in Boston. She sees her husband contented and says she is perfectly contented. Mr R is engaged in a saw mill which occupies all his time, he dines at one o'clock, though the usual hour of the place is two, because he wishes to be absent at the same time with his workmen. He is in partnership with a young man by the name of Gondoin a cousin of Mr L's classmates. Every body appears to be interested in the Rogerss. Ellen shewed me her children who are both pretty, the boy particularly and they are remarkably well behaved. While there Mrs Green the wife of Mr W. G. and Miss G. his sister called. They came to call for Ellen R. to go & see us. Miss G. is a lady I saw at Lebanon Springs six years ago. She was there with Mr Ward and Miss Cutler. Mrs Green invited us to take tea there tomorrow eveg with a small party. We accepted with pleasure. Sarah Crowninshield and her husband called just as we were coming away. Ellen's house is small and simply furnished but every thing is in very good style. They bear their reverses so cheerfully and live so consistently with their means that it is impossible not to feel interested in their success.

After dinner, Eliza and I took a carriage and accompanied by Dr Robinson rode up the river, we passed Mrs Kilgore's former residence and one or two other pretty houses, but in general the banks are settled by farmers, Cincinnati being too young a city for country seats. The ride was very pleasant. We went out about three miles and came in sight of the Miami. Our return gave us prettier views. I observed a small, rapid stream winding around the base of a hill into which some laborers were throwing earth which they dug from the side. Mr Lowell says that this is done as the easiest mode of carrying it off. Many of the hills have an appearance of having been cut away which is occasioned by digging for sand or limestone with which steps & facings of houses are made. I think it the most beautiful sort of stone for the purpose. It is so fine and of such a handsome brown color

This evening we have passed, stupidly enough, at Mr Flint's. We did not even get the information we anticipated about this part of the country for the old gentleman was so in raptures with the singing of a Miss Deranger who kept it up the whole time that he had not a moment to talk. Mrs Flint said she had heard a good deal of music in her life, in New Orleans and elsewhere, but she never heard any she considered equal to Miss Deranger's. The company consisted of Mr & Mrs Crowninshield, Mr Walker of Charleston who is here with his wife, Mr Peabody the clergiman about to be settled, a Mr Cranch, Mr Star & one or two other indescribables. Miss F. was talkative as usual. She shewed us a picture of her Father in water colors. We ordered the carriage a quarter before ten and were astonished to find it eleven when we reached home. The coachman neglected to inform us of his arrival. I had no idea Cincinnati was so large a place every body seems to live so far off. There was a proposal of walking to Mr Flint's but we could never have accomplished the distance before the eveg was through.

Friday This morng we received calls from Mr Hubbard, Mr Perkins, Mr and Mrs Walker. Mr W. is the gentleman who was tutor at Northampton at the time George was there; he has recently married to a Miss Bryant, originally from Philadelphia. She has resided in Cincinnati about a year. The parties which now render the city gay are made for her as bride. She is a pretty, delicate looking woman and was dressed this morng with great taste. Mr Walker has been here only a year and is getting as much business in the law as he wishes. He says there is not an idle man in the place, and had he been disposed to be one himself he should have found no companions. There is no such thing as a lounge. James Perkins is studying with him and he says he never knew a young man take hold of the law with the same energy & talent, he will undoubtedly succeed here. I have seen no place where I should like so well to have a friend reside who was going far from home. It is a large & growing place, there is no danger of growing rusty; there is constant intercourse with the west. Mrs Rogers says scarcely a week passes without bringing some of her acquaintances and the morals of the young men are said to be extremely good. The people here seem to be rational and although they visit considerably they are not exclusively devoted to fashion as in New York. We are all perfectly delighted with the place and although we had heard it extolled before we came are agreeably disappointed. New Orleans is the only place which having heard it much abused was even worse than we anticipated.

After our visitors had departed Mr L. Mr Sullivan and myself set forth upon some calls. We saw in fourth street the houses which were erecting, which struck us in very pretty taste. We went in & explored and were much pleased with the arrangement. All the smaller dwelling houses have some regard paid to ornament in the railings of the door steps which are usually of iron mounted with brass balls. We stopped at John Rogers's and saw Ellen & Mary Jane and the pretty children. Mr S. who had not been there before was quite charmed. We afterwards called upon Mrs Walker of Charleston but did not see her, and then at the Pearl St house to see Mr & Mrs Rogers of Philadelphia & Mr & Mrs Grosvenor our fellow passengers. In the eveg we went early to Mrs Green's having an engagement afterwards at Judge Millers We found a small, pleasant party of about thirty and were sorry not to stay until they broke up. E. Rogers, M. J. Derby, Mr & Mrs Pomeroy of Brighton Mr & Mrs Walker of Charleston, Mr & Mrs Hendez (she keeps school here) Mr Parkman of B. Mr & Mrs Foot and several others with whose names I am unacquainted, although most were introduced to me, comprised the company. Ellen talked about the schools in this place, she says there are no good ones for boys, but there are so many persons interested in having them, it is an evil which must soon be remedied.

As soon as the refreshments had been handed round we bid Mrs Green good eveg and rode to Judge Miller's where we found a larger party. The family itself is said to be a very agreeable one, they resided formerly in New Orleans & Philadelphia, and we were introduced to sundry very pleasant people. There seemed to be a feeling of cordiality and affability you do not always meet in larger cities and there is perhaps less formality of manner. Mrs Haynes a very pretty woman recently come here struck me as a remarkably attractive woman, we had a little dance on the carpet to music which was only tolerable. They usually here dance to the piano in private rooms. The band which is a fine one, plays only at public balls. Mr Walker was my partner, there was an attempt to have but two cotillions. The latter part of the eveg, the youngest Miss Miller, who has a good voice played and sang two or three songs, and we were quite delighted with the voice of a Mr Wheelock who after accompanying Mrs Haynes, who played, and Judge King in the song of "All's Well" gave us a simple scotch air with no instrumental accompanyment. He leant his head upon his hand and which is said to be his usual attitude on such occasions. Mr Wheelock was educated at West Point and married a Philadelphia lady whose father was very rich, but who, soon after the marriage, lost his fortune and Wheelock having nothing he became discouraged and fell into bad habits, his voice probably also aided in ruining him, it is a dangerous gift. He now edits the Evening bulletin a small sized paper here and his wife does something for their support. The party was, altogether, an extremely genteel one and in Boston we might take a lesson with respect to refreshments. Nothing was handed but ice cream which was served in large glass bowls or dishes from which you helped yourselves; this passed round but once or twice. We had also lemonade and different sorts of syrup mixed with water. The ladies were dressed in the New York style.

Saturday We sent for a carriage this morng and set forth on our calls. Miss Barton, who visited us with Mr Storey, was out. Mrs Green too indisposed to see us but we were received by Miss G. the sister. The house is finely situated. it forms part of Mr Foot's who built the whole. His house stands on an elevated position and is very large, Mr Green's on one side looking like a wing and on the opposite a corresponding wing is now erecting for Mr Walker. When finished the whole will look like a princely establishment; you reach the house by an immense flight of stone steps; beneath are offices which rent for a sufficient sum to pay for the other part. Parson Parkman is staying here and we had the pleasure of seeing him; he and Mr Walker of Charlestown [Charleston] have come on to settle Mr Peabody in the pretty little gothic church next John Rogers's house. I trust we shall not leave before the services tomorrow as it will be something to say we have been at the ordination of the first Unitarian clergiman on this side the Alleghanys.

When we reached Judge Millers we found himself on the steps; he ushered us in and shortly after Miss M. made her appearance; she conversed very pleasantly, and looked prettier than last night; her Mother and sisters were too much indisposed to see us. Mrs Walker, the bride, upon whom we next called, looked very well. She resides with her aunt Mrs Sawner to whom we were introduced last eveg and who is remarkably pleasing; she also was at home, and upon her horse Eliza Sullivan is to take a ride this afternoon. E's friend Mr Hubbard has kindly borrowed it. Mrs L. wanted us to take tea with her Monday eveg but we expect at that time to be on our way to Pittsburgh, the city of smoke. The ladies in Cincinnati universally ride on horseback. They are obliged to do so, for there are no good carriage roads. (I neglected to mention in my description of Mrs Miller's refreshments, that late in the evening two large cakes were handed round on waiters. They looked nice but I did not try them & cannot say whether they were sponge or some other.)

This afternoon at four o'clock a party which was arranged this morng rode up to the door on horseback. It consisted of M. J. Derby & Miss Pomeroy, Mr Hubbard, Mr Perkins and Mr Holbrook, formerly of Boston. Eliza mounted Mrs Sawner's horse and I stepped into a gig preferring to brave the bad road in this vehicle to mounting a nag of which I knew nothing. We set forth and when partly up the street, were joined by Miss Eliot, sister of Mrs Foot & Mr <*blank space*>. Mr Gourdoin shortly after added himself to our party and we proceeded in good spirits. The country all the way is beautiful. We ascended a hill very steep for the gig, but our horse being of good stuff, carried us up without panting. From the top the city can be seen to great advantage, and you can judge of its extent. I expected to return the same way and did not have the back of the chaise put wholly down and consequently had not so perfect a view as I should otherwise, but I saw enough to convince me that it is already a mighty city. Although not smooth, yet the road was by no means so rugged as to impair the pleasure of our ride and we enjoyed the delightful scenery. In the direction we took, we lost sight, for a while, of both the river & canal and there were few farms of any consequence along the road as there is no facility for getting the produce to market. The country is beautiful from its extreme irregularity, it breaks into hills & valleys alternately, all thickly wooded or covered with luxuriant vegetation. We passed through a most romantic wood. In one or two places I was obliged to get out & walk and emerging from this we came upon the canal.

Our ride into town was pleasant, we left the rest of the party to take another path through the woods and came ourselves, some time before dark, to the Broadway house. Mr & Mrs Rogers of Philadelphia called this eveg. Some one was saying today that 43 years ago this place was a wilderness, not a tree cut down, forty years since it was sold for forty nine dollars. It is a fact that no cords are now allowed to be sold in Cincinnati. Whenever it is done it must be by stealth.

There are three steam ferry boats and a dozen of other sorts. No bridge can be thrown across the river as no abutments can be made sufficiently strong to stand against the ice which floats down the river.

<half page is blank>

Eliza Sullivan asked Mr Hubbard about Mrs Kilgore with whom Mother was acquainted when she was in Cincinnati. She boarded at the house with her and gave E. a very circumstantial account of her engagements and marriage ("for she is now Mrs De Witt"). It seems she for some time received the attentions of Mr Starr a lawyer here also a boarder at Mrs Hamilton's, and it was supposed was engaged to him, although the match was not declared. He was obliged to go away for ten days to attend the court and during this time Mr De Witt who had before been rather attentive became devoted to her & the very day of Mr Starr's return she went into dinner with him arm in arm which was considered equivalent to a declaration of engagement. Mr S. was not in the room at the time and after dinner when Mr Hubbard was walking with him, he remarked "you came in too late to day." "Why so," said Mr S. Mr H. then related what had passed to which Mr S. said little at the time but upon returning home from the lecture where they had been together he entered the parlour where all the boarders were sitting and told Mr De Witt he should like to speak with him; they went into another room together and Mr Starr said "The subject upon which I wish to speak is Mrs Kilgore." "Stop sir," said Mr De Witt, before you proceed any further I will inform you that Mrs K & myself are engaged to be married. "After this declaration you are at liberty to say what you please." Mr Starr then related the terms upon which he was himself with the lady saying that they had been engaged several months and that letters had passed between them. "That is of no consequence," said Mr De Witt. "at present she is engaged to me."

They then returned to the parlour and Mr Starr marching up to Mrs Kilgore said "I will thank you for my letters madam." "Certainly sir," and they all three walked out of the room together. This was all that Mr Hubbard saw that night.

The next morng Mr H. took his usual place at table about half way down opposite Mrs Kilgore. Shortly after Mr S. came in & took the next place, Mr De Witt being at the bottom of the table. Just in the pause there always is before people begin to eat, Mr S said in a very loud tone of voice, "I wonder madam you can sit opposite me without blushing. "I have a great mind," putting his hand upon his pocket, to take out your letters & read them before the assembled company." "Do sir, do sir," said she in a very hurried tone of voice. He then called her the basest of women, told her she had conducted in an abominable, infamous manner &c. Mr Hubbard said he never heard such language used before to a female. Mrs K. beckoned to Mr De Witt & he came up & put his hand upon the back of her chair & said "I sir am the protector of this lady. Any thing said to her I consider addressed to me." "I congratulate you, sir, any body who is the protector of that lady has his hands full!" There was then some mutual recrimination and in answer to something said by Mr De Witt Mr Starr seized the carving knife & brandished it about. Mr H. said from the expression of his countenance he had no doubt he would have plunged it into his rival's heart if he could have got at him. Mr De Witt then made a movement to go round the table when the gentlemen interfered. Mrs Kilgore fainted & the ladies screamed. In a few days they were married.

Mr Hubbard said Mr De Witt was a little surly disagreeable man without any attraction and Mr Starr one of the first lawyers in the place and not withstanding his ungentlemanly conduct on this occasion the public feeling was so much in his favor that since the affair he has been invited every where and much cosseted while Mrs De Witt is almost excluded from society. Mrs Kilgore was an extremely vain woman & would swallow the grossest flattery and, Mr H. said, might be induced by a person who gave her a good dose to do almost any thing.

<half page is blank>

Sunday May 20th This morning, much to our discomfort, we received information, just as we were going to church, that the steam boat Sentinel upon which we had taken passage, would sail as soon as we could make ourselves ready, being only waiting for us; we accordingly dispatched packing as speedily as possible and came on board where we found Mr & Mrs Evans Rogers & Miss McCauley had preceded us. M J. Derby, Mr Perkins, J. Rogers & a Mr Appleton forming our escort, we left Cincinnati almost with regret and certainly none but favorable impressions. The river has been very beautiful though not more so than below Cincinnati. George has suffered exceedingly from his cold to day, it was more severe when he waked this morng. I do not know how to guard him from adding to his cold.

Monday The scenery is so fine on both sides the boat we hardly seat ourselves on one guard before we are called to admire something on the other. We stopped to take wood at a little spot upon a small creek in Virginia and, attracted by the beauty of the scene Eliza and I joined the gentlemen in their excursion on shore. The bank was very pretty and behind the house, which stood there was a dell finely wooded. We entered the negro part of the establishment where we saw "Sylvia" who was probably cook, and her child, "Delaware." We asked if she lived in the room we were in, she said yes, and pointing to the bed said "There is my scaffold." We afterwards went into the mansion house, a small hut the picture of neatness where we saw a pretty, trig looking woman with a child in her arms. We remarked that the situation was a pleasant one. Yes, said she, "but we did not think it quite so much so in time of the flood." I asked if she were alarmed and she replied that she was fearful the bank would be washed away; the family were seven days confined to the chamber. Captain Turnbull told us that all the log huts on the Mississippi are constructed with a chamber in the roof and furnished with a box of earth in which there can be put a fire, that the inhabitants may retire there in case of inundation. Capt T. passed a night in one of these huts and asked the man who owned it how high the water came, and he pointed to a spot over the door. We passed Guyandot the first town in Virginia. George's cold has oppressed him a good deal and he has been languid all day. He seems very delicate.

Tuesday Upon looking from my state room window this morng I observed we were passing the steam boat Transport. Mr Lowell was on deck and said after she had gone some distance there seemed to be an explosion of steam and he thought one of the pipes burst. They have a barbarous custom of waking every body at five o'clock on board this boat and the mulish chambermaid will not suffer any one to sleep later. The deck passengers breakfast after us and it is necessary to get through early. We passed Marietta which is beautifully situated at the mouth of the Muskingum. Its church with two towers its court house and other public buildings give it, for a little place, quite an imposing appearance, it is on one side the mouth of the river and another small village upon the other.

Previously we had passed Blennerhassetts island which I cannot better describe than in the words of the "Western Pilot."[32] "This beautiful island is celebrated as having formerly been the residence of Mr Blennerhassett an Irish emigrant of distinction, who built a splendid mansion upon it, the ruins of which are still to be seen. He possessed great wealth and expended a vast sum of money in decorating his residence, and in laying out his pleasure grounds with great taste and elegance. His lady was a very accomplished woman and his house the resort of the most literary & polished society. When Aaron Burr was projecting his famous expedition he called upon Blennerhassett, induced him to join in the conspiracy and to embark, with all his wealth, in his schemes.[33] They were detected, arrested and tried for treason. Blennerhassett was ruined. His splendid mansion was deserted & went to decay. His pleasure grounds were overrun with brush & weeds and it now presents but a mass of ruins." The island is most beautiful and peculiarly interesting from these observations. We could see only the ruins of some of the buildings, and these nearly gone. Of the mansion house there was no trace visible from the boat. A fine large orchard yet shews that it has been subject to cultivation.

The scenery today has been constantly changing and is quite as beautiful as my highly raised expectations warranted. Cottages situated in the most picturesque situations, hills covered with the thickest growth of wood with every shade of green beautifully blended, cultivated fields, sometimes the mountains nodding over the boat almost and then again forming only the back ground to wide fields and meadows. The little rivers with their rustic bridges and creeks running back into the hills add greatly to the scene. I have been sitting some time stern of the boat thus taking in both sides of the river, as well as the view down as far as the eye could reach. George has been quite indisposed this eveg. He was made sick by his cold and raised a good deal of phlegm. I trust he will be better tomorrow. Marrietta is the oldest town of any size on the river.

Wednesday The weather was dull, and part of the time rainy this morng

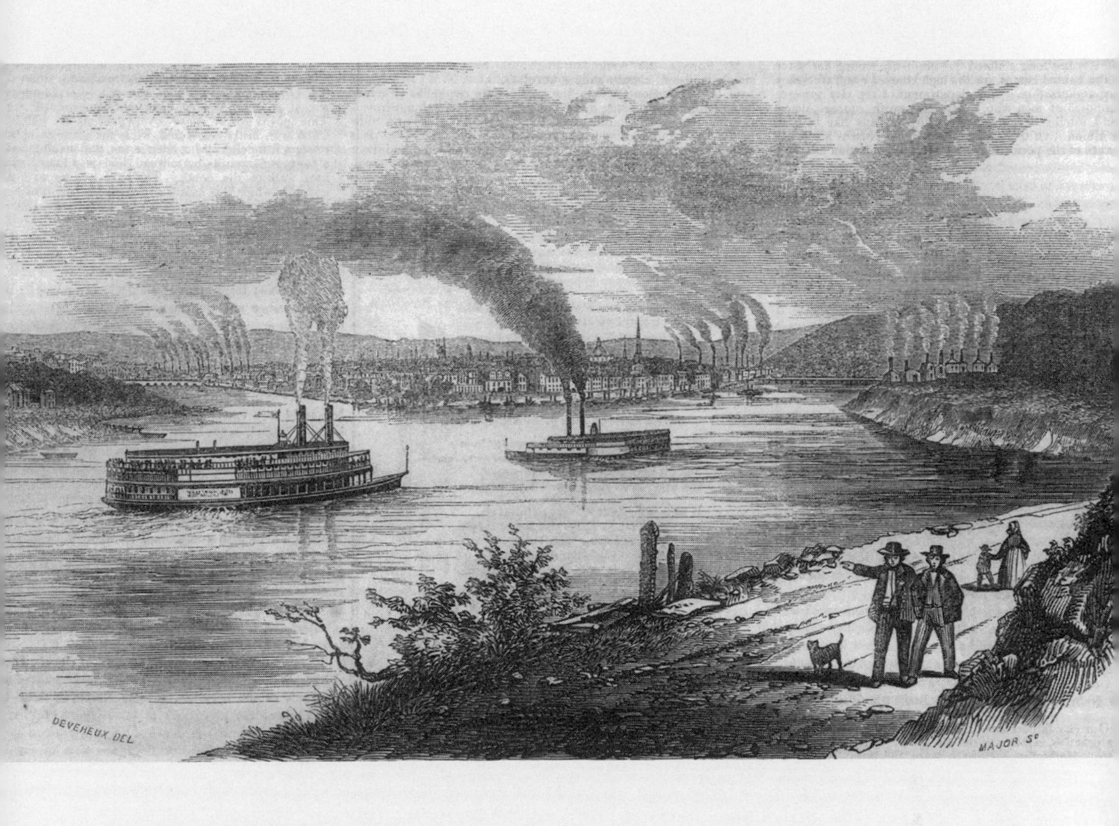

"View of the City of Pittsburgh, Pennsylvania." From GLEASON'S PICTORIAL DRAWING-ROOM COMPANION, *vol.* 4 (1853): 280. *Courtesy of the Massachusetts Historical Society.*

but the river so constantly becoming more beautiful and interesting, we did not feel disposed to keep in the cabin. We passed new Economy & an establishment of Count Leon's composed of seceders from Rapps, both poor looking places enough.[34] New E. being only purchased in March. We all felt a strong desire to go on shore at Old Economy but our captain who has made, he says, the shortest passage ever known did not like to spare us half an hour, as it would be so much taken from his laurels. The gentlemen, however, persuaded him with a bribe of five dollars and a certificate of the excellence of his boat, (which he well deserves) and he stopped. It rained quite fast, but that did not deter Mrs Rogers, Miss McCauley & myself, and we mounted a steep hill, rendered easy by the winding of the path.

The settlement looks much like any other little village, the tavern with its bar room like any other tavern, and the shop like any other country shop. The houses are all of about the same size, some of brick & others wood painted white with small gardens attached to each. We asked the tavern keeper what were the objects of curiosity and he said, "a great many," and mentioned a "labyrinth garden" half way up a picturesque hill back of the place, which we had not time to visit, & the museum which too we were forced to give up. A large building stands on the main street, probably the school and the church is directly opposite Rapps house which is the largest dwelling in the place and has an extensive garden. We could only see, peeping over the fence some high shrubbery and the tops of three small buildings looking like summer houses. Mr Sullivan rapped several times at the door of Rapps house but could not gain admittance.

As we approached Pittsburg the city at a great distance was recognized by the dense mass of smoke rising from its various forges. The country in its immediate vicinity is most beautiful and many pretty houses are dispersed among the hills. On the right bank the mountains rise precipitously and have a very extraordinary appearance with their coal mines and little black hovels and forges. Here and there you see a rail road which brings the coal directly from the mine into the furnace. The hills are all crowned with trees and a path or road winds round occasionally in a romantic manner. Pittsfield lies at the junction of the Alleghany & Monongahela rivers & has a background of towering hills. It would be a very pretty place, its locality is so good were it not completely obscured by smoke. Mr L. says it much resembles one of the English manufacturing towns. We left the boat after a short passage of three days and four hours, arriving at two o'clock, our passages from New Orleans to Pittsburgh have cost us $52 each a distance <*words missing*> miles, $35 to Louisville, $5 to Cincinnati & $12 to Pittsburg. The weather being rainy we did not receive a favorable impression of the place in coming up to the New Exchange. It looked black and old, every thing was penetrated with coal dust. We are all accommodated with good rooms here. Mr L. says it is much like the English inn.

This afternoon, as we are to leave early tomorrow, I resolved to see something, and as all the coaches were gone to the races I sallied forth with Mr Lowell on foot to see the glass works. It rained only a little when we set out but I was soon immersed in mud & clay. The glass cutting was precisely what I have seen at Letchmere's point, the pressing was new to me. Having got completely muddy I thought I might as well proceed to see the commencement of the tunnel through which the canal is to pass & accordingly waded through the clay to the place, a long distance, the rain pouring in torrents. It is a great curiosity; an excavation is made in the rock and after an arch of stone is formed, the earth is thrown back again. It is done by the proprietors of the canal. The state have no interest except as stock owners.

Having by some means got upon a hill in returning, the only mode of getting into the street was by descending a steep descent of clay. I accordingly attempted it Mr Lowell one side & a gentleman fellow passenger in steam boat on the other. I was in a perfect gale of laughter, every minute we were obliged to stop and pull up our shoes to which the mud laid claim & the elements above were in their most angry mood. Glad was I when wet through we reached the hotel. I was rejoiced to make myself dry. This eveg Eliza & I sat a short time with Mrs Rogers & Miss McCauley who are very pleasant women & retired early to our rooms to write.

Thursday At half past eight this morng, after breakfasting with Cooper the actor, who gave us some information respecting roads &c. we bade adieu to our late companions Mr & Mrs Rogers Miss McCauley W. Gorham & Mr Phillippi who are going to the falls, and set off in an Extra, Mr S. Eliza Mr L. myself Dr Robinson, George Lorenza & Margaret. George has seemed miserably, his cold does not appear to yield and he has been quite feverish all day. Immediately upon leaving Pittsburg we began to ascend the Alleghanies and have enjoyed all day the richest views—hills, valleys woods & fields of grain. The woods are all clear of underbrush a great beauty, immense fields of grain, wheat principally. This with smaller grain are the chief productions of these parts. The houses along the road are mostly log or rude frame huts, it seems singular that in a land apparently so rich we do not find better habitations. We stopped at Turtle Creek hill to change horses & entered a neat house where we were civilly received by a pretty looking woman who had two or three small children. We dined at Daily's at Stewartsville and have come to Greensburg to sleep. A good house, Tanner's I think, and a tolerably pretty place. 30 miles today.

Friday. We left Greensburg at ½ past eight and have proceeded a few steps when our fiery steeds not admiring the high hill in prospect before us turned into their stable in defiance of the driver and at considerable risk of breaking our necks. We escaped however unhurt, and getting out concluded to peditate the mountain in advance. The air was bracing and we enjoyed the walk. The ride has again been through a most beautiful country. The different points of the hills constantly varying our prospect. There are evident marks of coal mines all along and at one place where we stopped there was a mine close to the house which we explored. The excavation is small at present. We changed horses at Youngstown, which the landlord called a "considerable oldish sort of a place," and dined at Laganier where we found, as usual in Pennsylvania, good bread, butter, and well dressed meat, preserves made with maple sugar excellent. In the afternoon we had the misfortune to break the pole of our rickety old coach which occasioned a delay of more than half an hour and did not arrive at Storstown, where we are to lodge, until nine o'clock. The house promises well, we have had a good supper and the bed rooms look comfortable. In the tea room we found souvenirs, albums & scrap books, the two last in very good taste, belonging to "Miss May Graham" and a very tasteful glass of flowers on the window seat indicated a young lady of some pretensions. I hope we shall not be disappointed in the morng.

George was very feverish last night and this morng was fretful, but has been gradually growing better all day and this eveg he has brightened wonderfully. His cold is leaving him and in other respects within two days he is quite well. He has been in the habit all winter of drinking water frequently, and yesterday and today we have stopped often to give it him, there is no turning him off. He usually drinks two or three times in the course of the night & the last took it more frequently than common. perhaps it may have helped his fever. Lorenza has suffered for two days with a violent headach. We have collected some flowers in our rambles today. We walked up one very severe hill. We understand that this morng they had a frost here severe enough to kill the beans & cucumbers. 29 miles.

<very light pencil sketch>

Saturday. This morning after a comfortable night we rose early that we might be ready to set off early. The gentlemen had some conversation with the landlord Mr Graham, who said he kept the house for the amusement, having amassed sufficient fortune to live without the employment. He was landlord here for twenty years and became so fond of the life as to be unwilling now to relinquish it; he has a son settled in Cincinnati and a daughter married to Judge somebody, besides the Miss Mary Graham, whose tastes occasioned us some speculation last night. Mr G. says he has given all his children the best education the county affords.

We did not get away until a quarter before eight and then left in a hard rain which was only the precursor of a stormy day. We were very sorry to have our view from the top of the mountains interrupted by the mist and in consequence of the weather which, in addition to its effect upon the land scape, obliged us to shut up the carriage. Our glimpses of the beautiful scenery have been only occasional. Indeed, this morning I dozed away several hours. Our ride has been a great part of it along the edge of the precipice which must in the winter season be very dangerous, having the misfortune to have a leaky vehicle we some of us were wet, and altogether glad to stop. We changed horses at *<blank space>* and about four o'clock reached Bedford "Dillon's" to dine where we felt greatly disposed to pass the night but could not arrange the coaches so as to render it possible; here we had an excellent dinner in a hall hung with Indian ornaments of various sorts, pouches, wampum belts, beautiful pipe stems decorated with feathers, swords, birch canoes &c &c. all arranged with great taste.

Finding we were pleased with these affairs Mr Dillon desired his wife to shew us a complete dress made by the Indians. His son in law was an agent to some of the tribes and these things were presents to him, all but the dress which he had caused to be made, finding the materials. I had no idea that they could sew so well. it was executed as neatly as any white woman could have done it. We were also suffered to inspect a basket made by the daughter who lived two years among the Indians; it was made in their style with porcupine's quills and quite pretty. In a small room through which we passed, hung the skins of some small animals with fine fur, the feet adorned with beeds. We have been struck with the good taverns ever since we came into Pennsylvania, there seems to be a high tone about them.

Being shut up in a better carriage after dinner we travelled on through a lovely country, the latter part of the way on the borders of the Juniata, a little stream whose banks are extremely pretty, in some places the opposite shore quite perpendicular, covered to a great height with every shade & shape of trees. Here we are at length established at what seems a nice house, at the Juniata crossings. The situation is so beautiful we can only regret not arriving earlier and in a pleasanter day. Directly opposite flows the stream and on the opposite shore is the most splendid mass of foliage of every tint. A bridge & rapid on the left add much to the scene.

Since leaving Pittsburg we have continually encountered the large, covered Pennsylvania wagons loaded with the goods and chattels of emigrants, who were sometimes walking ahead and sometimes bundled in with their worldly goods. They are going to try their fortunes in the west. We talked with two good looking well dressed English women who said they came from Cambridgeshire and were going to Cincinnati to settle. The husband of one was a cooper, the other a farmer. They did not come to America so much on their own account as for the sake of their children. Every body along the road says that the number of emigrants this year is greater than ever before. We sometimes meet a row of five or six wagons together.

The Cornus Florida and wild honeysuckle are in bloom and constantly greet our eyes. I yesterday noticed many plants of Rhododendron but it is not in flower. George has seemed brighter & better today. 45 miles. There are the greatest number of chubby red faced children in these parts I ever saw.

Sunday May 27th Chambersburg. We arrived here just at dark and fortunately engaged our rooms before the "accommodation" came in. We are most comfortably established. The town we have had no opportunity of exploring and shall probably have to leave too early in the morning to go out. We left Juniata valley, where we passed last night almost with regret. The situation of the house so pleasant, and every thing inside so neat and so comfortable. The tavern keeper's daughters, nice looking little girls, waited upon us and seemed extremely desirous to please; the family have resided there about six weeks. It was peculiarly unfortunate yesterday that the rain prevented our seeing the entrance to the Juniata valley which is very beautiful, the part through which we passed after leaving the house, to day, was extremely fine. The ride has throughout been delightful, the scenery much like what we have had for a day or two, and even more varied. We dined at McConnell's town and after leaving there ascended the Cove a mountain and afterwards bade adieu to the Alleghanies. From its summit we had the finest view we have yet seen. I walked some distance with Mr Lowell and thus could command a more extensive survey. We have still encountered the wagons containing the emigrants and have been much struck with the size & fine formed, fat & sleek appearance of the horses, so different from the Cuba hacks. George has been quite bright & well to day, his cold hangs about him, but is lessened. We observed this eveg the death of Mrs Cunningham, in the paper, she died in this state at Somerset on her way home.

Monday. Last night after I had retired to my room, Mr Lowell came up and said Captain Welles & family had arrived in the accomodation stage, his wife and three little girls, the eldest about seven, and the youngest an infant. I did not go down, but this morng after breakfast encountered the Captain in the entry and was introduced to Mrs W. who is a pretty, lady-like looking woman. I was pleased with the glimpse I had of her. Captn W. brought me some shells which he had promised from the Alleghany & Monongahela rivers; he amused Eliza while I was up stairs with an account of his voyage from Cincinnati to Pittsburg and seems to have lost none of his drollery. They intend stopping at Chambersburg to day but expect notwithstanding to overtake us our motions are so much more leisurely.

I omitted to mention yesterday, the great beauty of the scenery after leaving McConnelstown when we were winding round the sides of the mountain, having this little village for miles on one side or the other beneath us. The road is necessarily very circuitous; the approach to it is also beautiful. To day before dinner the country was generally level and uninteresting, the houses being mostly log and these rudely patched together, some few frame or plaster. I am disappointed in this respect, having expected an air of comfort and ease in most of the habitations in Pennsylvania. We passed through Shippensburg a flourishing place and dined at Carlisle where there are several churches and an appearance of thrift. We observed a large building erected for a college, but which, our landlord informed us, was entirely unused, it proved to be an unsuccessful experiment.

Since dinner we have left the rough uninviting country and have been passing through the richest and finest looking farms possible. The fields of grain have borne the aspect of those I expected to see on the Ohio for I must confess in this I was greviously disappointed, having found on the river none of the luxurient cultivation I anticipated. Beautiful scenery, to be sure I saw, but no fields yielding the abundant produce I had imagined; those I presume, were back from the river. This afternoon we have been continually coming upon the famed Pennsylvania barns some of wood others of brick but the greater part of stone which have a very substantial appearance and as the stone and lime are at hand probably not the most expensive. They cost from $1000 to $1500. It strikes me as very singular that the houses to which these barns are attached are mostly very small and totally tasteless. I hope to see better things in this particular, tomorrow.

As we approached our journey's end we came upon the most beautiful scenery, a very picturesque river, a tributary of the Susquehannah. The distant Alleghanies, fields of waving grain, gentle hills and dales and finally the Susquehanna itself at this place a charming river. The pretty town of Harrisburg on the opposite shore and the bridges by which it is entered forming a fine picture. We felt chagrined to have our view intercepted by the covering of the bridge which only permitted us to look up & down the river at the windows placed at regular intervals. The carriage, on a penalty of a two dollar fine was obliged to go at a snail's pace and the bridge seemed to me interminable; there is an end however to all things, and we at length emerged on to a delightful little island from whence we could see the pretty islands with which the water was studded; our pleasure was, however, of short duration for we entered another long bridge by which we at last entered the town. We experienced a little delay in procuring lodgings for the legislature is in session and a national convention is to meet here tomorrow and in consequence the houses are quite full. We are now tolerably comfortable at the Harrisburg Inn but shall not feel sorry to leave in the morning.

Before tea we strolled up to the Capital in some respects a very fine looking building and the situation is perfect. There are three buildings, the centre containing the Senate & representative chambers and being higher & larger than the others & surmounted by a dome. They serve as wings though separated from the main building. The porticoes are extremely handsome, having tall Ionic pillars reaching to the roof. They are formed of freestone painted white, having much the appearance of marble. We ascended to the dome from whence there is a truly magnificent view, on the left the city which contains about four thousand inhabitants, all the houses are of brick and look new & pretty; there are eight or nine churches in the place some of every denomination almost, but no quakers. Before us was the river with its bridges & islands on the other side looking over fertile fields. We saw the high mountains through the gap of which the Susquehannah glides, and behind the canal leading to Philadelphia over which is thrown a pretty bridge and on this side also the fields were waving with a variety of colors. Just beneath us a little church and a few cottages clustered together formed a pretty group. On coming down we entered the senate chamber which is a very fine room, mahogany chairs & desks, crimson drapery, Brussels carpets. I observed prints of Judge Marshall & Stephen Girard.[35] From here to the representative chamber where we sat in a chair formerly belonging to William Penn and now the Speakers, and looked at a flag of American manufactured silk presented by Mr Duponceau.[36] The arms of Pennsylvania I observed to be a ship a plough & three trees.

Coming home we rambled down to the river, where we were kindly asked by a gentleman to sit upon his balcony which we did & enjoyed one of the prettiest scenes I ever witnessed. The hour was sunset and the river both up & down could not have been improved, coming down the street through one of the arches of the bridge, we saw a little island and a town on the opposite side. I observed a good many ladies and gentlemen sitting on the door steps or standing on the sidewalks with no covering to their heads. It seems to me they do this more every where than in Boston. After tea Eliza and I came up stairs and now at twelve o'clock I am writing up my journal. George rather languid to day. 50 miles to day.

Tuesday We left Harrisburg at ½ past eight this morning and riding a distance of nine miles by the side of the Susquehannah reached Middleton where we bade it adieu. The scenery thus far was very pretty. The canal ran between us and the river and with its little bridges added to the effect of the scene. After leaving Middleton we were disappointed in the country. We saw fine grain and immense fields of clover but there was nothing particularly picturesque on either side. The houses were ordinary although the barns denoted wealth; passing through Elizabethtown and crossing two or three creeks we reached Lancaster where we had an excellent well served dinner at the stage office. The houses are built in the German style and I observed on the signs principally German names.

For a mile before dinner & since leaving Lancaster we have been travelling through a most romantic highly cultivated country. There has not been a barren spot, immense fields of grain waving all around us and the distant hills encircling the landscape. Clumps of trees standing at intervals on either side and here and there a solitary and beautiful elm or oak. The houses have mostly been furnished with piazzas and although still tasteless structures, being built of stone have a comfortable appearance. The enormous stone barns struck us more than ever. It is really curious to observe the large fields of clover where cows are grazing half concealed by it; the butter, which is most delicious since we came into these regions, is no doubt rendered so by this sweet food. Everything has an air of plenty. Plaster of Paris seems in general use. The size and beauty of all the horses we have seen are very striking. A short time before reaching Sadsbury, where we are to sleep, we came upon the rail road which is making between Columbia and Philadelphia, it seems to be a stupendous work. We have come 50 miles today and intend to get to Philadelphia to dine tomorrow if possible. George had a violent coughing fit before he was up this morng but has since seemed pretty well. 50 miles.

Wednesday We were not particularly pleased with the house of Sadsbury being much struck with the want of attention we received. It was our intention to rise at ½ past five, breakfast at six and set off immediately after, but it rained severely and we postponed our departure until ½ past seven. Our ride was through a fine country and in sight of the rail road almost all the way. We stopped once or twice to take a little cake and bread and butter, and arrived at the Mansion house in Philadelphia about four o'clock. The environs of the city disappointed us. We saw no handsome houses and the cultivation was inferior to that upon the farms fifteen or twenty miles back. We have had the railroad in view almost all day, in some parts it is nearly completed and seems to be a stupendous undertaking.

Upon our arrival Mr Sullivan sent to the boarding house where he supposed his daughter Nancy was staying with Harriet Cutter &c, and learned the whole party had left about five days since for New York. This was a severe disappointment to Eliza who had been expecting all the journey to meet her sister. We sat down to a very good dinner and after it was over, Mr S. went to procure more information respecting Nancy, thinking it strange that no letters had been left for him; he shortly after appeared bringing Nancy with him to our very great joy. It seems the rest of the party had gone to New York and she had remained, waiting for her father, at Mr Walsh's.

Mr & Miss Walsh and Mr Poinsett called in the eveg. We have received letters from home and Mr Lowell considers it essential to his business to go to Baltimore to my infinite chagrin, as it will delay our return home three or four days. Little George has been in good spirits ever since our arrival. He slept most of the time in the carriage and is the better in some respects for the ride. We are most comfortably established here, fine bed rooms and a good parlour, where we have an excellect table. 57 miles.

Thursday The rain to day has prevented Mr Sullivan from going, and I have enjoyed it very quietly with the girls. We were informed this afternoon of the arrival of Mr Cushing and Mr Shepherd, but they have not favored us with a call although they both said they should do so. I feel a strong desire to see the nabob. Nancy says he has parted with his house to Mr Stephen White for which he deserves to be trimmed. This eveg old Mr. J. Vaughan called to see the Sullivans and afterwards Mr Furness and Mr Twyng, Stephen Perkins's partner. Mrs Elwyn sent for me to tea. Mr Lowber in reply to Mr Sullivan's note announcing our arrival said he regretted he was too ill to come out.

June 1, 1832

Friday After bidding the Sullivans good bye, they departed in the twelve o'clock boat, and receiving a call from Mrs Haven & her husband who invited us to take tea I walked forth with Mr L. We went to Mrs Elwyn's who was at home and welcomed us very kindly. her spirits were much depressed and she looked old and care worn. John is here, at present, on a visit. He came as a great man, one of the convention.[37] He went to Baltimore a few days since and was so much indisposed Mrs E. said he returned without going to Annapolis to see Emily who is pleasantly established at the barracks. This must have mortified his mother, though she spoke of it as unavoidable and as if that were his only object in going to Baltimore, but in conversation with my husband he suffered the truth to escape him that there were horse races there at the time he went & it is probable they were as attractive to him as Emily. Mrs E. sent up for Matilda who did not condescend to make her appearance. I am grieved that I shall not probably see E. if I go to Baltimore as the time is too precious to be spared.

This afternoon we went to the gallery of fine arts which greatly disappointed me. It is inferior to any exhibition at the Atheneum. Afterwards to see Mrs Derby who looks most wretchedly but who keeps up her spirits and goes out. She came down stairs to receive us and moves quickly and easily, but is no better for her winter in Charleston. From here we went to Mrs Elwyn's where we were engaged to tea. Mrs Alfred was there with her bonnet on being engaged to tea, and as the room was quite dark I could not distinguish her features. Matilda looked well. In the eveg Count del Verney or some similar name, called and another gentleman whose announcement I did not understand.

Saturday. This morng received a visit from Mr & Mrs Haven who asked us to tea but as we intend going early tomorrow and are engaged this afternoon we declined. We afterwards went to the water works, called at Mrs Elwyn's, Mrs R. S. Smiths upon Miss Harper and went to shops returning to a two o'clock dinner to be ready to attend Dr Hudson under whose hands I sat two hours while he was most thoroughly filling a tooth. He is the most satisfactory dentist in this particular I ever saw; he had not time for another which he said required attention and appointed tomorrow morng. As my husband has resolved to relinquish the expedition to Baltimore on account of his impatience to get home we shall take the boat which goes at ten o'clock on Sunday and go to Trenton to pass the night. Frederick Cabot called this eveg his wife being too much fatigued. They are at present at board here and are going to Germantown to pass the summer. The neighbourhood of Philadelphia has of late years been very unhealthy in the summer season, so much so that the handsomest country seats have been abandoned; fever and ague is the scourge of these parts

Sunday This morning I attended Dr Hudson, according to appointment, at seven o'clock. The good gentleman was not down and did not commence tormenting me until a quarter before eight; he was so long working upon my tooth that I did not leave him until nearly ten when it was raining and we concluded to take tomorrow's early boat. Mrs Smith called before my return to take us to church but I missed her & staid at home. She sent to request me to accompany her this afternoon and as it was raining hard after dinner we rode to her house and went with her to St. Peter's where we heard Mr Chatterton rather a dull preacher. I returned with Mrs Smith after church & sat with her waiting for the carriage. She was very civil to us. We afterwards drove to Alfred Elwyn's but did not find his wife at home. Saw her at Mrs E's where we passed a few minutes, & young Mr King was there. Charles Pickering called this morng.

NOTES TO THE DIARY

1. James Fenimore Cooper, *The Bravo*, 3 vols. (London: H. Colburn and R. Bentley, 1831).

2. Sir Walter Scott, *Anne of Geierstein; or, The Maiden of the Mist* (New York: J. & J. Harper, 1829).

3. Robert Plumer Ward, *Tremaine*, 3 vols. (London: H. Colburn, 1825).

4. Rev. Abiel Abbot, *Letters Written in the Interior of Cuba Between the Mountains of Arcana, to the East, and of Cusco, to the West, in the Months of February, March, April, and May, 1828* (Boston: Bowles and Dearborn, 1829).

5. Refers to a revolt of November 1830 in the Congress Kingdom of Poland, which was under Russian control. A Polish-Russian war ensued, ending in the defeat of the Polish rebels in September 1831.

6. Don Luis de las Casas (1745–1807), governor general of Cuba from 1790 to his death and successful sugar planter and promoter of Cuba's sugar industry at the turn of the nineteenth century. Jaime Suchlicki, *Historical Dictionary of Cuba* (Metuchen, N.J.: Scarecrow Press, 1988), 155–56.

7. Error in original.

8. February 3, 1832

9. Date probably incorrect.

10. Date probably incorrect. Possibly February 20, 1832

11. Date probably incorrect.

12. Date probably incorrect.

13. Appears as "compy" in the original.

14. A question mark appears here in pencil, apparently written in a different hand.

15. Error in original

16. In nineteenth-century Latin America a woman could be placed "on deposit" in cases of marital conflict and concern over family honor. See Kristin Ruggiero, "Wives on 'Deposit': Internment and the Preservation of Husbands' Honor in Late Nineteenth-Century Buenos Aires," *Journal of Family History* 17, 3 (1992): 253–70.

17. Lord Byron (Jan. 22, 1788–Apr. 19, 1824), one of the most famous English romantic poets, died in Missolonghi, Greece, after joining the Greek war for independence against the Turks.

18. Navigation station at the mouth of the Mississippi Delta.

19. General Andrew Jackson (Mar. 15, 1767–June 8, 1845), seventh president of the United States (1829–1837). This reference is to the headquarters from which Jackson had led troops against a British invasion of New Orleans in 1815. This famous victory against the British helped him win the presidency.

20. There appears here a half-page entry that has been partially erased and recopied following the entry for Wednesday, April 25.

21. Some of the first railways operated by animal power rather than steam locomotive. George Rogers Taylor, *The Transportation Revolution, 1815–1860* (New York: Rhinehart, 1951), 76.

22. General Wade Hampton (1751 or 1752–Feb. 4, 1835), sugar and cotton planter, congressman, soldier; reputed to be the wealthiest planter in the United States at the time of his death.

23. Thomas Moore (1779–1852), Irish romantic poet, friend of Lord Byron and Shelley.

24. Baron Edward Bulwer Lytton Lytton, *Eugene Aram* (New York: J. & J. Harper, 1832).

25. Lodovico Ariosto, *The Orlando Furioso*, trans. William Stewart Rose, 8 vols. (London: J. Murray, 1823–1831).

26. Constantin-François Volney, *Ruines, ou Méditation sur les révolutions des empires* (London: R. Carlile, 1827).

27. Robert Pollok, *The Course of Time, a Poem, in Ten Books*, 3d ed. (Boston: Crocker and Brewster, 1828).

28. Appears as "hdkf" in the original.

29. Error in original.

30. Unable to locate reference.

31. May 15, 1832.

32. Samuel Cummings, *The Western Pilot, Containing Charts of the Ohio River, and of the Mississippi from the Mouth of the Missouri to the Gulf of Mexico, Accompanied with Directions for Navigating the Same, and a Gazetteer, or Description of the Towns on Their Banks, Tributary Streams, &c. Also, a Variety of Matter Interesting to Travellers and all Concerned in the Navigation of Those Rivers* (Cincinnati: N. & G. Guilford, 1829).

33. Harman Blennerhassett (Oct. 8, 1765–Feb. 2, 1833), wealthy Irish immigrant and associate of Aaron Burr. He met Burr in 1805 and provided assistance and funding for Burr's plans to invade Mexico and bring about the separation of the Western states from the Union. He was indicted for treason and acquitted along with Burr in 1807. Blennerhassett's property was destroyed, and he returned to Europe in 1822.

34. Johann Georg [George] Rapp (Nov. 1, 1757–Aug. 7, 1847), German-born religious leader and founder of the Harmony Society, a communal society that established one of the most successful utopian communities in the United States. Economy, Pennsylvania, was their third settlement, founded in 1824. Rapp's leadership and enforced rules of celibacy fostered tensions within the community in the latter 1820s. In March 1832, 176 dissenters seceded from the community under the leadership of another German immigrant who called himself Count de Leon.

35. Judge John Marshall (Sept. 24, 1755–July 6, 1835), Chief Justice of the United States and principal founder of the American system of constitutional law. Stephen Girard (May 20, 1750–Dec. 26, 1831), French-born merchant, financier, philanthropist.

36. William Penn (Oct. 14, 1644–July 30, 1718), founder of Pennsylvania. Peter Stephen Du Ponceau (June 3, 1760–Apr. 1, 1844), French-born lawyer and author.

37. The Democratic Convention of May 21–May 23, 1832, which was called in order to nominate Martin Van Buren to the vice-presidency. Arthur M. Schlesinger Jr., ed., *History of American Presidential Elections*, vol. 1 (New York: Chelsea House, 1971).

Biographical Key

Anderson

Lars Anderson (1803/5–1878): "Lars"

Born near Louisville, Kentucky. Married to Catherine Longworth (1815–1893), of Cincinnati. By the end of his life, he was one of Cincinnati's wealthiest and most prominent businessmen, with major real estate holdings. Business associate to Francis Cabot Lowell II.

Cleveland

Richard Jeffry Cleveland (1773–1860): "Mr. Cleveland"

United States vice-consul at Havana, 1828–1833.

Dorcas Cleveland Hiller Cleveland (dates unavailable): "Mrs. Cleveland"

Wife and cousin to Richard Jeffry Cleveland, whom she married on October 12, 1804.

Horace Cleveland (1814–1900): "Horace"

Son of Richard Jeffry and Dorcas Cleveland, born in Lancaster, Massachusetts. He worked on a coffee plantation in Cuba during the period of his father's posting as vice-consul at Havana and later became a landscape architect and writer. In 1842 he married Maryann Dwinel.

Two other sons of Richard Jeffry Cleveland, one in France and one who arrived in Havana while the Lowells were there.

The Lowells socialized regularly with the Clevelands while in Havana.

Crowninshield

Sarah Gooll Putnam Crowninshield (1810–?): "Sarah Crowninshield"

Born into a leading merchant-shipping family of Salem, Massachusetts, she was the daughter of Hon. Samuel Putnam and Sarah Gooll Putnam. Sarah Crowninshield was an old friend of Mary's. They met in Cincinnati, where the Crowninshields were on their honeymoon.

Francis Boardman Crowninshield (1809–1877): "husband"

Married to Sarah Gooll Putnam Crowninshield (1831 or 1832?). His brother George C. later married Harriet Sears, who was part of the Lowell traveling party to Cuba (see below).

Derby

Mary Jane Derby (1807–1892): "Mary Jane"

Painter and lithographer, she was born into a leading Salem merchant-shipping family. She worked as a freelance artist in the late 1820s and married Rev. Ephraim Peabody (see below) on Aug. 5, 1833. Failing eyesight and family responsibilities forced her to give up her artistic career in the mid-1830s. She was an old friend of Mary's, whom she met in Cincinnati, where Mary Jane was visiting her older sister, Ellen Rogers (see below).[1]

DeWolf

James DeWolf (1764–1837): "Mr. James D'Wolf"

A Bristol, Rhode Island, senator and maritime trader, he captained a ship in the African slave trade as a young man before settling in Bristol, where he built a fortune as a merchant. His trading interests ranged from the Caribbean to Russia. One of the earliest American textile manufacturers, he owned the Arkwright Mills in Coventry, Rhode Island. DeWolf also owned the Mount Hope and San Juan sugar plantations in Cuba, and he traveled regularly to the island. Though the Lowells met DeWolf only briefly, Mary described in detail a conflict between DeWolf and Alexander Griswold (see below), administrator on the Mount Hope estate and a personal friend of Mary's husband, Frank. The Lowells also stayed on the San Juan plantation in Matanzas, which was administered for DeWolf jointly by Mr. Wilson and Mr. Smith.

General George DeWolf (dates unavailable): one of "two Mr. D'Wolf's"

Brother of James DeWolf, he moved to Cuba from Bristol, Rhode Island, in 1825 after a failed Cuban sugar investment. He had connections to James Monroe and Andrew Jackson

Governor Collins (dates unavailable): "Governor Collins"

Described in the diary as brother-in-law to James DeWolf and part owner of the Mount Hope estate.

Elwyn

Elizabeth Sherburne Langdon Elwyn (dates unavailable): "Mrs. Elwyn"

Born in New Hampshire, she was the only daughter of Gov. John Langdon (1741–1819), who was the first presiding officer of the United States Senate in 1789. She married Thomas Elwyn (d. 1816), born in England and graduated from Trinity College, Oxford. The Lowells visited her in Philadelphia.

Charles Langdon Elwyn (dates unavailable): "Charles Elwyn"

Elizabeth Sherburne Langdon Elwyn's son. Clearly an old friend, he met the Lowells in New Orleans.

Alfred Langdon Elwyn (1804–1884): "Alfred Elwyn"

Elizabeth Sherburne Langdon Elwyn's son, born in Portsmouth, New Hampshire. He was graduated from Harvard in 1823 and as a doctor of medicine from the University of Pennsylvania in 1831, though he never practiced medicine, dedicating himself rather to philanthropy and the study of natural history. He made his home in Philadelphia, where the Lowells visited him near the end of their trip.

John Langdon Elwyn (1801–1876): "John"

Elizabeth Sherburne Langdon Elwyn's son. He was the New Hampshire representative to the Democratic Convention of May 26, 1832. The Lowells saw him at his mother's home in Philadelphia.

Emily Langdon Elwyn (dates unavailable): "Emily"

Elizabeth Sherburne Langdon Elwyn's daughter. Married to Colonel Erving, she was living at Annapolis barracks at the time of Mary's trip. The Lowells did not manage to visit her.

Matilda Langdon Elwyn (dates unavailable): "Matilda"

Elizabeth Sherburne Langdon Elwyn's daughter.[2]

Fellows / Fellowes

Nathaniel Fellows (1780–1842): "Mr. Fellowes"

Born in Roxbury, Massachusetts, the son of Captain Cornelius Fellows, a sea captain, and Sarah Fellows. His parents died while he was a minor, and he came under the guardianship of his uncle Nathaniel Fellows, a prominent Boston merchant and owner of an important estate in Cuba. He lived also in Philadelphia and Cuba and was a merchant and slave plantation owner. The younger Nathaniel Fellows, who suffered from epilepsy, appears to have inherited his uncle's Cuban properties upon his death in 1806. He married three times and had nine children by his last two wives.

The Lowells visited Mr. Fellows in Cuba in 1832 after obtaining a letter of introduction through Mary's parents in Boston. He was then a widower for the third time. He owned 406 slaves and three estates outside Havana (Reserva, Fundador, Pequeña Cabaña). He rented a fourth estate (Silencio).

Matilda Fellows (dates unavailable): "Miss Matilda"

Daughter of Nathaniel Fellows by his second wife, Aglae Louise Auguste Hélène Graton de Chambellan. Educated in Philadelphia, Miss Matilda was described very favorably and in some detail by Mary.

Pauline Fellows (dates unavailable): "Pauline"

Daughter of Nathaniel Fellows by his second wife, Aglae Louise Auguste Hélène Graton de Chambellan.

Louise Fellows (dates unavailable): one of Mr. Fellows's "three little girls"

Born in Havana, Cuba, she was the daughter of Nathaniel Fellows by his third wife, Lucy Lambert.

Charlotte Fellows (1827–1906): one of Mr. Fellows's "three little girls"

Born in Havana, Cuba, she was the daughter of Nathaniel Fellows by his third wife, Lucy Lambert.

Susan L. Fellows (1829–1915): one of Mr. Fellows's "three little girls"

Born in Havana, Cuba, she was the daughter of Nathaniel Fellows by his third wife, Lucy Lambert.

Nancy Williams (1783–1858): "Mrs. Williams"

Born in Roxbury, Massachusetts, the sister of Nathaniel Fellows, she married John S. Williams. At the time of the Lowells' visit, she was living in Cuba on the Reserva estate along with Mr. Fellows, his daughters, and her daughter (identified only as "Miss Wilson"), who was away from the plantation.[3]

Gorham

Probably William Cabot Gorham (1810–1843): "W. Gorham"

A member of the Lowell traveling party from Boston to Cuba, he was possibly the cousin of Francis Cabot Lowell II through Benjamin Gorham, Francis Cabot Lowell II's uncle.

Benjamin Gorham (1775–1855): "Mr. Gorham"

Gorham, Francis Cabot Lowell II's uncle, saw the travel party off at Boston Harbor.

Griswold

Alexander Griswold (dates unavailable): "Mr. Griswold"

Mr. Griswold was the plantation administrator employed by James DeWolf (see above) on the Mount Hope Estate, Cuba, probably from Bristol, Rhode Island, like the DeWolfs. Mary's husband, Frank, met him on a previous trip to Cuba and they became friends. Two months before the Lowells' arrival in Cuba, Mr. Griswold had been attacked on the plantation and was in a legal battle with the DeWolfs for compensation.[4]

Jenckes / Jenks

Sarah Updike Crawford Jenckes (1768–?): "Mrs. Jenckes"

Mrs. Jenckes was an American plantation owner in Cuba. She married John Scott Jenckes, and the couple migrated to Cuba in 1796. On March 16, 1807, the Jenckes family was granted permanent residence in Cuba by the Marquess of Someruelos, governor and captain general of the island. They established a coffee plantation near the village of San Cyrilo, outside Havana. At the time of the Lowells' visit to the plantation, Mrs. Jenckes was a widow. Mary described her as a "remarkably fine looking old lady."

William Scott Jenckes (1794–?): "Mr. Jenckes"

A very prominent and wealthy figure in Matanzas, he was the son of John Scott and Sarah Updike Crawford Jenckes. Born in Rhode Island, he migrated to Cuba with his parents at age two. He became a citizen of Spain on January 31, 1825, and changed his name to Guillermo Scott Jenckes Updike. In 1829 he was named "interpreter of languages" and moved to Matanzas, where he and a cousin established two sugar mills ("Concepcion" and "La Victoria").

Mrs. Jenckes (dates unavailable): "Mrs. Jenckes"

A second Mrs. Jenckes, wife of William Scott Jenckes, is described by Mary as "a Spanish lady."[5]

Lowell

Mary Lowell Gardner Lowell (1802–1854): "Mary"

The diary's author, Mary Lowell was the daughter of Samuel Pickering Gardner (1767–1843) and Rebecca Russell (Lowell) Gardner. Born in Boston, she was a member of the city's rising merchant-industrial elite. She married her first cousin, Francis Cabot Lowell II, in 1826.

Francis Cabot Lowell II (1803–1874): "Frank"

Husband (and first cousin) to Mary, he was born in Boston, son of Francis Cabot Lowell I (1775–1817) and Hannah Jackson (dates unavailable). His father was the first industrialist in the United States. Francis Cabot Lowell II managed family trusts and real estate holdings and served on boards of Boston banks and insurance companies.

George Gardner Lowell (1830–1885): "George"

The son of Mary and Francis Lowell, born in Boston, he accompanied his parents on their trip to Cuba.

Lorenza Stephens (1806–1869): "Lorenza"

The Lowells' nanny and servant, Lorenza accompanied the Lowells on their trip to Cuba.[6]

Macleay

William Sharp Macleay (1792–1865): "Mr. Macleay"

A naturalist and diplomatic o<cial, born in London, England. In 1825 he was appointed to the Mixed British and Spanish Court of Commission for the Abolition of the Slave Trade in Havana, Cuba. While in Cuba, he collected crustacea, insects, and bats, which he donated to the British Museum. He returned to Britain via the United States in 1836 and migrated to Sydney, Australia, in 1839, where he remained until his death. He was introduced to Mary in Havana by their mutual friend, Mr. Ebenezer Sage.

Metcalf

Eliab Metcalf (1785–1835): "Mr. Metcalf"

Born in Franklin, Massachusetts, Metcalf was a portrait and miniature painter, resident in Cuba at the time of the Lowells' visit. He visited Guadeloupe (1807–8) and Halifax, Nova Scotia (1810). He studied painting and worked as an artist in New York City before moving to New Orleans for his health (1819). He moved to Havana, Cuba, in 1824, which he made his home for the rest of his life. Mary's husband, Frank, met him during a previous trip to Havana, and the Lowells saw him regularly during their Cuba visit.

Moreland / Morland

John Morland (dates unavailable): "Mr. Morland" (also "Moreland")

John Morland is probably the Mr. Morland with whom the Lowells socialized regularly in Havana. He was a partner in the Havana trading firm of Frías Morland and Co..

Mrs. Morland (dates unavailable): "Mrs. Morland" (also "Moreland")

The wife of Mr. Morland, she socialized regularly with the women of the Lowells' travel party in Havana.

Clara Morland (dates unavailable): "Clara"

The young daughter of the Morlands; Mary mentions that Mr. Morland had four more daughters at school in Brookline, Massachusetts.

Noyes

Mrs. Noyes (dates unavailable): "Mrs. Noyes"

Sister of Sarah Updike Crawford Jenckes (see above), she was staying with Mrs. Jenckes, along with her daughter (Miss Noyes).

O'Farrill / O'Farrell

Ignacio-Juan-Antonio-José-Doroteo de Montalvo y Nuñez del Castillo, O'Farrill y Espinosa de Contreras, Count of Casa-Montalvo (1795–1843): "Count O'Farrell"

This is the probable identity of the "Count O'Farrell" Mary mentions. He was a member of the Cuban nobility who was born and established in Havana. Powerful sugar planters and slave traders, the extended O'Farrill family counted itself among the leading families of the Havana nobility from the late eighteenth century. They were descendants of a Spanish noble family originally of Irish lineage.. Though Mary did not meet the count, she visited his palace in Havana, which she described in some detail.[7]

Peabody

Reverend Dr. Ephraim Peabody (1807–1856): "Mr. Peabody"

A Unitarian clergyman, married to Mary Jane Derby (see above) on August 5, 1833, he met the Lowells in Cincinnati.

Physick / Physic

Dr. Philip Syng Physick (1768–1837): "Dr. Physic"

A physician and surgeon based in Philadelphia, he studied at the University of Pennsylvania, St. George's Hospital, London, and University of Edinburgh. He is often referred to as the "father of American surgery" because of his innovations in surgical procedures and instrument design. Mary mentioned his medical advice to Eliza Sullivan (see below) regarding treatment of her tuberculosis, as well as a special trip made by Lars Anderson (see above) to Philadelphia for medical treatment.

Ramos

José-Antonio Ramos de Espitarte y Fernández, Fernández de Villamil y Agrela, Marquis of Casa-Ramos de la Fidelidad (dates unavailable): "Marquis Ramos"

This is the probable identity of the Marquis Ramos, whose daughters visited with Mary in Cuba. He was born in San Andrés de la Graña, Mondoñedo, Spain, and moved to Cuba before 1809. By profession he was a lawyer and received his noble title only in 1818. He was married twice, first to Josefa de Leon y Fantini and second, in 1809, to Josefa-Gabriela-Salvadora de Chaves y Bello, Trinquier y Garcia, who died in 1823.

Mrs. Hernandez and Mr. Hernandez (dates unavailable):

These are the daughter and son-in-law of Marquis Ramos. Eliza Sullivan (see below), of the Lowells' travel party to Cuba, socialized regularly with the Hernandezes, whom Mary described as "of the first rank." The Lowells visited the Hernandez sugar plantation in Matanzas with the Sages (see below).

Madame de Suzane (dates unavailable):

The daughter of Marquis Ramos, Mary described in some detail the controversy surrounding her marriage to a French officer, which was opposed by her sister, brother-in-law, and father.[8]

Robinson

Dr. Horatio Robinson (?–1849): "Dr. Robinson"

An unmarried doctor from Salem, Massachusetts, graduated from Harvard in 1822. He was a member of the Lowell party throughout most of the trip. He seems to have been traveling for health reasons and was probably suffering from tuberculosis.

Rogers

John Rogers (1800–1884): "John Rogers"

Born in Boston, Rogers was the son of Daniel Denison Rogers and Elizabeth Bromfield. Graduated from Harvard in 1820, he relocated to Cincinnati, where he was a partner in a sawmill.

Sarah Ellen Derby Rogers (1805–?): "Ellen"

Wife of John Rogers, daughter of John Derby (1767–1831) and Eleanor Coffin (1779–?), and elder sister of Mary Jane Derby (see above), who was visiting her in Cincinnati at the time of the Lowells' arrival. The Rogers were clearly old friends of the Lowells.

Two children: Ellen (b. 1828) and John (b. 1829).

Sage

Ebenezer William Sage (1788–1833): "Mr. Sage"

Born in Middletown, Connecticut, son of Ebenezer Sage (1754–1831), he moved to Cuba in the mid-1810s, where he established the Santa Ana coffee plantation in Lumidero, Matanzas region. He was also part owner of the

Ontario plantation with his brother-in-law Mr. Webster (see below). A slave insurrection occurred on the Santa Ana plantation in 1825, while the Sages were visiting the United States. He had no children.

Hepsey Howard Sage (c.1792–?): "Hepsy"

This is the probable identity of Ebenezer William Sage's wife. Married about 1813, the Sages appeared to have been old friends of the Lowells, and the two families visited regularly in Cuba.[9]

Sagra

Ramón de la Sagra (1791–1871): "Mr. Sagra"

Director of the Havana Botanical Garden and author of an early statistical work on Cuba in 1831.[10]

Sears

David Sears Sr. (1787–1871): "Mr. Sears"

Part of the Lowells' traveling party from Boston to Cuba, Sears was born in Boston and lived primarily on his inheritance. He was known for philanthropy through the Sears Fund and political service in the General Court and State Senate. He married Miriam Clarke Mason (1789–1870) in 1809. He built a home at 42 Beacon Street, Boston, in 1819, which later became the Somerset Club. He supported the abolitionist cause in the 1840s and 1850s.

Harriet Elizabeth Dickason Sears (1814–?): "Harriet"

The daughter of David Sears, she married George Caspar Crowninshield, of Salem, Massachusetts, after returning from Cuba.

Miriam Cordelia Mason Sears (1816–1850): "Cordelia"

The daughter of David Sears, Cordelia traveled to Cuba for her health, presumably suffering from tuberculosis. Mary reported that Cordelia was "greatly amused" by an incident in Havana when the two women received catcalls while riding unaccompanied in an open carriage.

Shaler

William Shaler (1773–1833): "Mr. Shaler"

A sea captain, U.S. consul in Algiers (1812–1824), and author, Shaler was born in Bridgeport, Connecticut. He was an old friend and business partner of Richard Jeffry Cleveland (see above), whom he had first met in 1800 during a shipping venture in Mauritius. The two men were active in shipping in South America, China, and the Pacific Coast of North America. Because of ill health, he resigned his post in Algiers and was named U.S. consul to Havana, Cuba, in 1830. He lived in Havana at the home of the Clevelands. He introduced the men in the Lowell travel party to the governor of Cuba, and the Lowells met him on several social occasions in Havana. Mary disapproved of his "cold, positive way." He never married and died in Cuba during a cholera epidemic.

Dr. Nathaniel Burger Shaler (?–1877): "Dr. Shaler"

A nephew of William Shaler, Dr. Shaler was graduated from Harvard in 1827 and from Harvard Medical School in 1829.

Silsbee

Nathaniel Silsbee (1773–1850): "Mr. Silsbee"

Seaman, merchant, and statesman, Silsbee was born in Salem, Massachusetts. As a young man he worked as a sailor and sea captain on voyages to the Caribbean, Asia, the Mediterranean, and Russia. He retired from the sea in 1801 and became a ship owner and leading merchant and financier in Boston and Salem. He was a representative in the United States House of Representatives from 1816 to 1820. He later served in the Massachusetts legislature and United States Senate. He married Mary Crowninshield in 1802 and was a business associate of Mary's husband, Frank.

Sullivan

Richard Sullivan (1779–1861): "Mr. Sullivan"

Lawyer and philanthropist, based in Boston and Brookline, Massachusetts, he was the son of Massachusetts Attorney General James Sullivan and Hetty Odiorne, whose family was connected to the leading families of New Hampshire. He married Sarah Russell (1786–1831) in 1804, one of several marriages between the Russell and Sullivan families. Richard Sullivan gave up practicing law, thanks to his wife's family fortune. He was a cavalry officer in the War of 1812. He had philanthropic interests in the Massachusetts General Hospital, the Massachusetts Agricultural Society, and Harvard University. Sullivan was related to Mary Gardner Lowell through her mother, Rebecca Russell Lowell Gardner. He was part of the Lowell traveling party to Cuba. Mary described the Sullivans as connected to the "best society" in Havana.

Elizabeth Lowell Sullivan (1805–1833): "Eliza"

A daughter of Richard Sullivan, Eliza never married. She traveled to Cuba for her health, presumably suffering from tuberculosis. Though Mary reported her condition improved during the trip, Eliza died one year after their return to Boston.[11]

Webster

Ephron William Webster (1782–?): "Mr. Webster"

This is the probable identity of the Ebenezer William Sage's brother-in-law (see above). He was co-owner of the Ontario plantation in Matanzas, Cuba. Born in West Hartford, Connecticut, he married Maria Sage in 1807 in Middletown, Connecticut. The Websters lived on the Ontario plantation. The Lowells met Mr. Webster at Mr. Sage's Santa Ana plantation in Cuba.

Maria Sage Webster (1787–?): "Mrs. Webster"

A sister of Ebenezer William Sage (see above), she was born in Middletown, Connecticut.

Frederick Webster (dates unavailable): "Frederick"

Mary reported that the Websters' son Frederick was a student at the private school run by Mr. Cubi y Soler, which the Lowells visited in Havana.

NOTES TO BIOGRAPHICAL KEY

1. Sally Pierce and Catharina Slautterback, *Boston Lithography, 1825–1880: The Boston Athenaeum Collection* (Boston: Boston Athenaeum, 1991), 170.

2. Langdon Family Papers, box 11, MHS; *Massachusetts Historical Society Proceedings*, ser. 2, vol. 1, pp. 145–47.

3. George Marshall Fellows, "A Genealogy and Partial History of Fellows Families in America," manuscript, 6 vols., Fellows SG FEL, boxes 1 and 2, New England Historic Genealogical Society.

4. For correspondence between James DeWolf and Alexander Griswold, see DeWolf Papers, vol. 2, Baker Library Historical Collections, Harvard University.

5. Information on the Jenckes family was supplied by Craig Reekie. Further information about Mrs. Jenckes and her son (identified only as Mrs. J. and Mr. J.) appears in Rev. Abiel Abbot, *Letters Written in the Interior of Cuba Between the Mountains of Arcana, to the East, and of Cusco, to the West, in the Months of February, March, April, and May, 1828* (Boston: Bowles and Dearborn, 1829).

6. On the Gardners and Lowells, see Elizabeth Gardner Amory, "The Gardner Family of Salem and Boston" (typescript, June 1908), Gardner Family Papers, Ms. S-4, MHS; Ferris Greenslet, *The Lowells and Their Seven Worlds* (Boston: Houghton Mifflin, 1946); Betty G. Farrell, *Elite Families: Class and Power in Nineteenth-Century Boston* (Albany: State University of New York Press, 1993).

7. Rafael Nieto y Cortadellas, *Dignidades nobiliarias en Cuba* (Madrid: Ediciones Cultura Hispanica, 1954), 145–46.

8. Nieto y Cortadellas, *Dignidades*, 165.

9. Sage Family Papers, MHS.

10. Ramón de la Sagra, *Historia económico-politica y estadística de la isla de Cuba, o sea de sus progresos en la poblacion, la agricultura, el comercio y las rentas* (Havana: Imprenta de las Viudas de Arazoza y Soler, 1831).

11. Thomas C. Amory, *Memoir of Honorable Richard Sullivan* (Cambridge, Mass.: John Wilson and Son, 1885).

Glossary

bohío	thatched-roof hut; slave dwelling
calesero	carriage driver
Creole	In Spanish America, a native descended from European ancestors; a person of mixed European and black descent; in Mary's descriptions of Cuban plantations, the term usually refers to the children of slaves who were born into slavery.
funche	cornmeal dish
mauvaise honte	self-consciousness
mayoral	plantation foreman
montero	member of rural poor or small farmer class in Cuba
Otaheitan [Otaheite]	a variety of sugarcane originally from Otaheite, an island in the South Pacific; planted in the Caribbean and Louisiana in the early nineteenth century
potrero	stock-raising farm
secadero	drying rack
trig	trim; neat
volante	two-wheeled horse-drawn carriage

Bibliography

Amory, Cleveland. *The Proper Bostonians*. New York: E. P. Dutton, 1947.

Bakan, Abigail B. *Ideology and Class Conflict in Jamaica: The Politics of Rebellion*. Montreal: McGill-Queen's University Press, 1990.

Bergad, Laird W. *Cuban Rural Society in the Nineteenth Century: The Social and Economic History of Monoculture in Matanzas*. Princeton: Princeton University Press, 1990.

Bergad, Laird W., Fe Iglesias García, and María del Carmen Barcia. *The Cuban Slave Market, 1790–1880*. Cambridge: Cambridge University Press, 1995.

Blake, S. "A Woman's Trek: What Difference Does Gender Make?" *Women's Studies International Forum* 13, no. 4 (1990): 347–55.

Bohls, Elizabeth A. *Women Travel Writers and the Language of Aesthetics, 1716–1818*. Cambridge: Cambridge University Press, 1995.

Blunt, Alison. *Travel, Gender, and Imperialism: Mary Kingsley and West Africa*. New York: Guilford Press, 1994.

Blunt, Alison, and Gillian Rose, eds. *Writing Women and Space: Colonial and Postcolonial Geographies*. New York: Guilford Press, 1994.

Coughtry, Jay. *The Notorious Triangle: Rhode Island and the African Slave Trade, 1700–1807*. Philadelphia: Temple University Press, 1981.

Crawford, Mary Caroline. *Famous Families of Massachusetts*. Boston: Little, Brown, 1930.

Dalzell, Robert F. *Enterprising Elite: The Boston Associates and the World they Made*. Cambridge: Harvard University Press, 1987.

Farrell, Betty G. *Elite Families: Class and Power in Nineteenth-Century Boston*. Albany: State University of New York Press, 1993.

Greenslet, Ferris. *The Lowells and Their Seven Worlds*. Boston: Houghton Mifflin, 1946.

Guicharnaud-Tollis, Michèle. *Regards sur Cuba au XIXe siècle: témoignages européens*. Paris: L'Harmattan, 1996.

Hahner, June E. *Women Through Women's Eyes: Latin American Women in Nineteenth-Century Travel Accounts*. Wilmington, Del.: SR Books, 1998.

Larkin, Jack. *The Reshaping of Everyday Life, 1790–1840*. New York: Harper and Row, 1988.

Levine, Robert M. *Cuba in the 1850s: Through the Lens of Charles DeForest Fredricks*. Tampa: University of South Florida Press, 1990.

Martínez-Alier, Verena. *Marriage, Class, and Colour in Nineteenth-Century Cuba: A Study of Racial Attitudes and Sexual Values in a Slave Society*. Cambridge: Cambridge University Press, 1974.

Martínez-Fernández, Luis. *Fighting Slavery in the Caribbean: The Life and Times of a British Family in Nineteenth-Century Havana*. Armonk, N.Y.: M. E. Sharpe, 1998.

Masur, Louis P. *1831: Year of Eclipse*. New York: Hill and Wang, 2001.

McEwan, Cheryl. *Gender, Geography and Empire: Victorian Women Travellers in West Africa*. Aldershot: Ashgate, 2000.

Méndez Rodenas, Adriana. *Gender and Nationalism in Colonial Cuba: The Travels of Santa Cruz y Montalvo, Condesa de Merlin*. Nashville: Vanderbilt University Press, 1998.

Mills, Sara. *Discourses of Difference: An Analysis of Women's Travel Writing and Colonialism*. London: Routledge, 1991.

Moreno Fraginals, Manuel. *The Sugarmill: The Socioeconomic Complex of Sugar in Cuba, 1760–1860*. Trans. Cedric Belfrage. New York: Monthly Review Press, 1976.

North, Douglass C. *The Economic Growth of the United States, 1790–1860*. New York: W. W. Norton, 1966.

Pérez, Louis A. *Cuba and the United States: Ties of Singular Intimacy*. Athens: University of Georgia Press, 1990.

———. *On Becoming Cuban: Identity, Nationality, and Culture*. Chapel Hill: University of North Carolina Press, 1999.

———, ed. *Impressions of Cuba in the Nineteenth Century: The Travel Diary of Joseph J. Dimock*. Wilmington, Del.: Scholarly Resources, 1998.

———, ed. *Slaves, Sugar & Colonial Society: Travel Accounts of Cuba, 1801–1899*. Wilmington, Del.: Scholarly Resources, 1992.

Pratt, Mary Louise. *Imperial Eyes: Travel Writing and Transculturation*. London: Routledge, 1992.

Robinson, Jane. *Wayward Women: A Guide to Women Travellers*. Oxford: Oxford University Press, 1990.

Index

Page numbers in *italics* indicate illustrations or their captions.

Index